BRITISH
ROYAL
BOOKPLATES

Tinted lithograph by Joseph Nash (1808–76) from his Views of the Interior and Exterior of Windsor Castle, *1848, a work dedicated to Prince Albert. Queen Victoria and the Prince are depicted in Queen Elizabeth's Gallery viewed from the west end. The Royal Library's appearance has changed very little since then.* © *1991. Her Majesty the Queen.*

BRITISH ROYAL BOOKPLATES

AND EX-LIBRIS OF RELATED FAMILIES

Brian North Lee

Scolar Press

Published by
SCOLAR PRESS
Gower House
Croft Road
Aldershot
Hants GU11 3HR
England

Ashgate Publishing Co.
Old Post Road
Brookfield
Vermont 05036
USA

British Library Cataloguing in Publication Data
Lee, Brian North
    British Royal Bookplates: and ex-libris of related
    families.
    1. Great Britain. Bookplates
    I. Title
    769.52

    ISBN 0–85967–883–0

Book design by Wileman Design. Typeset in Great Britain by Poole Typesetting (Wessex) Ltd., Bournemouth, Dorset. Printed in Great Britain at The University Press, Cambridge.

Contents

Acknowledgements — vii

Introduction — 1

The Royal Arms of Great Britain since 1603 — 11

Royal crowns and coronets — 13

The Prince of Wales's feathers, other badges and mottoes — 14

The Hessian and Battenberg arms — 15

Notes on the catalogue — 16

British Royal Bookplates — 19

Addenda — 185

Bookplates of grandchildren of Queen Victoria
of, or married into, European Royal Houses — 189

Bookplates of related families
I   By marriage — 199
II Illegitimate descendants of Charles II and James II and
    of marriages contravening the Royal Marriages Act 1772 — 207

Appendix: Armorials and other designs of questionable authenticity or
in the past wrongly recorded as bookplates — 229

Genealogical tables — 249

Select bibliography — 255

Index — 257

Acknowledgements

I am most grateful to Her Majesty the Queen for graciously permitting publication of this study of bookplates relating to the Royal family before 1952. For allowing their personal ex-libris to be illustrated I owe especial thanks to Her Majesty Queen Elizabeth the Queen Mother, Her Royal Highness Princess Alice, Duchess of Gloucester and Sir Henry and Lady May Abel Smith. Her Royal Highness the Princess of Hesse and by Rhine and Her Grace the Duchess of Beaufort also provided bookplates for illustration; a number of ex-libris from the Franks and Viner Collections are reproduced by courtesy of the Trustees of the British Museum; and examples from the Winterburn Collection are shown by courtesy of the Donohue Rare Book Room of the Richard A. Gleeson Library at the University of San Francisco. Sir Robin Mackworth-Young, Mr Oliver Everett, Miss Bridget Wright and Mr Stephen Patterson have most kindly assisted my researches at the Royal Library, Windsor Castle.

For information on bookplate usage I thank His Imperial Highness the Grand Duke Vladimir of Russia, Their Royal Highnesses Prince and Princess Michael of Kent, His Grace the Duke of Argyll, Mr and Mrs Patrick Manley, and Dr D. H. Newsome, Master of Wellington College. Gratitude is also due to the staff of the Department of Prints and Drawings at the British Museum, the Chief Executive of Book Trust, and the staff of Liverpool Public Library. Gratitude is also acknowledged to Mr Duncan Andrews, Miss P. Cooper, Principal of Queen Alexandra's House Association, Mr Stephen Corey, Sir Derek Hart Dyke, Bart., Mr Robert Golden, Mr H. W. P. Harrison, Mr Henry B. Muir, the late Mr Geoffrey Mussett, Mr George S. Swarth, Mr David Williamson, and the Ven. David N. Griffiths, Archdeacon of Berkshire.

Amongst friends who are collectors of bookplates I express my thanks for assistance to Mr Peter Allpress, Mrs Audrey Arellanes, Professor William E. Butler, Mr David Frean, Mr Paul Latcham, Dr Colin R. Lattimore, Mr Ernest Pearce, Mr Brian Schofield, Mr Peter Summers, Mr Bryan Welch and Mr Keith Wingrove. Finally, one could not but acknowledge a notable debt to those past collectors and documentors of ex-libris whose persistence and quiet researches have left record of investigation of the subject in past time. Any errors in the text are, of course, the author's alone.

Introduction

In view of the importance which ex-libris hold for bibliographers, historians and book and bookplate collectors it is surprising that no catalogue of British Royal bookplates has been published during the past century. Its first two decades witnessed the compilation of most bookplate reference works, and *The Ex Libris Journal* of the Ex Libris Society, 1891–1908, provides a record of diverse but by no means always scholarly research into the subject. Since then a small number of books and several hundred magazine articles have appeared, the latter being especially unmarked by seriousness and accuracy. Such diversification is daunting in itself, but anyone who diligently set about gathering printed documentation of Royal bookplates would have been largely disappointed. Nor can recourse to original prints in bookplate collections have assisted them much, for annotation is often lacking or sparse, and – as will be explained – not all examples included therein prove to be genuine ex-libris.

Only three twentieth century publications, all in limited editions, consider the question of Royal ex-libris in any quantity; and each is in some degree restricted in its usefulness. Christine Price's *Catalogue of Royal Bookplates from the Louise E. Winterburn Collection*, 1944, lists 103 examples relating to Great Britain. Of these, however, at least eight are not bookplates at all, two were for Indian princes, and the rest include variant states and an original drawing. It is none the less an attractive and intriguing book, and worth searching for. Percy Neville Barnett's *Australian Book-plates and book-plates of interest to Australia*, 1950, has a chapter on the subject, well illustrated; but Barnett indulges in a chattiness and lack of precision which would be out of favour today. Arvid Berghman's *Kungliga och Furstliga Exlibris*, 1955, includes fifty-one British examples, fourteen of them illustrated, but the text is in Swedish and the detail provided is scant. In view of the limitations these evidence, it seemed that a book specifically devoted to the subject might be of use to scholars and collectors; but it must be admitted that it was embarked upon with a degree of reluctance and reticence. There are diverse reasons why recording of Royal ex-libris has been neglected in the past, and detailing some of them will serve to explain one's diffidence and throw light upon the character and usage of the bookplates recorded.

First amongst the considerations which discourage a chronicler is the delicacy demanded by respect for privacy. A bookplate is *per se* a personal mark of ownership, having within the lifetime of its user no public purpose at all. It will be understood that for this reason bookplates of the present reign must lie beyond the scope of this book. Bookplates are nevertheless of much use to bibliographers and historians in later times in ascertaining the provenance of books, and they are of interest to serious collectors on this account and for the insights they offer into the style and quality of this minor branch of graphic art. Not unnaturally the ex-libris of Royalty, which are generally uncommon and in some instances extremely rare, have been prized by collectors fortunate enough to find them. They may turn up in old collections in the saleroom or bookshops, after the sale of old libraries, or amongst the studio effects of their engravers and artists. Bookplates are not, however, obtainable from living members of the Royal family by request; and past collectors, especially around the turn of the century, who bombarded not only Royalty but distinguished folk in all fields with demands for their ex-libris threatened to bring a scholarly and serious area of research into disrepute. A most courteous hand-written letter, in the writer's collection, from the King's Librarian at Windsor in 1910 to an unnamed correspondent details the situation perfectly:

> Sir, In reply to your letter to the King of 23rd ult. I have it in charge to inform you that His Majesty never, except in very special circumstances, gives away a copy of the Royal bookplates, & regrets that he is unable to depart from this rule in your case. You will see, I think upon reflection, that if His Majesty were to comply with one such request, it would be difficult for him to refuse to comply with all; in which case he would be obliged to distribute some thousands of bookplates every year.

Readers who examine, as they almost certainly will, the catalogue and illustrations before turning to this introduction may initially be surprised to discover how many Royal personages did not use bookplates and also that they are almost non-existent prior to the reign of King George III. The obvious conclusion that not everyone is a book lover and, indeed, that not all bibliophiles bother to use an ex-libris only partly accounts for this. Royalty has made much use in the past of bookbindings and book-stamps on bindings as an alternative, and often much grander, means of indicating ownership. The bookbinding has, in Royal circles, a much older history than ex-libris. Cyril Davenport's *Royal English Bookbindings*, 1896, shows sumptuous examples from the reign of King Henry VIII to that of King George IV. They tended to be, of course, adornments for individual books. In his *English Heraldic Book-Stamps*, 1909, the scope extends to the reign of King Edward VII; but these differ in being mainly stamps for general use when books were bound or rebound. Davenport comments that, 'Towards the end of the seventeenth century the popularity of the book-stamp was diminished by the growth of the use of adhesive book-plates.' Book-stamps have, nevertheless, continued in use in king's houses into this century, whereas — apart from an isolated example — use of bookplates by kings and queens is as yet unproven before King George III's reign. This is not surprising, for his immediate pre-decessors were not very keen book collectors. All our monarchs since have, however, used ex-libris.

Generosity hinders the chronicler of Royal ex-libris, for twice the Royal Library has been given to the nation. The earlier collection was predominantly the books of King James I, cared for and added to by his eldest son, Prince Henry, with books which King Charles I and King Charles II had acquired, though they were not major collectors. Small interest was taken in the Royal Library by the rulers from 1685 to 1757, when King George II gave it to the nation. King George III, after his accession in 1760, much regretted the loss and set about energetically re-forming the Royal Library, amassing some 65,000 volumes and 19,000 manuscripts and tracts. In 1762 he spent, for instance, about £10,000 on the fine library of Joseph Smith, many years British Consul at Venice, and thus added to the Royal Library some of the best and scarcest editions of Latin, Italian and French authors. A record of Joseph Smith's library and its dispersal is in W. Y. Fletcher's *English Book Collectors*, 1902. The King also, incidentally, purchased Smith's collection of coins, a collection indicated on the latter's bookplates, one of which (Franks Coll.27324) is shown here. George III's Library was greatly enhanced when (Sir) Frederick Augusta Barnard, his librarian, scoured the Continent for fine books on his behalf. This second Royal Library was presented by King George IV to the nation in 1823, and the King's Library at the British Museum was built to house it.

Whether there are Royal bookplates prior to those of King George III in the King's Library is not evident, but it seems unlikely. None has so far been located, and the usage of ex-libris to affix to books was in its infancy in Britain until the very end of the seventeenth century. The Royal Library at Windsor has, with the exception of the British Museum, the finest extant collection of Royal bookbindings, notably rich since the period of King James

The largest-sized bookplate of Joseph Smith

I; but these would not have called for an ex-libris as well. What appears to be a bookplate of King Charles I occurs in a copy of *Selden on Tithes*, 1618, at Windsor, and it is included here (33), though it was probably engraved for another purpose. It is, however, still in situ in a volume, and it is only where this is the case that one can assume a degree of confidence in authenticity before 1760. Such cautioning is needed because of the proliferation of Royal coats of arms.

Charles Hasler's *The Royal Arms*, 1980, is a valuable source of information on the diverse purposes for which such arms have been engraved or designed. They have been used on publications of diverse kinds, and even on occasion as specimens of an engraver's prowess. Inevitably, in the heady days of ex-libris collecting around the turn of the century, some found place in collections without any investigation of their authenticity. Gambier Howe's *Franks Bequest. Catalogue of British and American Book Plates*, British Museum, 1903–4, itself sufficiently reveals the problem. Of the seventy-eight compositions under the 'Royal Plates' classification, three are admittedly not ex-libris, eight are classified as 'probably not', five more are questioned, and nine are prints from bookstamps. Here alone, and in the classic British bookplate collection, is clear evidence of the uncertainty that has existed over the subject.

The seeking of a solution to questions including those noted above encouraged the idea of this book; but, having begun to research, a decision as to its scope had to be made. Where should a line be drawn so far as the classification 'Royal' is concerned? In other words, how close should those included be to the monarchy? So far as the book's first and principal section is concerned, you will find included the bookplates of monarchs and their consorts and all of the Royal family who bore the qualification of Serene Highness, Highness or Royal Highness, even if these were relinquished during their lives. His Serene Highness Prince Alexander of Teck, for instance, became Earl of Athlone in 1917, when in the First World War others of the Royal family in England who bore German titles were invited to relinquish them and adopt English surnames. He is thus within the first classification (10). Had he been, however, simply an English earl, or otherwise non-Royal, he would have been included – as the husband of Princess Alice – in the related families section. Then there was Princess Alice's brother, Prince Charles Edward, born 2nd Duke of Albany (his father having died before his birth). He became reigning Duke of Saxe-Coburg and Gotha, but, as a result of his First World War activities, his titles were removed from the Roll of Peers in pursuance of the Order of The King in Council in 1919. Since, however, he was for many years a Royal Highness it seemed proper to include him (34).

Consideration was also demanded by the marriages of Queen Victoria's children and grandchildren, some of whom became members of Europe's Imperial and Royal houses. Queen Victoria's eldest daughter, Princess Vic-

toria, for instance, became the Empress Frederick of Germany. It seemed entirely right to include not only her bookplate as Princess Royal of Great Britain but her plates as Dowager Empress (159–161). Her sons, Kaiser Wilhelm II and Prince Heinrich are also represented, the former by one of his several plates and with some reluctance (180 and 175). Any known bookplates of the children of Queen Victoria's second daughter, Princess Alice, who died so young and tragically, are included in view of their close links with Queen Victoria and the subsequent life of our Royal family, though they were Grand Ducal Highnesses. Of Prince Alfred's children, only Victoria Melita seem to have used a bookplate (179); and Princess Beatrice's daughter, Queen Victoria Eugenie of Spain, spent so much of her young life with her grandmother that one had no hesitation about her bookplate's inclusion (178). To have excluded such as the above would have been to ignore the place their owners had in our Royal family before their marriages; and their inclusion is a small evidence of Queen Victoria's unique position as the 'grandmother of Europe'.

To record properly the libraries in which the many bookplates shown here served would require a second volume. Whilst a small number of ex-libris were made for specific residences, such as Windsor, Balmoral, Osborne and Sandringham, the others have found home from time to time in some of several hundred houses and palaces in Great Britain and overseas which cannot obviously all be recorded here. The bookplates of individuals migrated with their books as their owners moved residence, sometimes not infrequently. It seemed appropriate in the following catalogue to cite in general at least one place where particular Royal personages, apart from monarchs and their consorts, lived for a significant time. To exceed this would have involved detailing individual's lives to a degree endangering the balance of documentation and biography for which a mere book on bookplates calls.

The subject is nevertheless fascinating and deserves a few observations and illustrations which may perhaps tempt the reader to research the matter more fully. Undoubtedly, the finest eighteenth century Royal bibliophile was King George III, and before presentation to the nation by his son his books were housed in the splendid old King's Library at Buckingham Palace, then called The Queen's House (see 77). They had apparently been kept at the old Palace at Kew until rooms were built for them at The Queen's House. Illustration of its Octagon Library indicates the importance the King attached to his books; and equally impressive is the access he afforded there to scholars. Dr Johnson was, amongst others, a welcome browser and adviser. King George III's considerable expenditure on books was eminently justified by his gladness in sharing his judiciously-assembled library with others.

An instance of the migration of books is afforded by the life of the Duke of Clarence, later King William IV. His ex-libris as Duke and King (169–170), together with his

King George III's Octagon Library at The Queen's House, now Buckingham Palace

regret at King George IV's disposal of the Royal Library, indicate that he was a book lover. Some were probably taken by him in his seafarings. It is likely that he had a modest library at Petersham, then after 1797 at Bushey Park, where he lived with Mrs Jordan and his children, but other books would have been at his apartments at St James's Palace. Maybe a few travelled with him to Hanover, whence he went for a year in 1818, or to the Royal Pavilion at Brighton when he became King (his Queen being much addicted to the bathing the place afforded). Windsor would then, doubtless, have been the home of most of them; and after his death Queen Adelaide had some of his books at her subsequent homes: Bushey Park; Witley Court, near Worcester; Cassiobury, near Watford; and finally Bentley Priory, near Stanmore in Middlesex. We know that a number of these books she bequeathed to his third son, Lord Frederick FitzClarence (193), and these assuredly had further peregrinations.

Whilst within Great Britain the tally of Royal residences is legion, some of our princes and princesses have made foreign marriages. Princess Elizabeth, the daughter of King George III, became Landgravine of Hesse-Homburg and her books, with their ex-libris made in Britain before her marriage (62–63) doubtless went overseas with her, and came back to be auctioned by Sotheby and Wilkinson in 1863. Another notable instance – referred to

earlier – was the Empress Frederick of Germany, Queen Victoria's eldest daughter, Victoria. She married in 1858 the future Friedrich III, German Emperor and King of Prussia. He, poor man, was stricken with cancer before he ascended the throne and reigned but three months; but his widow remained in Germany, where she suffered the egocentricity and unbalance of her eldest son, Kaiser Wilhelm II. The books of her youth, with her ex-libris as Princess Royal (159) found their eventual rest in the home she built for herself, Friedrichshof, in the Taunus Mountains. A residence she considered modest, it included a noble library, led to from the billiard-room by a small door with posts of fifteenth-century Venetian stonework. Bookshelves ran nearly all round the room, and in a Louis IX cabinet was a collection of beautifully arranged Royal and other autographs. Later volumes added to this library would have been marked by her Josef Sattler ex-libris (160–161).

It can be intriguing to take, as it were, another standpoint and consider bookplate usage in a single house. Claremont, near Esher, which is now a school, was for long a Royal residence. The present house, succeeding the one built in 1708 for his own use by Sir John Vanbrugh, was erected for Clive of India by 'Capability' Brown in the Palladian style. Whether Clive ever actually resided there is debatable, but if he did it was for a very short time, and

The Library at Friedrichshof

it is unlikely that his books with their Chippendale ex-libris (Franks Coll.6132) were ever there; but it is appropriate to limit mention here to Royal residents and their bookplates.

Claremont was the home of Princess Charlotte, King George IV's only child, and her husband, Prince Leopold of Saxe-Coburg-Saalfeld, for their short married life of eighteen months, 1816–17. To this house she would have brought books bearing her first ex-libris (37), and she and Prince Leopold had a joint bookplate (38) made for subsequent acquisitions. The library, with its lettered bookcases, led out of the hall. Following the Princess's death, shortly after giving birth to a still-born son, Prince (later King) Leopold retained the house, and it became something of a shrine to her. Her personal possessions, including a watch she had placed on a mantelpiece and the cloak and hat she flung over a screen as she came in for the last time, remained where they were, probably until 1882. Queen Victoria as a child often stayed with her uncle Leopold at Claremont, and indeed took lessons there in her governess's bedroom; so it is likely that books bearing her two earliest ex-libris (144 and 145) were there on occasion. The house was also a loved retreat for her and Prince Albert in their early married years. Then in 1848 King Louis-Philippe of France and Queen Marie Amelie came to live in exile at Claremont. They were parents-in-law to King Leopold, he having married their daughter Louise. The manner of their departure from France would not have given them chance to take their books, else the rather curious ex-libris Louis-Philippe put in his geography books would have been seen at Claremont. The King died two years later, but his widow remained at Claremont until her death in 1866.

The estate was settled on Prince Leopold, Duke of Albany, by the Queen in 1882 on his marriage to Princess Helen of Waldeck and Pyrmont, and Claremont was a much-loved home to them. Leopold's ex-libris as Prince and Duke (111) would be in his books there, but probably in his sitting-room, which he had fitted with bookshelves painted white and gold. This room, after his untimely death in 1884, became the Duchess's boudoir, but the books and shelves remained. He also had a special library for his servants (112). It is not surprising, for he was a real lover of books – Shakespeare and Sir Walter Scott were his favourite authors – and he had studied at Oxford. His thoughtfulness to servants recalls an incident in the life of his predecessor at Claremont, Princess Charlotte. She and her husband one day found an old lady on the estate, a Mrs Bewley, endeavouring to read a Bible with too small a print, and a little later they appeared at her door with a large calf-bound Bible, with a Prayer Book containing two pound notes.

When Prince Leopold, Duke of Albany died in 1884 his widow was left with a young daughter and expecting another child. The posthumous arrival was a son, Prince Charles Edward, who later became Duke of Saxe-Coburg and Gotha. There is a charming – if somewhat fulsome – account of Claremont, featuring the Albany children, in the *Strand Magazine* for 1895. There they were privately educated, their tutor a Miss Jane Potts, who was much admired by the young Princess Alice; and they took lessons in the schoolroom – a handsome apartment with a cream and gold ceiling, and walls in electric blue brocade of fern-leaf pattern. Rather overcrowded, as Victorian rooms were, with pictures, portraits and busts, armour and china, it also contained globes, maps, writing-tables,

The schoolroom at Claremont

patent desks and schoolbooks, with a 'perfect' toy store and singing birds in cages. It must have been delightful then, though it had in earlier days been the bedroom in which Princess Charlotte died, and had been shut up for years afterwards. Probably in this schoolroom Princess Alice, later Countess of Athlone, pasted her ex-libris into her books, for it was engraved by the time she was 13 (20). No other Royal bookplates relating to Claremont are known. Princess Alice thought an ex-libris was made for her mother at the same time as her own, but it seems unlikely: she was recalling in her letter on the subject a minor event some eighty-four years earlier; and further-more, a copy of Max Müller's *Auld Lang Syne*, 1898, in the author's collection contains Prince Leopold's plate as Duke of Albany. Surely the Duchess would have used her own ex-libris had she had one, for the volume is inscribed to her. It is interesting to note, however, that she conti-nued to use her husband's bookplate fourteen years after his death.

Though this book's scope is limited to Royal person-ages and their relations, we must not forget that their courts and households were numerous. Some of their retinues would be resident, others semi-resident. Courtiers have rarely indicated their station in the inscriptions of their ex-libris, but several instances may be mentioned in passing. Amongst the earliest is the bookplate of 'Dame Anna Margaretta Mason Relict of Sr. Richard Mason Kt. Late Clerke Comtroler of the Green Cloath [sic] to King Charles and King James the Second. 1701' (Franks Coll.19910 and *151). She was the daughter of Sir James Long of Draycot Cerne, Wiltshire. Of the same period are the bookplates of 'The Right Noble William Duke of

Devonshire Lord Steward of his Ma(jes)ties Household and Knight of the Most Noble Order of the Garter' (Franks Coll.5428, *18, 5429, *12, *16). William Cavendish, 1st Duke of Devonshire, occupied this import-ant office from 1689 until his death in 1707. 'Sr. Clement Cottrell Kt. Master of the Ceremonyes' (Franks Coll.7022) followed his father and grandfather in this function, as his son and grandson were to do after him; but Solomon Dayrolles, who became Master of the Revels in 1744 and was a great personal favourite at court, makes no mention of his office on his bookplate (Franks Coll.8264–5). There are four varieties of the bookplate of 'Sir Thos. Brand, Knt. Gentleman Usher of the Green Rod and Gentleman Usher Daily Waiter to His Majesty Anno 1735' (Franks Coll. 3544, Viner Coll.518–9 and private collection); and of several ex-libris of Henrietta Louisa Fermor, Countess of Pomfret (Franks Coll.10401–4, Viner Coll.1444–5), all of which name her as a Lady of the Bedchamber to the Queen, the largest one, by Samuel Wale, names Queen Caroline in its inscription. Perhaps modesty precluded reference to a 'place at court' on others' ex-libris, or contrariwise a feeling of certainty that their station was known to all. One realizes, however, what a fascinating record of court posts, many long since defunct or changed in title, more fully inscribed ex-libris could have provided.

The annals of the Royal family are inevitably records both of their service and that of those who served them, often beyond the strict bounds of the court. Collectors who investigate bookplate ownership are often led on to biographical concerns. It can be an absorbing pursuit, and the writer has found that not infrequently a bookplate recalls an anecdote relating to the Royal family. A couple

POB DAWNE   O DDUW

The R.ᵗ Hon.ᵇˡᵉ Henrietta Louisa Jeffreys, Countess of Pomfret,
Lady of the Bed-chamber to QUEEN CAROLINE

Samuel Wale's bookplate for the Countess of Pomfret

of instances spring to mind. The modest eared-shield armorial for the Revd William Gunn of Smallburgh, Norfolk (Franks Coll.13070) might easily pass unnoticed. Yet Gunn it was who, in 1793, whilst acting as chaplain in Rome, accompanied Prince Augustus Frederick (later Duke of Sussex) to a hotel and there, with no other witnesses, performed a ceremony of marriage between the Prince and Lady Augusta Murray. The Dean of Arches in 1794 dismissed Gunn's performance as 'a show and effigy of marriage', but the Duke was truly grateful to Gunn and made him his senior chaplain. An attractive anonymous allegorical bookplate for Majendie by William Henshaw of Cambridge (Franks Coll.19536) surely belonged to Henry William Majendie, who was at Christ's College from 1771. His father instructed Queen Charlotte in the English language and was sometime tutor to the Prince of Wales and the Duke of York. Majendie's first Royal appointment was somewhat more curious for a clergyman. King George III decided that his thirteen-year-old son Prince William (later King William IV), who was to begin a naval career, needed a classical tutor to accompany him on his voyages. The Revd Henry Majendie was chosen, and was made 'Midshipman'. Very odd the Prince's shipmates must have thought it, but the tutor flourished and later became Bishop of Chester and Bangor.

A heraldic way of acknowledging singular Royal service is by an augmentation of honour. A notable example of this is the arms of Lane, formerly of King's Bromley.

Colonel John Lane was instrumental in saving King Charles II after the Battle of Worcester. He received him at his seat at Bentley, and the Prince was taken in disguise by Miss Lane to Abbot's Leigh, and thence to Trent. For these signal services, as explained in Burke's *Landed Gentry*, 'the family was dignified with an especial badge of honour, viz., the Arms of England in a canton, in augmentation of its paternal coat, and a crest, a strawberry roan horse, bearing between its forelegs the Royal crown.' Two more modern instances, arising from medical services to King Edward VII, may be cited, but these include only elements of the Royal arms. Sir William Gull attended the King as Prince of Wales in 1871 during an attack of typhoid, and was created a baronet the following year with, as augmentation to his arms, a canton ermine thereon an ostrich feather argent quilled or, enfiled by the gold coronet which encircles the badge or plume of the Prince of Wales. A crest of augmentation was also granted: a lion passant guardant or (i.e. a lion of England), supporting with the dexter paw an escutcheon azure thereon an ostrich feather argent quilled or enfiled with a like coronet. No bookplate for Sir William has been seen, but the ex-libris of his son, Sir William Cameron Gull, beautifully depicts the augmentation of honour. Finally there is Sir Frederick Treves, Bart., who was Surgeon to the Royal Family. He it was who performed the operation on King Edward VII when he developed appendicitis just before his Coronation. Treves was created a baronet the same year, and was given as augmentation of honour to

THE REVᴰ Wᵐ GUNN, B.D.

SMALLBURGH, NORFOLK.

DELECTANT DOMI; NON IMPEDIUNT FORIS.

The bookplates of the Revds. William Gunn and Henry William Majendie

his arms a lion of the Royal arms. His home, Thatched House Lodge in Richmond Park, is now of course a Royal residence, for it is the home of Princess Alexandra and Sir Angus Oglivy.

The reader who studies the character of the Royal ex-libris in this book will observe that their users required of them first and foremost that they be serviceable. Few of them, apart from the four series for the Royal Library at Windsor and others engraved by Stephen Gooden and J. A. C. Harrison, are outstanding in the ambition of their design and the quality of their engraving. The three bookplates for the Teck family are superbly engraved and yet modest in composition. Throughout two hundred years our Royalty has tended to use just such bookplates as other people; and it is evident that they have not often felt it necessary to make undue display. If you were no less than second in line to the throne, as was Princess Charlotte as the only child of the Prince Regent, 'C P' with a coronet above would suffice (37). The Princess was not, in any case, given to grandeur. One could cite numerous instances of 'under playing' or modesty in the ex-libris before us. Doubtless the pure simplicity of Queen Victoria and Prince Albert's Balmoral bookplate (154) reflects the feelings they had for the place: it was a loved retreat, where they could be themselves and indulge in an unhedged life after the formal life at court. A similar lack of ostentation marks the Queen's later Balmoral ex-libris (155) and one for Osborne (134). Whilst formal splendour suited the Royal Library at Windsor, King George V chose the simplest of G. W. Eve's cypher plates (96) to adorn his personal books. A study of ex-libris of Europe's Royal families reveals the same tendency. Most of the more flamboyant plates encountered were made as gifts rather than commissioned – and nothing could be more modest than most bookplates which members of the Romanov dynasty used – despite the vast populace and territories over which they held sway.

A very considerable number of artists and engravers made Royal bookplates; and clearly ex-libris were generally ordered without fuss as required, from sources known to be capable of providing what was wanted. There were plenty of London engravers to choose from in the eighteenth and nineteenth centuries, and in the latter heraldic stationers abounded. The Royal family could choose from these or other sources. One has only to study, for instance, a book like *Louisa Lady in Waiting*, compiled and edited by Elizabeth Longford, 1979, to see the regular demands made on engravers, printers and lithographers for the supply of menus, invitation cards, concert programmes and the like. Seating plans for Royal banquets, the disposition of the Royal family and their attendants on railway journeys, and much else were needed with great regularity; and bookplates would on occasion be amongst the requirements.

Grouping ex-libris by style or artist is informative. There are few stylistic innovations worth remarking, but whilst King George III (75–77) and King William IV (169–170) were content to conform unambitiously to contemporary taste, King George IV was imaginative and innovative in commissioning bookplates in different sizes for Carlton House Library (80–83) and for the Royal Library (84–86), the latter series being very handsome. Queen Victoria and all successive monarchs have also opted for plates in three sizes for Windsor. Prince Albert's clever idea was to adopt ex-libris in different colours for classification (4 and 154). The competent but uninspired armorials, generally termed die-sinkers, for Prince George of Cambridge (87), King Edward VII as Prince of Wales (49), Prince Leopold (111), Prince Arthur (22) and King George V as Duke of York (88) were engraved over a period of about forty years and have kinship of style and manner. These are virtually the last Royal bookplates conforming to stereotyped tradition, for in the present century members of the Royal family have preferred individuality and distinctive character in the design of their ex-libris.

On the question of calling on established engravers or firms, it is likely that the Duchess of Teck had seen C. W. Sherborn's acclaimed bookplates in friends' libraries, and that her admiration led to his being commissioned by her, her daughter, and later the Duke. Probably for similar reasons the Battenbergs went to Acheson Batchelor of Margaret Street, who produced armorials which were equally worthy; but when Earl Mountbatten of Burma wanted a new bookplate after 1947 (116), Batchelor had retired and he employed a Bond Street stationer. That they called on the fine engraver George Taylor Friend was not known to the Earl for years; but engravers used by stationers were expected to remain anonymous. Eve's success with the Royal Library plates for Queen Victoria (156–158) led to his being called on to make invitations to the two following coronations, and the Prince of Wales's investiture in 1911, as well as the Windsor bookplates for King George V (91–93). (King Edward VII so liked his mother's series of Windsor plates that he had them re-etched with his cypher.)

In the period around the turn of the century members of the Royal family, like the nobility and others, went to the West End stationers J. & E. Bumpus and Truslove & Hanson for personal ex-libris; but – since, as noted above, the engravers called on always remained anonymous – it is unlikely they ever knew that J. A. C. Harrison engraved most of them until 1908, after which Robert Osmond succeeded him. Even here the groupings are interesting. Queen Alexandra, her daughters, her son and her daughter-in-law and the Duchess of Connaught went to Messrs Bumpus, whilst Princess Christian and her daughters sought out Truslove and Hanson. The series of gift ex-libris presented to the Royal family by the Australian Ex Libris Society is, frankly, of peripheral interest, for it is unlikely that they were ever used, although the acceptance of them both merits their inclusion here and indicates their owners' welcoming of such tokens from their antipodean subjects.

Apart from the recourse to engravers and stationers evidenced in the catalogue, two bookplate makers must be singled out as of note. One was Prince Louis of Battenberg, later 1st Marquess of Milford Haven, the only Royal personage known to have designed ex-libris included here (Queen Alexandra's claim to have 'designed' her ex-libris probably implied no more than detailing inclusions, the composition's arrangement being finalized by Scott and the engravers Syson and Harrison).

Prince Louis, who was most artistic, designed eight Royal bookplates, and possibly more. They are his own 'Royal Navy' plate (114), an armorial for his wife, Princess Victoria (162), an armorial for his son, George, as Earl of Medina (97), an octagonal armorial for his sister-in-law, Princess Beatrice (30), a lozenge with coronet and supporters for his sister-in-law, Princess Irene of Prussia (176), a quatrefoil composition for her husband, Prince Heinrich (175), a diamond-shaped plate for their son, Prince Waldemar, and a triangular design for his sister-in-law, Princess Anna of Montenegro, the last showing the arms of Battenberg and Montenegro on shields leaning left and right. The six illustrated here reveal the assurance, dignity and balance of his work, and the success with which he exploited shapes alternative to the rectangle – which has largely dominated bookplate design. He also saw the attractiveness of printing in colour, for his own plate is in brown and Prince Heinrich's and Princess Anna's occur in blue.

The second artist for mention is Lord Badeley (see 11). Though he was an amateur engraver and his work is of variable quality, his 220 bookplates include examples for Queen Mary (129), Queen Ingrid of Denmark, Princess Helena Victoria (165), Princess Beatrice (31), and Princess Alice, Duchess of Gloucester (21). Doubtless these were commissioned as a result of his long friendship with Queen Mary.

A tendency to encourage love of books by having bookplates made for princes and princesses as minors is also worthy of note. The earliest example is the joint ex-libris for the Prince of Wales – later King George IV – and his brother Prince Frederick, Bishop of Osnabrugh, bearing the date on which they began their formal studies in 1771 (78). They were then 8 and 7 years old respectively. A subsequent plate (79) was used later on in their education. The book labels of Queen Victoria as Princess (144 and 145) are most modest in composition and probably date from her years of study under her preceptor, the Revd George Davys, and numerous tutors. In 1904 ex-libris were engraved for the Princes Edward and Albert – later King Edward VIII and King George VI – when they were not more than 10 and 9 years old (58 and 99). Moreover, their sister Princess Mary was no more than 13 when the same design was copied for her by Robert Osmond (130) after J. A. C. Harrison's plates for her brothers. The much more recent bookplate for the little Welsh cottage in the grounds of the Royal Lodge, which Queen Elizabeth II and Princess Margaret enjoyed as children, must lie beyond the scope of this work. Reference has already been made to the ex-libris for Princess Alice (20), later Countess of Athlone, engraved when she was 12 or 13 years of age. It deserves at least a word on account of its long service. Apart from Princess Mary and Princess Alice, the childhood users of bookplates mentioned above all had others in later years; and one wonders how many people have lived to enjoy books bearing an ex-libris engraved for them practically eighty-five years earlier.

To make the text as comprehensive and useful as possible the catalogue has been divided into five parts. The first and principal of these comprises British Royal ex-libris as earlier defined, together with a handful of interesting 'association' items, such as the plate for the Royal Yacht *Victoria and Albert* (138) and several for Chapels Royal or 'Royal Peculiars'. Next follow a handful of bookplates of grandchildren of Queen Victoria of, or married into, European Royal houses. The third section shows bookplates of families closely related by marriage but not themselves Royal. This again is, understandably, a very small group, for it was customary during most of the period this study encompasses for princes and princesses to marry only into Royal houses. Indeed, there was no instance approved by the monarch contrary to this between the marriage of Henry VIII's sister to Charles Brandon, Duke of Suffolk and the marriage of Queen Victoria's daughter, Princess Louise, to the Marquess of Lorne in 1871; nor were there many other instances before 1952.

The fourth classification comprises the ex-libris of non-Royal but immediate illegitimate descendants of King Charles II and King James II. Joined with these are book-plates relating to later marriages in contravention of the Royal Marriages Act, 1772; and sons- and daughters-'in-law' — a not entirely apt term — are included. Finally, shown much reduced in size, is a group of armorials and pictorial plates of questionable authenticity or in earlier writings wrongly recorded as bookplates which have not been mentioned elsewhere in the text. In the light of the problems of ascription already referred to, it seemed that negative confirmation or a statement of doubt was to be preferred to the leaving of questions unanswered. In other words, the aim has been, wherever possible, to provide an answer to the question so often posed in correspondence: 'Is this a Royal bookplate?' Doubt will inevitably remain in respect of several armorial and pictorial plates; a small number of genuine bookplates may have eluded discovery; but if this book answers most of the questions which arise about the ownership of Royal bookplates it will have served its purpose.

The Royal Arms of Great Britain since 1603

In order to avoid undue repetition of the changes undergone by the Royal arms since 1603, the major alterations to them are detailed below:

1603–1689

The Royal arms were Quarterly, 1st and 4th, quarterly I and IV, Azure, three fleurs de lys or (France modern); II and III, Gules, three lions passant guardant or (England); 2nd, Or, a lion rampant within a double tressure flory counterflory gules (Scotland); 3rd, Azure, a harp or, stringed argent (Ireland).

1689–1702

On the accession of King William and Queen Mary, the lion of Nassau (Azure, billetty and a lion rampant or) was added in pretence. Their impaled arms as joint rulers need not concern us here.

1702–1707

Queen Anne returned to the use of the Stuart arms above (1603–1689) but with the motto which Queen Elizabeth I had used 'Semper Eadem'.

1707–1714

The Union with Scotland led to a rearrangement of the Royal arms, with the arms of France for the first time since the reign of King Edward III relegated to the second quarter. The blazon became: Quarterly, 1st and 4th, Per pale, dexter, Gules, three lions passant guardant or (England); sinister, Or a lion rampant within a double tressure flory counterflory gules (Scotland); 2nd, France; 3rd, Ireland.

1714–1800

The arms of the Elector of Hanover were added at the accession of King George I, and this was effected by dropping the fourth quarter (a repeat of the first) and replacing it with a simplified version of the Hanoverian coat. The Royal arms thus became: Quarterly, 1st, Per pale, England and Scotland; 2nd, France; 3rd, Ireland; 4th, Tierced per pale and per chevron, I, Gules, two lions passant guardant or (Brunswick); II, Or, semée of hearts gules, a lion rampant azure (Luneburg); III, Gules, a horse courant argent (Hanover); on an inescutcheon, Gules, the crown of Charlemagne proper (Arch-Treasurer of the Holy Roman Empire).

1801–1837

The arms of France were dropped, having become anachronistic as a result of the Revolution. The Royal arms thus became: Quarterly, 1st and 4th, England; 2nd, Scotland; 3rd, Ireland; overall, ensigned by the Electoral Cap or Bonnet, an inescutcheon of Hanover (as detailed immediately above) with the Electoral inescutcheon. From 1816 the Electoral Cap was replaced by the arched Royal crown of the Kingdom of Hanover, of the type elsewhere here referred to as a 'continental crown' (see p.13). Non-sovereigns used this form without *either* the Electoral Cap/Crown (depending on date) *or* the inescutcheon on the Hanoverian inescutcheon.

1837– the present

Owing to the Salic Law Queen Victoria could not succeed to the Kingdom of Hanover, which passed to the Duke of Cumberland, eldest surviving son of King George III. The arms of Hanover were thus removed from the Royal arms, which became: Quarterly, 1st and 4th, England; 2nd, Scotland; 3rd, Ireland. So they remain to this day.

Excepting where a monarch used or uses different arms as sovereign of Scotland (and this seems to have applied only to King James I of England and VI of Scotland and all the twentieth century monarchs), the crest remains as it has throughout the period detailed above: On an Imperial crown proper, a lion statant guardant or, imperially crowned proper.

The supporters, likewise, have remained the same: Dexter, a lion guardant or, Imperially crowned proper; sinister, a unicorn argent, armed, unguled and crined or, gorged with an open crown or coronet of crosses patée and fleurs de lys alternately and attached thereto a chain reflexed over the back also or.

The Royal mark of cadency, for both sons and daughters, is the label. Since the accession of King George III these have all been argent or argent with differences. They are of three points argent for sons and daughters of the sovereign, though Princess Charlotte was in 1816 assigned a label of three points when her father was Prince Regent, and the daughters of King Edward VII were assigned labels of five points, their grandmother still being Queen at the time. Grandchildren are assigned labels of five points generally, though there are exceptions.

Note: The inescutcheon of Saxony was placed on the Royal arms for descendants of the house of Saxe-Coburg until 1917. It was then dropped as a result of anti-German feeling.

Royal crowns and coronets

The 'Imperial crown', with two arches and four crosses patée alternating with four fleurs de lys, was introduced during the reign of King Henry VIII. King Charles I had a four-arched crown; King Charles II reverted to just two intersecting arches; but the four-arched variety was also used in heraldry by all the later Stuart monarchs. In the period which is chiefly our concern here, however, it is the shape of the crown's arches which has seen change, as will be observed from the armorials illustrated. Most depictions of crowns within this period have followed roughly the shape of St Edward's crown, but the official shape for crowns from the accession of King Edward VII to the death of King George VI was based on Queen Victoria's crown as Empress of India, with crescent arch. There are inconsistencies, however, and the term 'Royal crown' is used here throughout.

Coronets, by contrast, differ in order to indicate the relationship by descent of their users to the monarchy. Detail of the types of coronet appropriate to members of the Royal family was confirmed by a Royal Warrant of 19 November 1917 as follows:

> The heir apparent shall have a coronet composed of four crosses patée and four fleurs de lys surmounted by a single arch with orb and cross.
>
> The sons and daughters of the heir apparent shall have a coronet composed of two strawberry leaves, two crosses patée and four fleurs de lys.
>
> Younger sons and daughters of the sovereign, which includes brothers and sisters of the sovereign, shall have a coronet composed of four crosses patée and four fleurs de lys.
>
> Sons and daughters of younger sons and brothers of the sovereign shall have a coronet composed of four strawberry leaves and four crosses patée.
>
> Sons and daughters of daughters of the sovereign with the style of Highness shall have a coronet composed of four strawberry leaves and four fleurs de lys.

It seems that in the period around the turn of the nineteenth century there was some divergence of opinion on the coronet of strawberry leaves alternating with crosses patée and fleurs de lys – which we now associate with the children of the heir apparent. The bookplate of Princess Sophia (141), daughter of King George III, shows this form, as do the first bookplates of her sister, Princess Elizabeth, and her niece, Princess Charlotte, daughter of the Prince Regent (the second bookplates, however, of both the latter show the coronet of a child of the sovereign, though Princess Charlotte's father was still Prince Regent). *Kearsley's Peerage*, 1796, gives this as a princess's coronet, and *Debrett*, 1806 and 1827, gives it as the Princess Royal's coronet – which would be inappropriate to all three. King George III's eldest daughter, Princess Charlotte Augusta Matilda, who became Queen of Württemberg, apparently used this coronet as Princess Royal; but none of her successors – Princess Victoria, later the Empress Frederick, Princess Louise, Duchess of Fife, and Princess Mary, Countess of Harewood – did. They used the coronet appropriate to a child of the monarch. In the catalogue illustrations it will also be noticed that the coronets on the bookplates of Princess May of Teck, later Queen Mary, and Princess Alice, later Countess of Athlone, are also incorrect, being of four crosses patée and four fleurs de lys, and therefore proper only to sons and daughters of the sovereign.

Incidentally, in heraldry the velvet cap inside the crowns and coronets is always shown as crimson, whereas in the actual crowns and coronets as worn it is purple.

A considerable number of bookplates depict continental crowns or coronets. Apart from the Russian and German Imperial crowns, which are referred to where they occur, they are of two types:

1. A two-arched crown, the circlet obscured by a deep ermine border, such as that used by the first-generation Battenbergs. In order to standardize terminology this will here be called a 'continental coronet'.
2. A four-arched crown, as used by most of the German princes, and by Spain. This will here be called a 'continental crown'.

The Prince of Wales's feathers, other badges and mottoes

Though the term 'the Prince of Wales's feathers' is familiarly used, as here, the badge of three feathers enfiled by a coronet and with a scroll inscribed 'Ich dien' (I serve) is more precisely that of the heir apparent, whether he be Prince of Wales or no. Of course, he generally is, but King Edward VI – who was never Prince of Wales – used it. The point is academic in the period encompassed by this book, for none but Princes of Wales used the badge on bookplates. For details of the badge and its usage see Chapter 6 of John Brooke-Little's *Royal Ceremonies of State*, Country Life, 1980. The other Royal badges which appear on the bookplates include the compound badge of rose and pomegranate used by King Henry VIII and Queen Catherine of Aragon (L), the white rose of York (88 and 89), and the Tudor rose of King Henry VII, in which the roses of York and Lancaster were united (GG). The Tudor rose over the 'sunburst' badge generally ascribed to King Edward III appears on Eve's largest bookplates for the Royal Library at Windsor in the reigns of Queen Victoria and King Edward VII (156 and 54). It has been suggested that the 'sunburst' actually represents 'Winds or', a pun on the Royal residence.

Of the Royal mottoes on the bookplates, 'Dieu et mon droit' (God and my right) has been used since the time of King Henry V. 'Semper eadem' (Always the same) was used by Queen Elizabeth I, and was adopted by the next Queen Regnant but one, Queen Anne. It occurs here (B). 'In defence' was used by King James I as James VI of Scotland (O). 'Je maintiendrai' (I shall maintain) was the motto of King William III (HH); 'Treu und fest' (True and faithful) of Prince Albert, the Prince Consort; and 'Ich dien' is referred to above. The princes of Battenberg used 'In te Domine spero' (In thee, O Lord, I trust), but after 1917, when they took the surname Mountbatten, they adopted 'In honour bound' – though the Marquess of Carisbrooke retained the earlier motto. The Duke of Sussex, always an individualist, used Chapter 8, verse 31 of the Epistle to the Romans, 'Si Deus pro nobis quis contra nos' (If God be with us, who can be against us?). The ancient motto of the Most Noble Order of the Garter, 'Honi soit qui mal y pense' (Evil be to him who evil thinks), founded by King Edward III about 1348, has since the time of King Henry VIII appeared encircling the arms of the Sovereign and Knights Companion of the Order. The motto of the Most Ancient and Most Noble Order of the Thistle, 'Nemo me impune lacessit' (No one provokes me with impunity) also occurs here (183), as does 'Nec aspera terrent' (Difficulties do not daunt), the motto of the Royal Guelphic Order (191 and 193).

Other mottoes which will be found in this book are as follows:

'Aequabiliter et diligenter' (By consistency and diligence). Truro.

'Auspicium melioris aevi' (A pledge of better times). St Albans.

'Caelum non animum' (Heaven not courage). Countess Waldegrave.

'Comiter se fortiter' (Courteously but firmly). Buckingham and Normanby.

'Fato non merito' (By fate not desert). FitzGeorge.

'In solo Deo salus' (Salvation is in God alone). Harewood.

'In te Domine speravi' (In thee, O Lord, have I put my trust). Strathmore.

'Ne obliviscaris' (Do not forget). Argyll.

'Nec temere nec timide' (Neither rashly nor timidly). Fitz-Clarence.

'Pax in bello' (Peace in war). Plymouth.

'Secundis dubiisque rectus' (Upright both in prosperity and in perils). Cleveland.

'Steadfast and true'. Princess Christian.

'Tenax in fide' (Steadfast in faith). Abel Smith.

'Tenax propositi' (Firm of purpose). Gibbs.

'Ung roy ung foy ung loy' (One king, one faith, one law). Harewood.

'Virtute et opera' (Virtue and service). Fife.

The Hessian and Battenberg arms

The arms of Hesse, as borne by Louis IV, Grand Duke of Hesse and by Rhine, depicted on his stallplate as a Knight of the Garter, were: Azure, a lion rampant queue fourchée barry argent and gules crowned or holding in the dexter paw a sword argent, hilt and pommel or. The supporters were: Two lions queue fourchée Royally crowned or. He was the husband of Queen Victoria's daughter Princess Alice (19), and the father of Victoria, Marchioness of Milford Haven (162), the Empress Alexandra Feodorovna of Russia (173), Ernst Ludwig, Grand Duke of Hesse and by Rhine (174), and Irene, Princess Heinrich of Prussia (176).

The Battenberg arms, granted as a result of the marriage of Louis IV's uncle, Prince Alexander of Hesse, to Julie von Hauke, were: Quarterly, 1st and 4th, Azure, a lion rampant queue fourchée barry of ten argent and gules, crowned or (Hesse), within a bordure componée of the second and third; 2nd and 3rd, Argent, two pallets sable (Battenberg); with the crests of Hesse and Battenberg and the supporters of Hesse. These arms were later modified in the grants of Milford Haven and Mountbatten of Burma.

In order to avoid unnecessary confusion in the detailing of arms here, those incorporating the bordure componée will be referred to as 'Hesse modified'. There is one detail of the arms which requires explanation: the lions' tails. In both of the instances above they are queue fourchée. However, Prince Louis of Battenberg (later Marquess of Milford Haven), husband of Victoria, Princess of Hesse and eldest son of Prince Alexander, above, was in 1917 granted a modified version of the Battenberg arms, in which the lion rampant is double queued. The heraldic distinction depends, of course, on whether the doubleness begins at the tail's root (double-queued) or higher up (queue fourchée). Study of the bookplates shown reveals a lack of uniformity on this matter in respect of the supporters and the lions of the arms themselves. The term 'double-queued' will, therefore, be used for sake of convenience whatever the depiction evidences, or indeed on occasion fails to evidence, the bookplates being mostly small and lacking in clarity. 'Double-queued' is the form given in *Burke's Peerage*, 1970, for both Milford Haven and Mountbatten.

Notes on the catalogue

Deciding the most useful way to arrange the catalogue of bookplates called for much deliberation, for no alternative is entirely satisfactory. A purely chronological sequence would readily have given insights into stylistic changes and the fluctuations of ex-libris usage. However, in a book of this size it could confuse anyone unversed in Royal genealogy. Christine Price's comment, in introducing the Winterburn Catalogue, that 'Royal bookplates, except for England, are in a fair way to become museum pieces' implies more than recognition that some of our Royal ex-libris are commonly found in collections. The fact is that more of our Royal family have used bookplates than any foreign Royal house. Of 181 worldwide examples Miss Winterburn amassed, over a hundred relate to Great Britain (see p.1).

Here, of course, the number is greater, and — since easy reference should be the primary criterion — it seemed best to order the bookplates by the Christian names of their owners. After all, most Royal ex-libris are inscribed with baptismal names or initials. Thus, for instance, all the plates of Princess Beatrice are shown in a sequence, as are those of King George IV from 1771 until the 1820s. Where, however, a name like George recurs over generations, the bookplates are placed by the year of birth of their owner. There are, inevitably, small snags even in this arrangement. King George VI was as a child known as Prince Albert, and so his first ex-libris bears an initial 'A'; and 'D Y' stands for Frederick, Duke of York. Though these must be borne with, the genealogical tables and index will help with such problems.

The genealogical tables will help both to make clear wider family relationships and, by the numbers in brackets, direct readers immediately to the bookplate or bookplates used by the individual. Though this duplicates the index's information, it has the added advantage of indicating members of the Royal family who are not known to have used ex-libris. The tables and index will guide the reader to bookplates. Wider changes of style and title are indicated in the catalogue.

The form in which individual entries are ordered is in general as follows: the inscription as it occurs on the bookplate, with fuller detailing in brackets where required; the artist's or engraver's signature, or indication that the plate is unsigned; a summary description of the arms or design; brief biographical details of the owner, or a cross-reference to them (they generally accompany his or her first ex-libris); and brief details of the engraver or artist, or a cross-reference to them. For the benefit of bookplate collectors, examples in the Franks or Viner collections are noted after the description of the design, and there, too, the rarity of some items is noted. It must, however, be understood that the latter refers to the frequency with which bookplates, in books in non-Royal private collections or loose, have been found by the author. It bears no relation, of course, to the frequency with which they may — happily and rightly — occur in the British Library, the Royal Library at Windsor, other Royal libraries or those of descendants of their owners.

All bookplates are illustrated, except where there are several states from one copper, or a copy or facsimile has been made, and in these instances minor differences are detailed in the text. Since nearly all the illustrations are actual size, dimensions are indicated only where a reduction has been necessary. The only general exceptions to this are the armorials of questionable authenticity or in the past wrongly recorded as bookplates. As these are only of peripheral interest, and yet it is useful to know what they look like, they have been shown much reduced.

'Franks Coll.', followed by a number, indicates the presence of a bookplate in the collection of Sir Augustus Wollaston Franks, bequeathed to the British Museum. In E. R. J. Gambier Howe's *Franks Bequest. Catalogue of British and American Book Plates*, British Museum, 1903–4, the Royal examples are in Volume III. 'Viner Coll.' indicates the presence of a bookplate in the collection George Heath Viner gave to the British Museum to supplement the Franks Collection. Part of this is bound and numbered, but the Royal bookplates tend to be in the boxed or unmounted section. The Perez Collection, formed by Marino Luiz Perez, a Cuban who lived for some years in London, belongs to the Book Trust (earlier the National Book League), in London. The Edith Emerson Spencer Collection, referred to several times, is now in the possession of Mr George S. Swarth. Miss Spencer, of Los Angeles, amassed *c.* seventy Royal ex-libris. Miss Louise E. Winterburn was also a Californian, and 'Winterburn

16

Coll.' refers to bookplates in her collection which now belongs to the Richard A. Gleeson Library at the University of San Francisco. References to 'Fincham' indicate that the artist or engraver is recorded in Henry W. Fincham's *Artists and Engravers of British and American Book Plates*, London, 1897. Most of the bookplates recorded here were engraved on copper, so only where recourse to other reproductive processes can be identified will the medium be stated.

The aim throughout is to provide an informative and readable text without subjecting the reader to the tedium implicit in dwelling on trivia. We know, for instance, that though heraldry is both precise and exacting there are bound to be infelicities of depiction on the bookplate's modest scale. There seems, moreover, no good reason to debate such matters as Fincham's attributions of approximate date. His book is wondrously inaccurate, though we bless him for having written it. Had the bookplates not been illustrated then full verbal descriptions would have been essential. Since they are, it is possible and advantageous to focus on what the reader will want to know, not least amongst which is something of the life of the bookplate's user. In the main part of the catalogue the names of all whose bookplates are illustrated are given in English form, but foreign parents and others mentioned are not.

BRITISH
ROYAL
BOOKPLATES

1

A R (Queen Adelaide)

Unsigned. Joined initials (for Adelaide Regina) beneath a Royal crown within a very faint single-line octagonal border. Very rare. Perez Coll. (Book Trust, London) and author's coll.

Her Highness Princess Adelheid (Adelaide) Luise Therese Caroline Amalie was born at Meiningen on 13 August 1792, the elder daughter of Georg I, Duke of Saxe-Meiningen, and Luise Eleonore, Regent of the Duchy of Saxe-Meiningen 1803–21. Her amiability commended her to Queen Charlotte, and in 1818 she was married at Kew Palace to the Duke of Clarence, later King William IV (169–170). She bore him two daughters, both of whom died in infancy. The Duke and Duchess spent the first year of their marriage in Hanover, and thereafter until he came to the throne lived at Bushey Park. Small, slight and very graceful in figure, she was musical, took great pleasure in riding, was a fine needlewoman, and dressed in a modest and quiet fashion. She was also a good linguist, and read Greek. Her undeserved unpopularity as Queen was later changed to gratitude for her generosity and good works. The Queen was also exceptionally kind to her husband's natural children by Mrs Jordan. She willed some of the books William IV had as Duke of Clarence to his natural son, Lord Frederick FitzClarence, as his ex-libris declares (193); but he was only one of over a hundred legatees. Adelaide was the first Queen Dowager since Catherine of Braganza, who took herself off to Portugal after Charles II's death. We should recall, however, that, though her health was on occasion precarious, she was only 44 when William IV died. In her widowhood she seemed to find no home which entirely suited her. From Bushey she moved in 1843 to Witley Court, near Worcester, and then moved to Cassiobury, near Watford, which she rented for three years though it disappointed her. Finally she moved to Bentley Priory, near Stanmore in Middlesex, which she rented for three years from the Marquess of Abercorn. Here she died on 2 December 1849. She was buried at St George's Chapel, Windsor. For an account of her life see Mary Hopkirk's *Queen Adelaide*, John Murray, 1946.

2

Anonymous (Prince Albert of Saxe-Coburg and Gotha)

Signed 'M BYFIELD Sc'. Armorial: within the ribbon of the Garter, the Prince's quarterly arms as granted on his marriage to Queen Victoria in 1840: 1st and 4th, the Royal arms (as borne by Queen Victoria) with over all a label of three points argent charged on the centre point with a cross gules; 2nd and 3rd, Barry of ten or and sable, a crown of rue in bend vert (Saxony); continental crown above; the Royal supporters charged on the shoulder with a label as in the arms. The smaller and unsigned armorial which follows is quite similar to and probably contemporaneous with the above, and almost certainly by the same hand. Most prints encountered are on very thin paper. Uncommon. Winterburn Coll.15.

His Highness Prince Francis Albert Augustus Charles Emmanuel was born at Schloss Rosenau near Coburg on 26 August 1819, the second son of Ernst I, Duke of Saxe-Coburg-Saalfeld and later Duke of Saxe-Coburg and Gotha, and Dorothea Luise Pauline Charlotte Friederike Auguste, only child of August, Duke of Saxe-Gotha. He was created a Royal Highness days before his marriage in 1840 in the Chapel Royal, St James's Palace, to his first cousin, Queen Victoria (144–158). She bore him four sons and five daughters. Prince Albert was enlightened and artistic; he had a head for business, and organized the 1851 Great Exhibition, the surplus profits from which went to set up the Victoria and Albert Museum. He was created Prince Consort of Great Britain and Ireland in 1857, died at Windsor Castle on 14 December 1861, and was buried at the Royal Mausoleum at Frogmore.

Mary Byfield (1795–1871) was the daughter of James Byfield. One of six children, three of whom became engravers, she was an excellent facsimile engraver and her work for the Chiswick Press is justly renowned. The same age as Whittingham, who ran the Press, she probably taught his two elder daughters to engrave on wood. She lived in Islington, and continued working into her sixties. There is an article by Judith Butler on the Byfields in *The Private Library*, Winter 1980, and it includes details of Mary and a portrait. Fincham lists four Byfield bookplates, including (151), but not this or (3).

3

Anonymous (Prince Albert)

Unsigned. In its components this is identical to the foregoing bookplate, but the arms are in an oval and the motto and base are re-ordered. For smaller books. It was almost certainly also Mary Byfield's work (see (2)). Scarce. Winterburn Coll.14.

4

PRINCE ALBERT'S LIBRARY

Unsigned. The inscription in a garter, with continental crown above. It occurs in two sizes, the larger 38mm high, and was pasted at the bottom of the spines of the Prince's books. Several dozen volumes scattered throughout the Royal Library at Windsor still bear this ex-libris, which was probably made at the same time as the Balmoral ones (154). It is printed in gold on different coloured papers, the central circle being occupied by a number in ink. The colours indicated classification, and though too few books are extant to evidence how the system worked, it seems to have been on the following lines: numbers about 100 (russet), literary ephemera and astronomy; 200–300 (pink or white), literature; 400–700 (yellow), art and architecture; 800 (blue), exploration and travel; 1,300–1,500 (pale green), history and geography; 1,600–1,700 (bright green), science; 2,100 (red), cookery and sports; 2,300 (brown), theology; and 2,600 (orange), politics and ceremonial. (A manuscript list of the Balmoral Library categories, brought to the author's attention by the bibliographer in the Royal Library shortly before this book went to press would give fuller details of the colour-coding system.) It seems quite possible that these bookplates were process-produced by Andrew Gibb of Aberdeen. Gibb's own ex-libris, a print of which is in the Butler Collection, is similar and of comparable date, with his name and address on a garter and a crown above. It is, however, printed in black on green paper and has a tiny single-line octagonal border. One bookplate by Gibb is listed by Fincham, an armorial for Aberdeen Public Library, *c.*1885, signed 'Andrew Gibb & Co. Litho. Aberdeen'; and his own bookplate gives the address 40 Victoria Road, Aberdeen. Aberdeen is little more than fifty miles from Balmoral, and it seems entirely likely that the Queen and Prince would have favoured a local man to make their little ex-libris. For a note on the probable period of usage of the 'Prince Albert's Library' bookplate, see the following.

5

PRINCE CONSORT'S LIBRARY (Prince Albert)

Unsigned. Of virtually identical composition to the foregoing. Prints in gold on dark brown are in the Royal Library at Windsor, but it is also seen in gold on red and on green papers. One might have expected this plate for the spines of books to have been used between Prince Albert's being granted the title Prince Consort in 1857 and his death in 1861, but this does not seem to have been the case. There is a ten-year sequence of *Revue des Deux Mondes* in the Library at Windsor, vols 31–94, 1861 Pt.1–1871 Pt.4 (6 parts a year). The first nineteen of these, 1861–1864 Pt. 1, have 'Prince Albert's Library' ex-libris, numbered '63' and in russet, of the smaller size (see the foregoing). From 1864 Pt. 2 onwards they have 'Prince Consort's Library' plates of the larger size (for this bookplate also occurs in two sizes), printed in gold on dark brown, also numbered '63'. The inference is that the 'Consort' type was not used until after the death of Prince Albert, and that additions to his Library continued to be made for perhaps a decade after 1861. Incidentally, his eldest son, the future King Edward VII, as Prince of Wales used a similar ex-libris on the spines of his books (48), but all prints are in dark brown.

The 'Prince Albert's Library' and 'The Prince of Wales's Library' ex-libris have been seen only in the Royal Library at Windsor. The 'Prince Consort's Library' plate is most rarely encountered in collections, as is the comparable one for Balmoral.

NB   A portrait plate in memory of Prince Albert, with the additional inscription 'Always Labouring for the GOOD of others', is No. 13 in the Winterburn Collection. Since, however, its usage as a bookplate is unascertained, it is included in the final section here (A).

6

The Prince Consort's Military Library. (Prince Albert)

Unsigned. Armorial: within the ribbon of the Garter, quarterly arms as on (2), identical in their detail and very similar in conception. It differs notably in incorporating six crests: 1. A bull's head cabossed gules armed and ringed argent, crowned or, the rim chequy gules and argent (Marck); 2. Out of a coronet or, two buffalo's horns argent, attached to the outer edges of each five branches fesswise each with three linden leaves vert (Thuringia); 3. Out of a coronet or, a pyramidal chapeau charged with the arms of Saxony ensigned by a plume of peacock's feathers proper out of a coronet also or (Saxony); 4. A bearded man in profile couped below the shoulders clothed paly argent and gules, the pointed coronet similarly paly terminating in a plume of three peacock's feathers (Meissen); 5. A demi griffin displayed or, winged sable, collared and langued gules (Julich); 6. Out of a coronet or a panache of peacock's feathers proper (Berg). Franks Coll.33222. Winterburn Coll.103. Royal Library Coll., Windsor.

7

Presented to The Prince Consort's Library By

Unsigned. Armorial: identical to the foregoing, for it is printed from the same copper or steel plate, though the inscription below has been re-engraved. A line of dots follows 'By' in order for a name to be inserted, and a print in the author's collection indicates in blue type a presentation from Lady Fortescue; so evidently the bookplate was in use and the library was added to long after the Prince's death. Like (6), this was for the Military Library. Uncommon.

8

Presented to the Boys' Library, Wellington College, by H.R.H. The Prince Consort (Prince Albert)

Unsigned. Armorial: virtually identical to the foregoing, though it is almost certainly separately engraved and not a reworking of the copper. There are a number of small differences, including the more upright letters of the motto. Very rare.

Queen Victoria and the Prince Consort were, with the Prime Minister, Lord Derby, instrumental in the foundation of Wellington College as a memorial to the 'Iron Duke'. Intended for 'the education of orphan children of indigent and meritorious officers of the army', the Prince took a close supervisory interest in its first years, and gave books to establish a library there. The College Rolls of Midsummer 1860 and 1861 record the titles of 337 volumes so given, of which *c*.200 survive.

9

Presented to the Boys' Library, Wellington College, in the name of H.R.H. The Prince Consort [Prince Albert] by The Queen

Unsigned. Armorial: identical to the above but for its amended inscription. Queen Victoria presented books in memory of the Prince Consort first in 1862, and the titles were listed in the Christmas 1862 College Roll. Amongst the Prince's original gifts was a set of bound half-yearly volumes of *The Illustrated London News* from 1842. This gift was continued by Queen Victoria and, indeed, by all succeeding sovereigns to the present. Re-engraving of the gift ex-libris has thus been further necessary five times, involving of course only the name of the donor. Later varieties read as follows:

a)   'Presented to the Boys' Library, Wellington College, in memory of H.R.H. the late Prince Consort, by King Edward VII'.
b)   As above, but 'George V' below.
c)   As above, but 'Edward VIII' below.
d)   As above, but 'George VI' below.
e)   As above, but 'Elizabeth II' below.

Prints of all of these except Queen Victoria's gift plate are unknown in bookplate collections. It is touching to think that the Prince Consort's interest in Wellington College continues to be commemorated more than a century and a quarter after his death.

10

Alexander George of Teck (later Earl of Athlone)

Signed 'S DYKE 1910'. Armorial: Per pale, dexter, Or, three stags' attires fesswise in pale points to the sinister sable (Württemburg); sinister, Or, three lions passant in pale sable, their dexter fore-paws gules (Swabia); over all an inescutcheon, Paly bendy sinister sable and or (Teck); a mullet for cadency; crest and continental coronet. Very rare. Author's coll.

His Serene Highness Prince Alexander Augustus Frederick William Alfred George was born at Kensington Palace on 14 April 1874, the third son of Francis, Duke of Teck (68) and Princess Mary Adelaide (123), second daughter of Adolphus Frederick, Duke of Cambridge. He married in 1904 at St George's Chapel, Windsor Princess Alice (20), the only daughter of Prince Leopold, Duke of Albany. She bore him two sons and a daughter, Lady May Abel Smith (133). In 1917 Prince Alexander relinquished his German titles and the qualification Serene Highness and assumed the surname Cambridge, being two days later created Earl of Athlone. He was Governor-General of South Africa 1923–31, of Canada 1940–46, and was sometime Constable of Windsor Castle, Chancellor of London University and A.D.C. to four monarchs. Lord Athlone died at Kensington Palace on 16 January 1957 and was buried at Frogmore.

There is a brief illustrated article on Miss Dyke's bookplates in *The Ex Libris Journal*, Vol. 17, 1907, pp. 162–3. She started designing them in 1901, and fifteen designed in the next six years – most of them for ladies – included four engraved by Downey and one cut on wood by W. Harcourt Hooper. The article lacks biographical details, but there are enough clues to identify this gentle amateur as Sydney Margaret Eleanor (1881–1963), the third daughter of Sir William Hart Dyke, 7th Bart., of Lullingstone Castle, Dartford, Kent. Relatives had close links with the Royal family. Her grandfather was the 7th Earl of Sandwich, Captain of the Corps of Gentlemen-at-Arms; an aunt was lady of the bedchamber to Princess Helena, and cousins had Queen Alexandra and the Kaiser as sponsors at baptism. Relations in the Marquess of Anglesey's family, including her aunt Guinevere's sisters, had similar ties. One can understand, therefore, how the bookplate came about. She probably did no engraving herself; but the above could perhaps be by Scott-Gatty, to whom she was related, and who made a number of ex-libris.

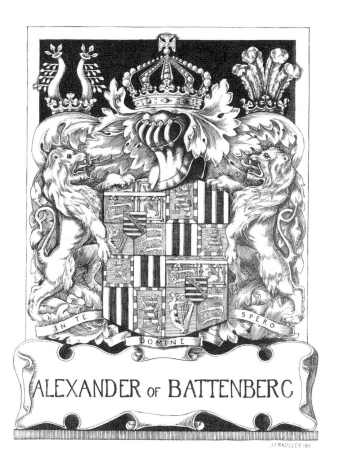

11

ALEXANDER OF BATTENBURG (later Marquess of Carisbrooke)

Signed 'J. F. Badeley 1911'. Armorial: quarterly, 1st and 4th, the Royal arms with an inescutcheon of Saxony and over all a label of three points argent the centre point charged with a heart and each of the others with a rose gules; 2nd and 3rd, quarterly I and IV, Azure, a lion rampant double-queued barry of ten argent and gules, crowned or within a bordure componée of the second and third (Hesse modified); II and III, Argent, two pallets sable (Battenberg); helm, crests (Hesse and Battenberg), motto (Battenberg) and supporters (Hesse, but uncrowned). There are two states, both uncommon:

a) With continental crown above. Author's coll.
b) With Royal coronet (four strawberry leaves and four fleurs de lys) and narrow shading introduced around the inner border at the top etc. The engraver's signature and date remain unchanged. Author's coll.

Henry John Fanshawe Badeley, 1st Baron Badeley (1874–1951) in 1897 won first place in a civil service competition for a clerkship in the Parliament Office, and he rose to occupy the position of Clerk of the Parliaments in 1934. An amateur engraver, he studied under Sir Frank Short, and he made *c.* 220 ex-libris. Several of them for members of the Royal family are illustrated here; but there was also one for Her Majesty Queen Ingrid of Denmark (daughter of King Gustaf VI Adolf of Sweden, and thus a great-grand-daughter of Queen Victoria, her mother being Princess Margaret, elder daughter of Queen Victoria's third son, Prince Arthur, Duke of Connaught and Strathearn). See also p.9.

For a note on Prince Alexander's life see (12).

12

Alexander Mountbatten First Marquess of Carisbrooke

Signed with monogram, probably 'A C K' (unidentified). Armorial: the arms are identical to those of the foregoing plate, except that the inescutcheon of Saxony no longer appears. Royal coronet, the crests as before, the lion supporters double-queued proper as before but now guardant. The bookplate occurs printed in black and in brown. Uncommon. Winterburn Coll.53 and author's coll.

His Highness Prince Alexander Albert of Battenberg was born at Windsor on 23 November 1886, the eldest son of Prince Henry of Battenberg (27–28) and Princess Beatrice (29–31), the youngest child of Queen Victoria. Educated at Wellington College, after serving in the Royal Navy he transferred to the Grenadier Guards and later became Hon. Colonel of the Isle of Wight Volunteers. In the Second World War he served in the Royal Air Force. He renounced the title of Prince of Battenberg and the qualifi-

cation Highness in 1917, when he was created Marquess of Carisbrooke etc., with the name Mountbatten. Lord Carisbrooke married in London in the same year Lady Irene Frances Adza Denison, only daughter of the 2nd Earl of Londesborough, by whom he had one daughter, Lady Iris Victoria Beatrice Grace Mountbatten. He died in London on 23 February 1960 and was buried at Whippingham.

NB   The coronet here – four strawberry leaves and four fleurs de lys – is the only example illustrated of the coronet appropriate to sons and daughters of daughters of the sovereign with the style of Highness. It occurs, however, on the two later states of Princess Helena Victoria's plate (165). She, however, retained the title Highness, whereas Alexander relinquished it in 1917.

13

A (Queen Alexandra, as Princess of Wales)

Signed 'DESIGNED BY KERBY & CO. OXFORD STREET'. Initial under two oval armorials: dexter, the Royal arms with the Prince of Wales's label in the Garter; sinister, in a decorative oval the arms of Denmark: A cross patée throughout argent fimbriated gules (Dannebrog) between 1st, Or, semée of hearts gules, three lions passant azure crowned or (Denmark); 2nd, Or, two lions passant azure (Schleswig); 3rd, Per fess, in chief, Azure, three crowns or (Sweden); and in base Per pale, dexter, Gules, a stock fish erect argent, crowned or (Iceland); sinister, per fess, in chief, Azure, a ram or (Faroes); in base, Azure, a polar bear sejant rampant argent (Greenland); 4th, Per fess, in chief, Kingdom of the Goths and in base, Kingdom of the Vandals. On an inescutcheon quarterly, I Holstein; II Stormarn; III Ditmarsken; IV Lauenburg; and over all an inescutcheon Oldenburg impaling Delmenhorst. Prince of Wales's coronet and badge with Royal crest above, in a rectangle with diaper ornament. Royal Library Coll., Windsor.

14

A virtually identical version, a little more strongly engraved, signed 'HATCHARDS. PICCADILLY' (see below). Royal Library Coll., Windsor. Her Royal Highness Princess Alexandra Caroline Marie Charlotte Louise Julie was born at Copenhagen on 1 December 1844, the eldest daughter of the future King Christian IX of Denmark, and Louise, third daughter of Landgrave Wilhelm of Hesse-Cassel and Princess Charlotte of Denmark. In 1863 her father ascended the throne, only months after Princess Alexandra married at St George's Chapel, Windsor, Albert Edward, Prince of Wales, who became King Edward VII in 1901 (48–57). They had three sons and three daughters. Her Majesty was made a Lady of the Garter in 1901, the first female appointment since 1488. A loved Queen and mother, and of remarkable beauty, she devoted herself largely to charitable work in widowhood and lived much at Sandringham. She died there on 20 November 1925 and was buried in St George's Chapel, Windsor.

Kerbys were over forty years in Oxford Street, for John Kerby & Son were booksellers and general stationers at No. 190 by 1856. Between 1869 and 1872 Endean became partner there, and they became publishers and printers etc. From 1883 only Kerby & Co. are recorded at No. 440, where they remained until the last years of the century. Fincham records no bookplates by them, but an 1873 memorial crest bookplate (J. W. Ayre) is signed 'Kerby & Endean', and doubtless like other big stationers of the time they provided ex-libris. The Princess's earlier plate cannot have been made before 1882. The famous, long-established booksellers, Hatchards of Piccadilly, must have been asked to copy the plate later. They were founded by John Hatchard in 1797, and were booksellers to Queen Charlotte and others of the Royal family.

15

ALEXANDRA (Queen, as Princess of Wales)

Signed 'W P B(arrett)', and thus commissioned from Messrs J. & E. Bumpus of London. It was designed by Scott and engraved partly by Syson and partly by Harrison. Pictorial. Winterburn Coll.20.

The subject of this bookplate is described in *The Ex Libris Journal*, Vol. 14, 1904, p. 108 and in Sir Frederick Ponsonby's *Recollections of Three Reigns*, 1951, in the chapter headed 'Life on the Royal Yacht', p. 143. Sir Frederick told how,

> After dinner the Queen took me down and showed me her cabin, which was lovely and not in the least like a cabin, but more like a drawing room. It was painted white and panelled with bookcases, with a boudoir grand piano and very comfortable armchairs around what looked like a fireplace. She was in great form and full of jokes. She showed me with pride her bookplate which she had designed herself. On it were her favourite books, her favourite music, her favourite dogs, a picture of Windsor, a picture of the Palace at Copenhagen, and a little strip of music, the first bars of her favourite song; a most elaborate bookplate, and she said she had been told it would be quite impossible to have so many different things portrayed, yet there it was.

The lines of music are the opening bars of Gounod's 'Romeo and Juliet'; the spaniels were called Billie and Punchie and the borzoi Alix; the favourite writers include Shakespeare, Shelley and 'John Inglesant'; and the composers represented by books are Brahms, Gade, Rubenstein, Schumann and Wagner.

The initials 'W P B', which occur on this and hundreds of bookplates including others for the Royal family, are those of William Phillips Barrett (1861–1938). A New Zealander, born at Christchurch, the son of a hotel keeper, he worked for Messrs J. & E. Bumpus from the early 1890s, and was responsible for the bookplate orders. Ex-libris consequently bore his initials and not those of their engravers. Indeed, engravers called on by West End stationers for bookplates in this period and since by tradition remained anonymous. Until 1908 Barrett added 'Inv' (for Invenit) to his initials — which had rankled much with Harrison over the years, and Barrett's loss of his services that year probably led to 'Inv' being dropped. Nothing is known of Scott, who designed many Bumpus ex-libris. John Edward Syson, engraver, was at 4A St Paul's Churchyard, London, EC in 1891. In 1893 he was at 22 Coleman Street, and in 1895 at 1 Bow Churchyard. By 1897, when he described himself as a heraldic engraver, he was at 22 Furnivall Street, but by 1906 had moved to 6 Greville Street, and to 50 Bow Lane in 1909. John Augustus Charles Harrison (1872–1955) was an outstanding engraver of postage stamps and banknotes. For many years chief portrait engraver for Waterlows, he made over 350 bookplates of high quality. Eight Royal plates of his engraving are shown here, and he also made an ex-libris for the Grand Duke Michael of Russia. There is a monograph on his work by the present writer, *J. A. C. Harrison Artist & Engraver*, The Bookplate Society & Forlaget Exlibristen, 1983. After 1908 Robert Osmond (see 64) became the engraver Messrs Bumpus principally called on.

The bookplate shown below with the monogram 'A H', for Alexandra House, Kensington Gore, dated 1884 on the central ribbon, is interesting for incorporating a portrait of Queen Alexandra as Princess. She laid the foundation stone in that year, and was the first Royal President of this residence for women students of the Royal Colleges of Music, Art and Science. This ex-libris is No. 19 in the Winterburn Collection, and is illustrated in Christine Price's *Catalogue of Royal Bookplates from the Louise E. Winterburn Collection*, 1944; but since it is not a Royal bookplate it is not catalogued separately here.

16

Anonymous (Prince Alfred, Duke of Edinburgh)

Unsigned. Armorial: the Royal arms with an inescutcheon of Saxony, and overall a label of three points argent charged on the centre point with a cross gules and on each of the others with an anchor azure, within the ribbon of the Garter; coronet above. This bookplate was engraved between 1863 (when he became a Knight of the Garter) and 1893 (when he became Duke of Saxe-Coburg and Gotha), and differs from others of its period for Royal princes, full armorials with supporters being favoured. Very rare. Franks Coll.33227.

His Royal Highness Prince Alfred Ernest Albert was born at Windsor Castle on 6 August 1844, the second son of Queen Victoria (144–158) and Prince Albert of Saxe-Coburg and Gotha (2–9). He entered the navy as a boy; and in 1862 was elected King of Greece, but refused the crown on political grounds. He continued to pursue his naval career, rising to Admiral of the Fleet in 1893.

Created Duke of Edinburgh in 1866, two years later there was an attempt on his life when he was visiting Australia (see 17). The Duke married at St Petersburg in 1874 the Grand Duchess Marie Alexandrovna, second daughter of Tsar Alexander II of Russia, and they made their home at Clarence House. A son and five daughters were born of the marriage, but the son, Prince Alfred, predeceased his father. The bookplate of the second daughter, Princess Victoria Melita, as Grand Duchess of Hesse and by Rhine is (179). In 1893 Prince Alfred succeeded his uncle, Ernst II (brother of the Prince Consort) as reigning Duke of Saxe-Coburg and Gotha. He was less outgoing than his brothers, but won the respect of the people of his Duchy. The Duke died suddenly at Schloss Rosenau on 30 July 1900 and was buried at Coburg. His successor as reigning Duke was his nephew, Charles Edward, Duke of Albany (34).

17

The Donation of H.R.H. The Duke of Edinburgh, to the SYDNEY SAILORS HOME. Sydney, March 12, 1868. (Prince Alfred)

Unsigned. Engraved label with coronet above. Very rare. Author's coll.

Unusual in being precisely dated, this ex-libris is of singular interest on account of the date it records. Prince Alfred entered the navy as a boy and travelled much of the world. In January 1867 he commissioned the *Galatea* and journeyed to Rio de Janeiro, the Cape, Adelaide, Melbourne, Tasmania and Sydney. At the last of these an attempt was made on his life. On Thursday 12 March 1868 the Duke attended a public picnic at Clontarf, on the shore of the Middle Harbour at Port Jackson, in aid of the Sailors' Home. Tickets were £1 and 10 s., and about 1,500 people were present, having travelled from Sydney and its environs by water. His Royal Highness and his party arrived in the steamer *Fairy* about 2.15pm. They were met by the President, Sir W. Manning, the Chief Justice, and others; they had lunch, after which they went out, the Prince intending to present a cheque for the Institution to Manning. At this point an Irishman named O'Farrell shot him from a position four to six feet behind him. The first bullet wounded him, a second misfired, and a third was deflected by the efforts of a Sydney coachman named Vail. The Prince, who showed great self-possession, was taken to Government House, where the bullet was removed two days later. O'Farrell was tried, convicted and executed. In a very short time £10,000 was subscribed towards erecting the Prince Alfred Hospital at Sydney, as a memorial of the Prince's escape.

It is unlikely the bookplate was presented with a gift of books on the day of the picnic, for the event had once been postponed due to weather and twice for the religious observances of Jews and Roman Catholics who wanted to attend; but it records the Prince's generosity and that day's events. Interest in bookplates later became strong enough for the Australian Ex Libris Society to be formed in 1923. Percy Neville Barnett, whose *Australian Book-plates and book-plates of interest to Australia* appeared in 1950, wrote extensively on bookplates. He was not, however, aware of this plate.

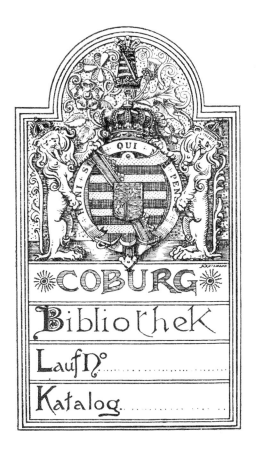

18

COBURG Bibliothek (Prince Alfred, as reigning Duke of Saxe-Coburg and Gotha)

Signed 'A Z Bilmann'. Armorial: Within the ribbon of the Garter, Barry of ten or and sable, a crown of rue in bend vert (Saxony) with over all the Royal arms differenced by the Prince's label (see 16) on an inescutcheon; crest of Saxony (see 6), supporters of same (Two lions reguardant crowned or) and continental crown. It occurs printed in black with the floral ornament and lettering in green, blue or red, and was probably made soon after 1893. Leiningen-Westerburg, in *German Book-plates*, 1901, p. 452, indicates that it also occurs with variant arms, but what they are is not evident. As Duke he elsewhere used the same arms as his predecessors: Quarterly of twenty-three: 1st, Julich; 2nd, Cleves; 3rd, Berg; 4th, Brehna; 5th, Westphalia; 6th, Coburg; 7th, Landgravate of Thuringia; 8th, Meissen; 9th, Roenhild and Hennenberg; 10th, Lichtemberg; 11th, Palatinate of Saxony; 12th, Palatinate of Thuringia; 13th, Landsberg; 14th, Engern; 15th, Orlamunde; 16th, Pleissen; 17th, Altenburg; 18th, Eisenberg; 19th,

Marck; 20th, Ravensberg; 21st, Sovereign rights; 22nd, Tonna; 23rd, Ravenstein; over all an inescutcheon of Saxony. The crests would be the same as those on the Military Library plate of Prince Albert (6), who bore the same arms as his elder brother Ernst II, whom Prince Alfred succeeded. Uncommon. Author's coll.

On becoming reigning Duke, after the death of his uncle and the renunciation of the Prince of Wales, the question of His Royal Highness's privileges as an English peer etc., was raised. It was understood that he would no longer sit in the Lords, but he was allowed to remain Admiral of the Fleet. Despite misgivings in Germany, he proved a popular ruler, very adaptable, cultured, concerned for agriculture and industry, and a good sportsman. The bookplate of his nephew, Prince Charles Edward, Duke of Albany, who succeeded him as reigning Duke, is heraldically simpler and lacks British characteristics (34).

19

ALICE (Princess, later Grand Duchess of Hesse and by Rhine)

Signed: 'C:A:FERRIER Sc.' Pictorial lozenge engraved on wood in two blocks and printed in black with the background in red; the name on a ribbon at centre, with Royal coronet above and rose, thistle and shamrock around the ribbon. It is listed by Fincham and referred to in *The Ex Libris Journal*, Vol. 6, 1896, p. 107, having been included in the Society's Fifth Annual Exhibition. Very rare. Author's coll.

Her Royal Highness Princess Alice Maud Mary was born at Buckingham Palace on 25 April 1843, the second daughter of Queen Victoria (144–158) and Prince Albert of Saxe-Coburg and Gotha (2–9). She married at Osborne House, Isle of Wight, on 1 July 1862, as his first wife, Ludwig IV, Grand Duke of Hesse and by Rhine 1877–92. There were two sons and five daughters of the marriage: Victoria, later Marchioness of Milford Haven (162); Elizabeth, later Grand Duchess Serge of Russia; Irene, later Princess Heinrich of Prussia (176); Ernst Ludwig, later Grand Duke of Hesse and by Rhine (174); Friedrich, who died as a child of haemophilia, as the result of a fall; Alix, later Empress of Russia (173); and Marie, who died as a child of diphtheria in 1878. Virtually the whole family were ill with it, and the Grand Duchess succumbed as a result of kissing her son Ernst in his distress on being told of his sister's death. The Grand Duchess died on 14 December 1878. Her burial was at Rosenhöhe. Perhaps the most outstanding of Queen Victoria's children, Alice was accomplished, very attractive, an advanced thinker and a born nurse. She nursed her dying father, probably saved her mother from breakdown after his death, and her works in Hesse were almost as celebrated as those of Florence Nightingale elsewhere. Indeed, she consulted her. Concerned also with education, housing, the role of women, and the care of orphans and the insane, she tired herself out for others' good – as her saintly daughter, Elizabeth, was to do in Russia a generation later.

For a note on Charles Anderson Ferrier see (153). Though only his name is on the plate, it was commissioned from James West, probably at about the same time (1860) that he was asked to supply designs for ex-libris in three sizes for the Royal Library at Windsor (151–153). In 1953 Sir Owen Morshead purchased for the Royal Library an album of West's bookplates and designs, and therein are several preliminary contrasting designs for Princess Alice's ex-libris.

20

ALICE MARY VICTORIA AUGUSTA PAULINE (Princess Alice, later Countess of Athlone)

Unsigned, but ascribed to Culleton. Armorial: the Royal arms with over all an inescutcheon of Saxony, but no label (Princess Alice was not assigned one until 1934). There are four varieties of colour: black, red–brown, orange–brown and very pale brown, the first and last having a single line rectangular border. It was listed in 1896 in an article by J. Carlton Stitt on English ladies' armorial bookplates in *The Ex Libris Journal*, Vol. 6, p. 103. Numerous books bearing the bookplate were in the saleroom and bookshops after the Princess's death. For a note on the coronet see p. 13. Winterburn Coll.39.

Her Royal Highness Princess Alice was born at Windsor Castle on 25 February 1883, the only daughter of Prince Leopold, Duke of Albany (111–112) and Princess Helen, third daughter of Georg Viktor, Prince of Waldeck and Pyrmont. As a child she lived at Claremont (see p. 4ff), once the home of Princess Charlotte (37–38) and Prince Leopold. She married at St George's Chapel, Windsor, in 1904 Prince Alexander of Teck (brother of Queen Mary), later Earl of Athlone. There were three children of the marriage, their daughter being Lady May Abel Smith (133). Princess Alice's memoirs, *For my Grandchildren*,

1966, recall the years when her husband was Governor-General of South Africa and Canada etc., and she was Chancellor of the University of the West Indies 1950–71. The longest-lived member of the Royal family, she appeared in Tuxon's well-known painting of Queen Victoria's Golden Jubilee, and was also able to take an active part in the 1977 Silver Jubilee celebrations of our present Queen. She was also present – the widow of a great-grandson of King George III – at the christening of Peter Phillips, Queen Victoria's great-great-great-great-grandson and her own great-great-great-nephew. Princess Alice died, aged 97, at Clock House, Kensington Palace – her home for many years – on 3 January 1981 and was buried at Frogmore.

Thomas Culleton, a London heraldic stationer, had premises at 2 Long Acre by 1856, but by 1861 was at 25 Cranbourn Street. Here his firm remained until the present century, but had moved to 32 Piccadilly by 1913, two years later disappearing from London trade directories. Fincham lists thirty ex-libris by Culleton, but there were many more – signed or unsigned – from their engraving shop.

21

A (Princess Alice, Duchess of Gloucester)

Signed 'H J B(adeley) 1949'. Initial within a scrolled cartouche which supports and frames the collar of the Royal Victorian Order (Princess Alice was made G.C.V.O. in 1948); coronet above. Depiction of the collar of the Order on a bookplate is singular. Though not very clear here, the inscription reads: 'VICTORIA BRITT. REG. DEF. FID. IND. IMP.' (See (32)). Royal Library Coll., Windsor.

Her Royal Highness Princess Alice,* formerly Lady Alice Christabel Montagu-Douglas-Scott, was born at Montagu House, London on 25 December 1901, the third daughter of the 7th Duke of Buccleuch and (9th Duke of) Queensberry, and Lady Margaret Alice Bridgeman, second daughter of the 4th Earl of Bradford. Her childhood was spent in the annual round of family homes: Montagu House, Eildon Hall, Drumlanrig Castle, Dalkeith House, Bowhill and Boughton. She married in 1935 at Buckingham Palace Prince Henry, Duke of Gloucester (109–110), the third son of King George V (88–96) and Queen Mary (124–129). There were two sons of the marriage: Prince William, who was killed in an aircraft accident in 1972, and Prince Richard, the present Duke of Gloucester. Their homes were Barnwell Manor, Northamptonshire and St James's Palace. Princess Alice has always enjoyed travel and country pursuits, and writes of these and her happy family life in *The Memoirs of Princess Alice, Duchess of Gloucester*, 1983. The book also gives a lively account of their years in Australia when her husband was Governor-General, 1945–47.

For a note on Lord Badeley see (11).

---

* Normally if the wife of a Prince is not herself of Royal birth she receives the style of Royal Highness and the 'female form' of his title, but does not, however, become a Princess in her own right. Thus, for instance, 'H.R.H. Diana, Princess of Wales' is the correct form. The only official exception to this is in the case of Princess Alice.

Library

22

Anonymous (Prince Arthur, Duke of Connaught and Strathearn)

Unsigned. Armorial: within the ribbon of the Garter, the Royal arms with over all an inescutcheon of Saxony and a label of three points argent charged on the centre point with a cross gules and on each of the others with a fleur de lys azure; with coronet, Royal crest and supporters charged on the shoulder with a label as in the arms; 'Library' below. Uncommon. Royal Library Coll., Windsor.

His Royal Highness Prince Arthur William Patrick Albert was born at Buckingham Palace on 1 May 1850, the third son of Queen Victoria (144–158) and Prince Albert of Saxe-Coburg and Gotha (2–9). He was named after his godfather, the Duke of Wellington. Created Duke of Connaught and Strathearn in 1874, he was appointed Field Marshal in 1902, and was Personal A.D.C to five monarchs. He married at St George's Chapel, Windsor, in 1879 Princess Louise Margaret (118), the fourth daughter of Prince Friedrich Karl of Prussia and Maria Anna, youngest daughter of Leopold IV, Duke of Anhalt. They had one son, Prince Arthur of Connaught (who predeceased his father), and two daughters: Margaret (d.1920), who became Crown Princess of Sweden, and Lady Patricia Ramsay (135). The Duke of Connaught was Governor-General of Canada 1911–16. He died at Bagshot Park, Surrey, on 16 January 1942, and was buried at Frogmore. His books were sold from Bagshot Park soon after his death, and some of them – including a finely bound edition of Shakespeare in nine volumes edited by Alexander Dyce – bore his bookplate. He was not apparently, however, an avid bookman, for some books in the sale were still in the original boxes in which Bumpus's and others had delivered them as wedding presents sixty-three years earlier, and they still had their cards in them.

23

Anonymous (Prince Augustus Frederick, Duke of Sussex)

The Royal crest within the collar of the Garter, coronet above, a leaf-fringed cartouche with helmet and owl below for shelf-mark. There are three varieties:

a) Unsigned, with horizontal shading of the cartouche. Franks Coll.33205.
b) As above, but the shading of the cartouche either worn or, more likely, largely erased. Author's coll.
c) From a different copper, of identical composition but differing in that the cartouche is unshaded, the collar is more robust and neatly rounded, etc. Signed 'Perkins and Heath Patent Hardened Steel Plate'. Franks Coll.33204. Winterburn Coll.71.

His Royal Highness Prince Augustus Frederick was born at The Queen's House, St James's Park, on 27 January 1773, the sixth son of King George III (75–77) and Queen Charlotte (35–36). He was educated by tutors and at Göttingen University, and was created Duke of Sussex in 1801. He married first (in contravention of the Royal Marriages Act) at Rome in 1793, and later at St George's, Hanover Square, Lady Augusta Murray, second daughter of the 4th Earl of Dunmore; she assumed the surname of de Ameland by Royal Licence in 1806. The marriage was declared null and void (see p. 7) by the Prerogative Court in 1794, but he had by her two children, Sir Augustus Frederick d'Este (1794–1848) and Augusta Emma d'Este (1801–66), who married as his second wife Thomas

Wilde, 1st Baron Truro (209). Prince Augustus Frederick married secondly, in like contravention, probably at her London house in 1831, Lady Cecilia Letitia Underwood (1785–1873), widow of Sir George Buggin and daughter of the 2nd Earl of Arran. She was created Duchess of Inverness in 1840. The Duke of Sussex died at Kensington Palace on 21 April 1843 and was buried at Kensal Green Cemetery.

Amongst King George III's sons only the Duke of Sussex fully inherited his father's love of collecting books, and he had a superb library at Kensington Palace. Of its more than 50,000 volumes, almost a quarter were theological, and these were kept in the 'Divinity Room'. They included rare Hebraica and manuscripts, as well as 5,000 editions of the Bible. Some of his treasures, including manuscripts of Italian opera and Bibles, he brought back from Rome in 1806. His librarian and surgeon was Dr Thomas Joseph Pettigrew, who catalogued a portion of his library under the title *Bibliotheca Sussexiana*, 1827 and 1839. The liberal-minded and philanthropic Prince wrote comments in his books. As Roger Fulford records, in *Royal Dukes*, Duckworth, 1933:

> Much of his time was spent in his Library and, as he read, he would sketch in ink an elaborate hand pointing to any passage he thought memorable or with which he disagreed. In the British Museum is his own copy of Gladstone's *Church and State*, decorated with these pointing hands and covered with such comments as 'A most mischievous argument', or

'This is merely declamatory – no argument'. But far worse for the Duke's reputation, a gentleman bought one of his prayer-books at the sale after his death, and found the fatal pointing hand against the Athanasian Creed with the comment: 'I don't believe a word of it'.

His library was, after his death, sold by Evans of Pall Mall in six sales between July 1844 and August 1845. There were 14,107 lots and they realized a total of £19,148.

No other bookplates by Perkins & Heath are recorded. Angier March Perkins (c. 1799–1881), who was born at Newbury Park, Massachussetts, was an engineer and inventor. He came to England in 1827 and for a time helped his father Joseph perfect a method of engraving banknotes. He also introduced a method of central heating. Perkins, Bacon & Co. specialized in banknote engraving at 69 Fleet Street from 1856 to 1871.

24

Anonymous (Duke of Sussex)

Armorial: the Royal arms as borne 1801–37 without an inescutcheon in the Hanoverian inescutcheon and over all a label of three points argent charged on the centre point with two hearts in pale and on the others with a cross gules, the arms in the Garter ribbon and collar, the George depending; with coronet, Royal crest and supporters charged on the shoulder with a label as on the arms. The motto, in translation 'If God is for us, who can be against us', is draped over a bracket below which has a blank oval

for the shelf-mark. There were two varieties used (but see the following plate):

a) The letters of the motto are shaded etc. Unsigned. Franks Coll.33203. Winterburn Coll.68.
b) The motto lettering is open, the 'sun's rays' shading is lighter, etc. Signed 'Perkins and Heath Hardened Steel Plate'. Franks Coll.33202. Winterburn Coll.69.

25

Anonymous (Duke of Sussex)

Unsigned, but almost certainly by Perkins and Heath (see the foregoing). Armorial: the Royal arms as on the last, to which this composition is very similar above the motto ribbon. The wreath below is sketched in, and it is quite possible that this was a trial state for the preceding ex-libris. The only example seen is in the Perez Collection at The Book Trust in London.

Duke of Sussex. K.G.

26

Duke of Sussex. K.G.

Unsigned. Armorial: within the ribbon of the Garter, arms as above, but on a spade shield; coronet, Royal crest and supporters charged on the shoulder with a label as on the arms, but the collar of the Garter and the George are lacking. Probably engraved for another purpose, but a note in pencil with it stated that it had been removed from a book. It was perhaps used before the foregoing were engraved, for the spade shield suggests a date not much later than 1800; but it cannot be earlier than 1801 when he was created Duke of Sussex. Only one print has been seen. Author's coll.

A & C. DOWNEY.

27

FÜRSTLICH BATTENBERGSCHE BIBLIOTEK (Princely Library of Battenberg)

Unsigned, but of English engraving and probably by A. & C. Downey (see (28) below). Seal armorial: Quarterly, 1st and 4th, Azure, a lion rampant double-queued barry of ten argent and gules (should be crowned or), within a bordure componée of the second and third (Hesse modified); 2nd and 3rd, Argent, two pallets sable (Battenberg); with the crests of Hesse and Battenberg and the supporters of Hesse (but uncrowned), a continental coronet above, motto below. It is virtually the same in composition as Prince Louis of Battenberg's first bookplate (113). Rare. Author's coll.

This is surely the plate identified in *German Book-plates*, by Leiningen-Westerburg, translated by G. Ravenscroft Dennis, 1901, as 'temporarily in the possession of Prince Alexander of Battenberg, Prince of Bulgaria, Count of Hartenau', though it is not as early as the 187- date suggested there. Had it been used only by Alexander I (1857–93), who was elected Prince of Bulgaria in 1879 but abdicated in 1886, it would have lain outside the scope of this study; but he probably did not use it, for his grandson, Dr Wilhelm Hartenau, who possesses many of his books, confirms there is no ex-libris in them. It was certainly used by others of the family, however, and perhaps by Prince Henry, who is ascribed with use of the following bookplate.

28

FÜRSTLICH BATTENBERGSCHE BIBLIOTEK (Princely Library of Battenberg)

Signed 'A. & C. Downey'. Seal armorial: the arms are here single and lacking the bordure, with crests of Hesse and Battenberg and the supporters of Hesse (again uncrowned), a continental coronet above, motto below. The design of this and (113) are clearly related to the above. This is No. 52 in the Winterburn Collection, where it is attributed to Prince Henry of Battenberg, though it is stated that it was also used by others of the family. Fincham also lists it, not ascribing it in the text but to 'Prince H' in the index. The general designation of a bookplate to a princely library is, of course, not uncommon in Germany.

His Serene Highness Prince Henry Maurice was born at Milan on 5 October 1858, the third son of Prince Alexander of Hesse and Julie Therese von Hauke (who in 1858 was created Princess of Battenberg), the daughter of Johann Moritz, Count von Hauke. Known as 'Liko' in the Royal family, he fell in love with Princess Beatrice (29–31) at the marriage of Prince Louis and Princess Victoria of Hesse in 1884; but Queen Victoria did not wish to lose her youngest daughter and companion, and for months spoke not a word to her, communicating only by notes. At last, on an assurance that the couple would live with her, she relented, and they were married at Whippingham Church on the Isle of Wight in 1885. There were four children of the marriage, including the Marquess of Carisbrooke (11–12) and Princess Victoria Eugenie, later Queen of Spain (178). The Queen rejoiced in the presence of the handsome and lively Prince in the home, and from the time the marriage was imminent he had favours showered on him: he was created a Royal Highness, made a

Knight of the Garter and Privy Councillor, and was Governor and Captain of the Isle of Wight and Governor of Carisbrooke Castle. Eventually, however, he longed for activity and, having obtained the Queen's reluctant permission, set out on the Ashanti Expedition to subdue King Prempeh of Ashanti in the Gold Coast. Here he contracted fever, and was returning home, but died on board ship on 20 January 1896. He was buried at Whippingham Church.

The Downeys were for almost eighty years engravers in London, and there were two quite distinct businesses which ran for many years, as well as shorter lived individual ventures in separate premises. As they are scarcely recorded in works on bookplates, a general note of them may be useful. The earliest establishment was that of William Henry Downey, who was at 51 College Place, Camden Town, in 1861, and was joined by Henry Downey in 1866. Their names remain as proprietors of the College Place business until 1883. In 1884 Alfred and Charles Downey had taken over there, and about a year later they moved to 47 Tottenham Court Road, where they remained until 1887. The only other Downey prior to that date recorded was Thomas, who had premises at

39 Great Castle Street, Oxford Street, from *c*.1874 to 1885. The Battenberg ex-libris, above, attributed to Prince Henry, was therefore engraved 1884–87, and probably soon after his marriage in 1885. Only a couple of bookplates by Alfred and Charles Downey are recorded by Fincham. The second substantial Downey business may have been started by Thomas Downey at 2 Tudor Street in 1884. By the following year he was no longer there, but Thomas and Edward had premises at 47 Berwick Street, Soho. They were joined in 1889 by Alfred Dyer Downey (who engraved (183)), and the former also became publishers in the last years of the century. In 1901 they removed to 63 Berners Street, where Alfred Dyer Downey described himself as a heraldic engraver, and there they remained until 1915. From 1916 only Downey & Co. 'copper and steel plate and die engravers' are recorded, at 84 Great Portland Street. They moved *c.* 1934 to 187 Wardour Street, and last appear in the *Post Office London Directory* (Trades) in 1940. Alfred Dyer Downey was the father of the well-known – and presumably freelance – bookplate engraver, Alfred James Downey (1882–1944) who made well over a hundred fine ex-libris. These are recorded in the *1929 Year Book* of the American Society of Bookplate Collectors & Designers, with a checklist.

29

BEATRICE (Princess, later Princess Henry of Battenberg)

Unsigned, but Sir Augustus Franks noted that it was engraved by Edward Whymper. Armorial used before her marriage: the Royal arms with an inescutcheon of Saxony and over all a label of three points argent the centre point charged with a heart and each of the others with a rose gules; coronet above and lac-d'amour around, in a decorative rectangular frame incorporating roses, thistles and shamrock. It occurs printed in black and in a pale grey-brown, generally on a rather flimsy paper. In recent years prints have turned up, notably in volumes of French literature – perhaps from amongst the effects of Princess Alice (20), at whose home Princess Beatrice spent her last two years. Franks Coll.33231.

Her Royal Highness Princess Beatrice Mary Victoria Feodore was born at Buckingham Palace on 14 April 1857, the fifth daughter and youngest child of Queen Victoria (144–158) and Prince Albert of Saxe-Coburg and Gotha (2–9). The Queen's favourite daughter, she became her secretary and constant companion, and the Kaiser referred to her as the 'petticoat' around 'my unparalleled grand-mamma'. Though the Queen was – to say the least – reluctant that Princess Beatrice should marry (see (28)), agreement that the couple should live with her won the day; and Beatrice was married at Whippingham Church on the Isle of Wight in 1885 to Prince Henry Maurice of Battenberg (27–28), third son of Prince Alexander of Hesse and by Rhine by his morganatic wife Julie, Princess of Battenberg. The four children of the marriage included the Marquess of Carisbrooke (11–12) and Princess Victoria Eugenie, later Queen of Spain (178). Prince Henry died from fever contracted in the Ashanti Expedition, in 1896. Princess Beatrice nursed her mother in her last years, became Captain and Governor of the Isle of Wight, and wrote *A Birthday Book*, 1881, and *In Napoleonic Days*, 1941; she also translated *The Adventures of Count Albert of Erbach*, 1898, and worked much on Queen Victoria's letters and papers. She died at Brantridge Park on 26 October 1944 and was buried in the Battenberg Chapel at Whippingham.

Edward Whymper (1840–1911) was the second son of Josiah Wood Whymper and brother of the artist and illustrator Charles Whymper. In the family's flourishing London wood engraving business he illustrated many 1860s books, but was more famed for his work and writings as an alpinist. No other Whymper bookplates are recorded. This one is wood engraved.

30

BEATRICE (Princess Henry of Battenberg)

Unsigned, but designed by Prince Louis of Battenberg (113–114 & p. 9) and engraved by P. C. Baker. Armorial: six single coats all facing to the centre, clockwise from the top: Hesse modified (see below); Saxony (Barry of ten or and sable, a crown of rue in bend vert); Scotland; Battenberg (see below); Ireland; and England. Coronets surmount each coat, and the circular armorial is within a hexagonal architectural frame, with name at centre. Franks Coll.33232.

The Franks Collection Catalogue notes 'R. C. Baker sc.', so it may be that prints not cut close (most are) bear a signature; more likely Franks was given by Baker bookplates of his engraving, and simply noted the fact. The artist was, however, surely P. C. Baker, a London engraver late in the last century. Few plates signed by him are recorded, but many were evidently unsigned.

Beatrice

31

Beatrice (Princess)

Signed 'J. F. B(adeley) 1928'. Lozenge armorial: the quarterly arms of Hesse modified and Battenberg (1st and 4th, Azure, a lion rampant double-queued barry of ten, crowned, within a bordure componée argent and gules (Hesse modified); 2nd and 3rd, Argent, two pallets sable (Battenberg) impaling the Royal arms with a label for difference as detailed already (29), within a festooned Jacobean cartouche, coronet above. Winterburn Coll.51.

Lord Badeley (see (11)) had as early as 1911 engraved an ex-libris for Princess Beatrice's eldest son, Prince Alexander, later the Marquess of Carisbrooke (11).

32

CHAPEL ROYAL. SAVOY

Unsigned. Seal armorial: Argent a cross gules charged with an ostrich feather and scroll argent between in chief a sword or on the dexter a house proper or on the sinister a lion of England and in base a fleur de lys and a millrind and a chief paly of four azure and purpure thereon a holy lamb proper between two Tudor roses with Royal crowns proper. A slightly modified version of these arms now in use seems to have been introduced late in the nineteenth century. The arms are held, on the bookplate, by an eagle, with Royal crown above, and the inscription is around the inner border of the seal. Franks Coll.33830.

The Chapel Royal of the Savoy is a private Chapel of the Queen in right of her Duchy of Lancaster, and thus a Royal Peculiar, extra-provincial and extra-diocesan. King Henry IV in 1399 annexed the Manor of the Savoy and all the estates of the House of Lancaster to the Crown as a separate inheritance, and the early sixteenth-century Chapel, in Savoy Street, London, WC2, is a link with the old Manor, Palace and Chapel of the Savoy. See Robert Somerville's *The Savoy, Manor, Hospital, Chapel*, A. R. Clark, Edinburgh, 1960, for fuller information. The Queen is Lord of the Manor of the Savoy, and as a separate inheritance of the Duchy the form of the National Anthem sung at every service varies from the norm in its second line:

> God save our gracious Queen,
> Long live our noble Duke,
> God save the Queen.

Since 1937 it has also served as the Chapel of the Royal Victorian Order;* and an Ante-Chapel, Robing Room for the Queen and Royal family, and a Chaplain's Room were added in 1958. It is administered through the Chancellor and Council of the Duchy, and its ordinary Sunday and weekday services are open to the public. It is also currently open to visitors from 10am to 4pm on Tuesdays, Wednesday and Thursdays.

NB   There is also a prize book label dated 18[80] reading 'Her Majesty's Schools of the Chapel Royal, Savoy'.

* The Royal Victorian Order was instituted by Queen Victoria on 21 April 1896, and its Anniversary is celebrated on 20 June, the date upon which she ascended the throne. There are five classes, and the Order is bestowed on those who have rendered extraordinary or important or personal services to the sovereign. Foreign Princes and persons may be favoured by Honorary Membership. The collar of the Order is depicted on (21).

33

Anonymous (King Charles I, as Prince of Wales)

Unsigned. The Royal arms as borne by James I as King of England (Quarterly, 1st and 4th, quarterly I and IV: Azure, three fleurs de lys or (France); II and III, Gules, three lions passant guardant or (England); 2nd, Or, a lion rampant within a double tressure flory counterflory gules (Scotland); 3rd, Azure, a harp or, stringed argent (Ireland), with over all a label of three points argent, on a shaded ground within the ribbon of the Garter. The coronet above rightly has four crosses patée and four fleurs de lys, but it is not the normal Prince of Wales's coronet, for it lacks the arch, orb and cross. The only print seen is in the Royal Library at Windsor Castle in a copy of *Selden on Tithes*, 1618 (II 70 Gall. C), which bears the arms of King James I upon the boards. It appears, from its placing, to have been used as a bookplate by Prince Charles, and the label indicates that it was engraved after the death of his elder brother, Prince Henry, in 1612.

His Royal Highness Prince Charles was born at Dunfermline on 19 November 1600, the second son of King James VI of Scotland and I of England (O) and Queen Anne, the second daughter of King Frederick II of Denmark. He became Duke of York in 1604, the year after his father's accession to the throne of England, succeeded his brother, Prince Henry, as Duke of Cornwall and Rothesay in 1612, and was created Prince of Wales and Earl of Chester in 1616. He came to the throne as King Charles I in 1625, and married in the same year Princess Henrietta Maria, the youngest daughter of Henry IV, King of France and Navarre, and Marie de Medici. There were four sons and five daughters of the marriage, including the future King Charles II (F and G) and King James II (P and Q), but three died in infancy and four others before the age of thirty. The Civil War blighted the latter part of his reign, and he was beheaded – dying with great courage and dignity – before the Banqueting Hall in Whitehall on 30 January 1649. He was buried in St George's Chapel, Windsor.

The Charles I armorial (E) engraved by Will Marshall is No. 30 in the Winterburn Collection, in the Catalogue of which it is rightly acknowledged not to be a bookplate.

34

**Ex libris Caroli Eduardi ducis Saxoniae. Privat-Bibliothek COBURG (formerly
Prince Charles Edward, Duke of Albany)**

Unsigned. Armorial: single coat of Saxony (Barry of ten or and sable, a crown of rue in bend vert), helm and Saxony crest (see (6)), within a decorative art nouveau frame. It probably dates from *c.* 1910, and was reproduced by process. Winterburn Coll.132. Rare.

His Royal Highness Prince Leopold Charles Edward George Albert was born at Claremont House, near Esher (for an account of which see p. 4ff) on 19 July, 1884, the only son of Prince Leopold, Duke of Albany (111–112), who had died almost four months earlier, and Princess Helen, third daughter of Georg Viktor, Prince of Waldeck and Pyrmont. He was therefore 2nd Duke of Albany at his birth. Educated at Eton and Bonn University, in 1900 he succeeded his uncle Prince Alfred, Duke of Edinburgh (16–18) as Duke of Saxe-Coburg and Gotha, reigning under the Regency of Prince Hermann of Hohenlohe-Langenburg until 1905. He married in that year at Glücks-

burg Princess Victoria Adelheid, the eldest daughter of Friedrich Ferdinand, Duke of Schleswig-Holstein-Sonderburg-Glücksburg. There were three sons and two daughters of the marriage. As a result of his activities in the First World War his titles were removed from the Roll of Peers in pursuance of the Order of the King in Council in 1919; and he had already in 1915 been struck off the Roll of the Order of the Garter, to which he had been admitted in 1902. Despite his views, however, his sister, Princess Alice, Countess of Athlone (20), retained her affection for him, and visited him until his death. He was obliged to abdicate his Dukedom of Saxe-Coburg and Gotha in 1918, and died at Coburg on 6 March 1954. His uncle, Prince Alfred, had included the Royal arms on an inescutcheon on his bookplate (18), but no grant of arms was ever made to Prince Charles Edward – hence the single coat depicted on his ex-libris.

35

Anonymous (Queen Charlotte Sophia)

Unsigned. Armorial: the Royal arms as used 1714–1800, impaling the arms of Mecklenburg-Strelitz: Quarterly of six, 1st, Or, a buffalo's head cabossed sable, armed and ringed argent, crowned and langued gules (Mecklenburg); 2nd, Azure, a griffin segreant or (Principality of Wenden); 3rd, Per fess, in chief azure, a griffin segreant or, and in base vert, a bordure argent (Principality of Schwerin); 4th, Gules, a cross patée argent crowned or (Ratzeburg); 5th, Gules, a dexter arm argent issuant from clouds in sinister flank and holding a finger ring or (County of Schwerin); 6th, Or a buffalo's head sable, armed argent, crowned and langued gules (Lordship of Rostock); over all an inescutcheon, per fess gules and or (Stargard). The armorial is within a Chippendale festooned frame on a mantle with Royal crown above. Franks Coll.33186. Winterburn Coll.62. Uncommon.

Her Serene Highness Princess Charlotte Sophia (some authorities reverse the order of the names) was born at Mirow on 19 May 1744, the fifth and youngest daughter of Karl Ludwig Friedrich, Duke of Mecklenburg-Strelitz and Elizabeth Albertine, the third daughter of Ernst Friedrich I, Duke of Saxe-Hildburghausen. She lost her father in 1752, and he in any case was a younger son, so she had no great aspirations in marriage. None the less the sentiments of a letter she sent to Frederick the Great of Prussia came to the notice of King George III's mother, who showed it to him – and shortly Princess Charlotte was leaving for England to become Queen. She married King George III (75–77) at St James's Palace on 8 September 1761, and she bore him nine sons and six daughters, including the future Kings George IV (78–86) and William IV (169–170). An excellent, unpolitical and domestic consort, Queen Charlotte was an invalid in her later years, and predeceased the King, dying at Kew Palace on 17 November 1818. She was buried at St George's Chapel, Windsor. See (36) for comment on her love of books.

The above bookplate occurs in two works in the Royal Library at Windsor Castle: Catherine Jemmat, *Miscellanies in Prose and Verse*, 1766; and a manuscript account of St Katherine's Hospital.

36

S (Queen Charlotte Sophia)

Unsigned. Initial on a shaded ground within a beaded oval, Royal crown above. Franks Coll.33185. Winterburn Coll.61.

The style of this ex-libris, with its beaded oval, indicates that it was engraved some years later than the foregoing; and its initial suggests that the Queen was known as Sophia within her family. The design's modesty is not surprising in view of her life of unfeigned domesticity. This, together with her recognition of the needs of her young family etc., led to a change in Royal residences — and consequently to the whereabouts of the family's libraries. King George I and King George II had lived at St James's Palace, and used Kensington Palace and Hampton Court as country retreats. King George III in 1762 bought Buckingham House (now Palace), similar then to Marlborough House today, and this was called The Queen's House until 1818. Queen Charlotte shared her husband's interest in books, and — on the evidence of Dr Croly — used to visit, with a lady-in-waiting, Holywell Street and Ludgate Hill, where second-hand books were on sale. Olwen Hedley's excellent *Queen Charlotte*, John Murray,

London, 1975, gives information on the Queen's libraries and books. At first, in The Queen's House 'mazarine blue' library in the new wing was a modest collection including works on the diseases and education of children, Italian, German and French literature, theology, the natural sciences, history and geography. To Fanny Burney, who lived at court five years and shared her love of literature, she remarked of a book: 'I picked it up on a stall. Oh, it is amazing what good books there are on stalls' (a servant had done the 'picking up' no doubt). Later, some of her books would have been at Kew, at Windsor and at Frogmore. At the last there was also a printing press, under the imprint of Queen Charlotte's librarian, Edward Harding, but its productions were undistinguished. The Queen's English and continental book collection continued to grow; poetry was an especial favourite, including contemporary writers; and there was drama and an abundance of novels. Though Frogmore House was recently opened to the public, restoration of the library has hardly begun. Her Majesty's books were sold in two parts in June–July 1819. The sale occupied twenty days and realized £4,540. The auction was at Christie's.

37

C P (Princess Charlotte)

Unsigned. Entwined initials with Royal coronet above. For a note on the coronet see p. 13. A print in the Perez Collection at The Book Trust has a manuscript note on it reading 'Library on the stair-case', and another from the E. M. Spencer Collection is annotated 'Bookcase. Warwick House', probably in the same hand. These may well have been added after disposal of her books, for Warwick House, St James's Stable Yard, was built for Henry Errington, who died in 1819, and the crown lease was then bought by the Earl of Warwick, whose family occupied the house until 1907. Neither bookplate the Princess used shows the arms assigned to her in 1816: the Royal arms without the electoral inescutcheon, with over all a label of three points argent, charged on the centre point with a rose gules; the lozenge ensigned by a Royal coronet and the Royal supporters charged on the shoulders with a label as on the arms. The dexter supporter was also crowned with a Royal coronet. Franks Coll.33212. Rare.

Her Royal Highness Princess Charlotte Augusta was born at Carlton House, London on 7 January 1796, the only child of George, Prince of Wales, later Prince Regent and King George IV (78–86) and his first cousin Princess Caroline, the second daughter of Karl II, Duke of Bruns-wick. She married at Carlton House in 1816, as his first wife, Prince Leopold of Saxe-Coburg-Saalfeld, Duke of Saxony, later King Leopold I of the Belgians (38). The joint bookplate used after their marriage follows. They lived at Claremont House, near Esher, an account of which will be found on p. 4ff. The Princess died there, giving birth to a stillborn son, on 6 November 1817, and was buried at St George's Chapel, Windsor. Princess Charlotte's death brought a fresh feeling of urgency to the question of the succession. The Prince Regent no longer had an heir; the Duke of York had been married since 1791, but childless; the Duke of Cumberland had married in 1815 a wife who was not expected to produce another child after the death of her daughter in 1817; and the Duke of Sussex had 'wedded' Lady Augusta Murray. As a result, 1818 witnessed the nuptials of no fewer than three of the Royal Dukes: the Duke of Clarence married Princess Adelaide, the Duke of Kent parted company with Madame St. Laurent — reluctantly, after twenty-seven years — and married Princess Victoria of Saxe-Coburg and Gotha, widow of Prince Emich Karl of Leiningen; and the Duke of Cambridge married Princess Augusta of Hesse-Cassel.

38

C L (Princess Charlotte and Prince Leopold of Saxe-Coburg-Saalfeld, later King Leopold I of the Belgians)

Unsigned. Monogram of entwined Cs and Ls on a ground shaded to represent clouds, continental crown and coronet above. For a note on the coronet see p. 13. Only one print has been seen, but the Princess's married life was very short: she married on 2 May 1816 and died on 6 November 1817 (see the foregoing for biographical details). The use of a background to represent clouds is not unfamiliar during this period, but it occurs on no other British Royal bookplate. The Princess was not, in any case, given to ostentation, as her earlier ex-libris evidences. Author's coll.

His Highness Prince Leopold George Christian Frederick of Saxe-Coburg-Saalfeld was the fourth of five sons (two of whom died young) of Franz, Duke of Saxe-Coburg-Saalfeld. He was born at Coburg on 16 December 1790. In 1814 he visited London, accompanying Tsar Alexander I of Russia, and very soon he and Princess Charlotte were in love. His marriage to her, though brief, was most happy, but the only issue of the marriage was stillborn. He married secondly in 1832 Louise Marie, the eldest daughter of Louis Philippe, King of France, and by her had three sons and a daughter. A powerful influence on his niece Queen Victoria (whose father died when she was only eight months old), he singled out Prince Albert as a suitable husband for her, and his judgement proved right. King of the Belgians from 1831 to 1865, he died at Laeken on 10 December 1865.

The home of Prince Leopold and Princess Charlotte was, as has already been indicated, Claremont, near Esher (for an account of which see p. 4ff). The Princess's architect, John William Hiort, with J. B. Papworth built the Cobham Road lodges, together with cottages, kennels, an aviary, and a 'retreat' later adapted as a memorial cenotaph. Many reminders of Princess Charlotte were retained at Claremont, including a mural decoration by a local sculptor named Williamson, and a piano made for her in 1817 by Broadwood.

39

Anonymous (Prince Christian of Schleswig-Holstein-Sonderburg-Augustenburg)

Unsigned. Armorial: Quarterly, 1st, Gules, a lion rampant crowned or, holding in his paws the long handled axe of St Olaf blade argent, handle or (Norway), all here reversed; 2nd, Or, two lions passant azure (Schleswig); 3rd, Gules, (should be) an inescutcheon per fess argent and of the field between three demi-nettle leaves and as many passion nails in pairle of the second (Holstein); 4th, Gules, a swan argent, beaked, membered and Royally gorged or (Stormarn); enté in point Gules, a knight in armour or on a horse and holding a sword argent and a shield azure charged with a cross patée of the second (Ditmarsken); over all an inescutcheon, quarterly, Or, two bars gules (Oldenburg) and Azure, a cross patée or (Delmenhorst). Above are four helms and crests, and descending from the mantling to surround the arms are the collars and badges of the Prussian Order of the Black Eagle and of the Garter. The bookplate, which may be of English engraving, was therefore made between 1866, when he was made a Knight of the Garter, and 1901, when he became Knight Grand Cross of the Royal Victorian Order, which subsequently would surely have been depicted. Royal Library Coll., Windsor.

His Highness Prince Frederick Christian Charles Augustus of Schleswig-Holstein-Sonderburg-Augustenburg was born at Augustenburg on 22 January 1831, the third son of Christian, Duke of the same, and Luise Sophie, daughter of Christian Konrad Sophus, Count of Danneskjold-Samsoe. He had, however, British ancestry, for his great-grandmother was Caroline Matilda, sister of King George III (75–77). She was Queen of Denmark, was known as the 'Queen of Tears', and married her first cousin, King Christian VII, whose mother was a daughter of King George II (J). Prince Christian married at the Private Chapel, Windsor Castle in 1866 Princess Helena Augusta Victoria (107–108), the third daughter of Queen Victoria and Prince Albert of Saxe-Coburg and Gotha. Granted the qualification of Royal Highness by Queen Victoria (as well as becoming K.G.) at that time, the Prince was a general in the British Army, High Steward of Windsor and Ranger of Windsor Great Park. He died at Schomberg House, Pall Mall on 28 October 1917 and was buried at Frogmore. Prince and Princess Christian had three sons and two daughters, Princess Helena Victoria (164–165) and Princess Marie Louise (who recalls the sad story of the 'Queen of Tears' in her *My Memories of Six Reigns*, 1956).

40

Anonymous (Prince Christian)

Unsigned, but clearly by the engraver of the foregoing, and probably made at the same time for larger books. Armorial: as the last in arms and other details but on a mantle; continental crown above as appropriate to the Schleswig-Holstein arms. Author's coll.

Prince Christian (for biographical details see the foregoing) was – his daughter Princess Marie Louise tells us, in her *My Memories of Six Reigns*, 1956 – a lover of literature and of poetry, knowing the whole of Gray's 'Elegy' by heart. He gave his children German lessons by means of German fairy-tales.

41

CHRISTIAN HELENA (Prince and Princess Christian)

Unsigned. Label: the two names forming a rectangle, continental crown above; printed embossed in blue, probably soon after their marriage. Rare. Author's coll.

See (39) and (107) for biographical details.

LIBRARY of the DUCHY of CORNWALL,
Founded by his Royal Highness
GEORGE PRINCE of WALES,
1783.

42

LIBRARY of the DUCHY of CORNWALL, Founded by his Royal Highness GEORGE PRINCE OF WALES, 1783. (Later King George IV)

Unsigned. Armorial: the Royal arms as borne 1714–1800, differenced by a label of three points argent, within the ribbon of the Garter; with the Royal supporters charged on the shoulders with a label as on the arms, the Prince of Wales's motto depending from a festoon below, with his coronet and feathers (see p. 14) above. The inescutcheon gules plain in the Hanoverian quarter was from 1708 proper to the heir to the dignity of Arch-treasurer of the Holy Roman Empire, and was thus borne by Princes of Wales (and, it is interesting to note, by the future King George III before 1751, when he was only the eldest grandson of the sovereign). Franks Coll.33196.

His Royal Highness Prince George, Prince of Wales, later Prince Regent and King George IV (for biographical details see (79)) became Duke of Cornwall and of Rothe-

say at birth. The bookplate's inscription indicates the year of the foundation of the Duchy's library, and the ex-libris was no doubt engraved shortly thereafter to dignify its volumes. See also (43) and (44).

The Duchy was instituted by King Edward III in 1337 in support of his elder son, Edward, the Black Prince; and since the Act of Parliament of that year the eldest surviving son of the sovereign has, as heir apparent, succeeded to the Dukedom by inheritance. King George III, not being 'filius regis', was the only heir apparent not to be Duke of Cornwall. In the parallel case of a grandson and heir apparent, Richard II was created Duke of Cornwall, as was Richard, Duke of York, when declared heir apparent in 1460. The fifteen bezants of the Duchy's arms (see (44)) derive from the arms of Poitou, borne by Richard, Earl of Poitou and Cornwall and King of the Romans, 1209–72.

The Library of the Duchy of Cornwall.

Albert Edward Prince of Wales.

43

The Library of the Duchy of Cornwall. Albert Edward Prince of Wales.
(later King Edward VII)

Unsigned. Armorial: the Royal arms, for detailing of which see (49), but with motto 'DIEU ET MON DROIT'. There have been at least two different printings: Franks Coll.33226, on grey or faded blue paper; and on a paper of deeper blue. The future King George IV (see (42)) and the future King Edward VII were the first Princes of Wales to have opportunity to have ex-libris made specifically for the Duchy of Cornwall Library; and they were also, incidentally, the two Princes of Wales who waited longest to become monarch. No subsequent holder of the dignity is commemorated by a Duchy bookplate.

44

Anonymous (The Duchy of Cornwall)

Unsigned. Armorial: the arms of the Duchy (Sable fifteen bezants, five, four, three, two and one) with the Prince of Wales's feathers and motto 'Ich dien'. (See (42).) Winterburn Coll.76. Rare.

45

DUCHY OF LANCASTER

Signed: 'W. Alexander, sc. 50 Strand, London'. Armorial: Gules, three lions passant guardant in pale or, a label argent (the arms of the Duchy), within a garter; Royal crown above. Winterburn Coll.77.

46

DUCHY OF LANCASTER

Unsigned. Similarly composed but of quite different engraving, the Royal crown being less angular etc. Franks Coll.33197.

The Duchy of Lancaster became a county palatine in 1351. It had its own courts beyond the Royal jurisdiction – but these rights have appertained to the Crown since Henry IV became King. The dignity of Chancellor of the Duchy of Lancaster is generally conferred on a member of the Cabinet, and the office of the Duchy is now in Lancaster Place, London, WC2. In earlier times the Duchy's offices were at Gray's Inn, situated between the Hall and the Chapel (see (106)), but they were moved from there just before 1788. The Queen's Chapel of the Savoy (32) is also closely associated with the Duchy of Lancaster, and the Chapel is administered through the Chancellor and Council of the Duchy. In September 1905 in the *Westminster Gazette* controversy arose on whether the reigning monarch is Duke of Lancaster, the question being whether the title belonged to John of Gaunt's descendants or the sovereign – in whom is vested the Duchy lands. Weinreb and Hibbert in *The London Encyclopaedia*, 1983, record that on a letter about this subject King Edward VII scrawled: 'I have always imagined that I was Duke of Lancaster, as the Sovereign of England always is. Queen Victoria considered herself so, just as the heir to the throne is Duke of Cornwall, and I have no wish to give up my rights.' Queen Victoria used to travel incognito as the Countess of Lancaster, and King Edward VII used the title of Duke when in Paris.

William Alexander was a trade engraver who had premises first at 1 York Street, Covent Garden (and probably also for a time at 7 Chandos Street, Covent Garden), but by *c.* 1830 he was at 50 The Strand. Only a handful of ex-libris signed by him are recorded.

47

E (Probably Prince Edward, Duke of Kent and Strathearn)

Unsigned. Initial on a shaded oval ground, with wreath, roundel and rectangular frame, coronet above. It is ascribed to Princess Elizabeth in Gambier Howe's *Franks Bequest. Catalogue* (33211). This is, of course, absurd, for she was not a Lady of the Garter and had, moreover, her own ex-libris (see (62) and (63)). With the coronet of a sovereign's younger child, and the ribbon of the Garter, this bookplate could have belonged only to the Duke of Kent or Prince Ernest Augustus, Duke of Cumberland, both of whom became K.G. in 1786. Sir Owen Morshead, sometime Royal Librarian at Windsor, believed it to be the Duke of Kent's; and its style suggests it was engraved not many years later than 1786. Very Rare. Royal Library Coll., Windsor.

His Royal Highness Prince Edward, the fourth son of King George III (75–77) and Queen Charlotte Sophia (35–36), was born at The Queen's House, St James's Park on 2 November 1767. He was educated at the house at Kew he shared, until 1779, with his brother William, later King William IV (169–170). Subsequently a frighteningly severe military officer, he became Commander-in-Chief of the forces in North America and Governor of Gibraltar. For twenty-seven years he lived happily with his mistress, Madame Alphonsine Therese Bernardine Julie de Montgenet de St. Laurent, Baronne de Fortisson, known as Madame St. Laurent. She bore him children given the surnames of Wood and Green (see 'The Parentage of Queen Victoria and Prince Albert', Appendix A to David Duff's life of Princess Beatrice, *The Shy Princess*, 1958). Following the death of Princess Charlotte (37–38) in 1817, however, he married – the succession being in question – in 1818 at Coburg and Kew Palace Princess Victoria, widow of Emich Karl, 2nd Prince of Leiningen, fourth daughter of Franz Friedrich Anton, Duke of Saxe-Coburg-Saalfeld. The Duchess of Kent (143) bore him one daughter, the future Queen Victoria (144–158), in 1819. His Royal Highness died eight months later at Sidmouth in Devon on 23 January 1820. He was buried at St George's Chapel, Windsor, but his body was later transferred to the Kent Mausoleum at Frogmore.

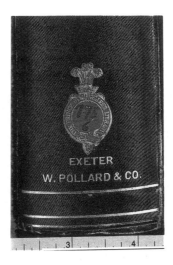

48

The Prince of Wales's Library (Later King Edward VII)

Unsigned. Label printed in gold on dark brown paper for use on the spines of the Prince's books. The only examples seen are still on volumes in the Royal Library at Windsor. It is of the same pattern as the spine labels for Balmoral Library (154) and Albert as Prince (4) and Prince Consort (5), though they were in various colours to indicate classification.

His Royal Highness Prince Albert Edward was born at Buckingham Palace on 9 November 1841, the second child but eldest son of Queen Victoria (144–158) and Prince Albert of Saxe-Coburg and Gotha (2–9). He was Duke of Cornwall and Duke of Rothesay, etc., at birth, and was created Prince of Wales when one month old. Educated privately and at Edinburgh University and Christ Church, Oxford, he had a starkly severe upbringing at home, his father and Baron Stockmar having devised a curriculum for him. He married at St George's Chapel, Windsor, in 1863 Princess Alexandra Caroline Marie Charlotte Louise Julie (13–15), the eldest daughter of Christian IX, King of Denmark, and Louise, third daughter of Landgrave Wilhelm of Hesse-Cassel. There were three sons of the marriage: Prince Albert Victor, Duke of Clarence and Avondale (d. 1892), Prince George, later King George V (88–96), and Prince John, who lived but a day; and there were three daughters: Princess Louise, later Duchess of Fife and Princess Royal (119), Princess Victoria (163) and Princess Maud, later Queen of Norway (132). Thwarted in his efforts to be of real use, the Prince of Wales found solace and pleasure in his social life, and the 'Marlborough House set' came in for censure. As King – he was by then sixty – he travelled much, as he had before. Edward VII was a popular monarch, and his efforts contributed to the 'Entente Cordiale' with France in 1904 and the Anglo-Russian agreement of 1907. He died at Buckingham Palace on 6 May 1910, and was buried at St George's Chapel, Windsor.

The Prince of Wales's Library

49

The Prince of Wales's Library (Later King Edward VII)

Unsigned. 'Die-sinker' armorial: Within the ribbon of the Garter the Royal arms with over all an inescutcheon of Saxony and a label of three points argent; with helm, Prince of Wales's coronet and feathers and Royal crest, the supporters charged on the shoulder with a label as on the arms, the lion crowned and the unicorn gorged with the coronet of his rank. From the Garter ribbon depend the George at centre and the badges of the Order of the Star of India, left, and of the Golden Fleece, right. The dates of His Royal Highness's election to the two latter orders – 1861 and 1852 – indicate that this bookplate cannot be earlier than 1861. In the Winterburn Collection Catalogue (No. 65) it is mysteriously ascribed to King George IV, despite its Saxony inescutcheon and the Star of India – the badge of which of course depicts Queen Victoria. Franks Coll.33225.

*The Prince of Wales's
Library.*

50

The Prince of Wales's Library (Later King Edward VII)

Unsigned. Almost identical to the last, though differing in many details. It lacks, for instance, the six pearls on the outer edges of the coronet, has a full stop after 'ICH DIEN', and the lion's tail has a larger tuft, etc. Since it was most probably from a different copper or steel plate it is numbered separately here. Author's coll.

The anonymous armorial shown will be seen to be virtually identical in design to (49) and (50) from the Garter ribbon upwards, but the ribbon below is differently shaped and there are no orders depicted. The print in the author's collection (illustrated) is a proof before the Garter motto and 'ICH DIEN' were engraved; a print in the Viner Collection includes these, and their lettering is virtually identical to that of the above. It does not, however, bear an inscription below, and we may thus probably conclude that both were preliminary proofs, discarded (or the plate amended) when it was decided to incorporate the orders' badges. That would inevitably necessitate reshaping of the motto ribbon.

See p. 8–9 for a comment on Royal die-sinker armorials.

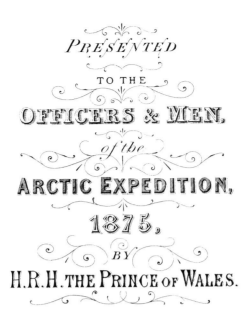

PRESENTED
TO THE
OFFICERS & MEN,
of the
ARCTIC EXPEDITION,
1875,
BY
H.R.H. THE PRINCE OF WALES.

51

PRESENTED TO THE OFFICERS & MEN, of the ARCTIC EXPEDITION, 1875, BY H.R.H. THE PRINCE OF WALES. (Later King Edward VII)

Unsigned. Engraved label with ornament and varied lettering. Only two prints seen: E. E. Spencer Coll. and author's coll.

Arctic exploration over the centuries was a matter of pressing ever farther, and there were many expeditions before R. E. Peary finally reached the North Pole on 6 April 1909. It is not surprising that a British expedition was marked by Royal favour, for expansion and discovery were impressive in this period. The 1875–76 expedition was under the command of (Sir) George Strong Nares (1831–1915). He entered the Royal Navy in 1845, and within nine years had had valuable experience – through journeys by sledge – of Arctic travel. He later briefly visited the Antarctic, his steamship being the first to cross the Antarctic Circle. Recalled in 1874 to lead the Arctic expedition (encouraged by the success of American expeditions) he set off with his party on 29 May 1875 with the *Alert*, in which he travelled, and the *Discovery*, with the intention of reaching the Pole. The Smith Sound route had seemed best, and the men were able to winter on the coast of Grant Land. The following spring, after dreadful ordeals with pack-ice and sufferings from scurvy, Albert Hastings Markham achieved the northern record latitude of 83° 20′ 26″ N, longitude 64° W, without the help of dogs. Lieutenant Pelham Aldrich, of the *Alert*, discovered and rounded Cape Columbia, Grant Land's most northerly point, and reached Cape Alfred Ernest; and Lieutenant Lewis A. Beaumont, in the *Discovery*, traced the coast of Greenland to Sherard Osborn fiord. Anything further was impossible, and Nares brought the expedition back to Portsmouth by October 1876. That year he was created K.C.B., and several geographical locations were named after him. Sir Albert Hastings Markham (1841–1918) had studied ice conditions before 1875. He returned to Arctic discovery in 1879, going with Sir Henry Gore-Booth to Novaya Zemlya, and in 1886 he surveyed the ice conditions of the Hudson Strait and Bay.

52

E R ROYAL LIBRARY WINDSOR CASTLE (King Edward VII)

Signed with monogram 'G W E(ve)' at lower right, and undated. As (158), but the cypher is changed from 'V R I' to 'E R', though the King was also Emperor of India. Significant shading has been added to the scroll below the Royal crest. For octavo books. Winterburn Coll.18.

The series of three bookplates by George W. Eve for the Royal Library at Windsor had been etched for Queen Victoria as late as 1897–98. Perhaps partly on this account, but also because they pleased him, King Edward VII had them amended by the artist for continued use throughout his reign. This octavo plate occurs also in a process reproduction; but process prints of the two larger sizes, which follow, have not been seen.

NB   Virtually as soon as amendment of the plates was completed in 1902 the King conceded to the organizing committee of King Edward's Hospital Fund the right to issue fifty sets of proofs to be sold at eight guineas a set for its benefit. The idea originated with Eve himself, as recorded in *The Ex Libris Journal*, Vol. 12, 1902, p. 51. To differentiate them from the Royal bookplates as used, each was given the Union Badge as a remarque. King Edward VII's Hospital for Officers had its origin in 1899 at the suggestion of the King, as Prince of Wales. His friends Miss Agnes Keyser and her sister Fanny started the hospital at their home, 17 Grosvenor Crescent, for officers injured in the Boer War. After the War the King insisted on its continuation, in 1903 giving the hospital his name and patronage. It has moved several times, and is now at Beaumont House, Beaumont Street, London W1.

See (53) for a note on George W. Eve.

53

ROYAL LIBRARY WINDSOR CASTLE E R (King Edward VII)

Signed 'G W E(ve)' in the shading between the Garter and the border at its narrowest point. Like the last this is a reworking of the bookplate used during Queen Victoria's reign. The cypher has been changed, the harp has been decorated with interlaced Celtic ornament, the shading has been amended, and the date (18)'97' is retained. (See (157)). For quarto books. Winterburn Coll.17.

For a note on proofs bearing a remarque see (52).

George W. Eve (1855–1914) entered the College of Arms, where his father had worked, early in life. He was the author of *Decorative Heraldry*, 1897, and *Heraldry in Art*, 1907, and he etched *c*. 250 bookplates of high quality.

He generally eschewed the use of tinctures in his armorials, on occasion achieving an almost three-dimensional effect. His bookplate work is recorded in G. H. Viner's *A Descriptive Catalogue of the Bookplates designed and etched by George W. Eve, R.E.*, published by the American Bookplate Society, Kansas City, 1916; and there is an article on his ex-libris in *The Ex Libris Journal*, Vol. 5, 1895, pp. 205–12. His Queen Victoria Royal Library series of plates are (156–158), and his later, and different, series for King George V (91–93). Eve also, incidentally, etched the invitation cards for the coronations of King Edward VII and King George V, and the invitation card for the investiture of the Prince of Wales (later King Edward VIII) in 1911.

54

ex bibliotheca regia in castel de windesor E R (King Edward VII)

'Signed G W E(ve)'. Like the foregoing this is a reworking of the bookplate used during Queen Victoria's reign. The cypher is changed, the harp is decorated with interlaced Celtic ornament, a considerable amount of shading has been added to the cross of St George, and the date '1898' is retained at lower right. A description of these plates in *The Ex Libris Journal*, Vol. 12, 1902, p. 53, comments that 'Above the shield on either side, and each within the (G)arter, are the badges of St. George, Patron Saint of the Order, and the Tudor rose of Henry VII over the "sunburst" badge of Edward III, its founder, both being symbolical of the fact that Windsor is the special home of the Knights of the Garter.' It is observed in Pinches, *The Royal Heraldry of England*, 1974, that there is no contemporary evidence for the sunburst or gold rays issuing from clouds as a badge of Edward III; but that it has been suggested the rays do not represent the sun but 'Winds or', a pun on Edward's birthplace, Windsor. The Tudor rose occurs again as ornament at centre of the base of the composition. For folio books. Winterburn Coll.16.

For a note on proofs bearing a remarque see (52) and for a note on George W. Eve (53).

SANDRINGHAM.

SANDRINGHAM.

55

E VII SANDRINGHAM. (King Edward VII)

Unsigned. Armorial: the Royal arms within the Garter, with helm, Royal crown, crest, supporters, mantling, and motto on a ribbon, in a rectangular border. Presumably produced from two line blocks, it is printed in black with its pounced ground in pink. Winterburn Coll.87.

56

A smaller version of the same. It is of slightly different design, not photographically reduced. Author's coll.

For biographical details of King Edward VII see (48). These ex-libris were made especially for Sandringham House in Norfolk, six miles from King's Lynn, a favourite residence of Edward VII and of later sovereigns, except Edward VIII. He purchased the estate as Prince of Wales in 1862 from Spencer Cowper for £220,000. Originally 7,000 acres, he extended it to 11,000, and it offered opportunity for sport and society. Here he could live the simple life of a country gentleman, but the old house proved inadequate and he had a new one built, 1869–71. There was a deer park with Japanese deer, and it was and is a superb venue for game shooting. The ballroom (1883) and additions to York Cottage, five minutes' walk away – where King George V (88–96) lived as Duke of York and King for thirty-three years – were the work of the architect Colonel Sir Robert William Edis. Also on the estate was Appleton Cottage, the home of Princess Maud (132) which she retained as Queen of Norway, and where her son King Olav V was born; and Her Royal Highness Diana, Princess of Wales, was born at Park House, only half a mile away, on the Sandringham estate. Ever a stickler for punctuality, King Edward VII kept all the clocks at Sandringham House an hour earlier than other people's time, as did King George V. It was the home of Queen Alexandra in her widowhood. She died there, as did King George V and King George VI. Still a dearly-loved home of the Royal family, Her Majesty Queen Elizabeth II and members of her family traditionally spend the six weeks after the Christmas holiday there.

BUCKINGHAM PALACE LIBRARY.

57

E R VII BUCKINGHAM PALACE LIBRARY. (King Edward VII)

Unsigned. E & R entwined and incorporating VII with Royal crown above and inscription below, within a rectangular border of ornaments. Process reproduced on gummed paper. Rare.

The modesty of this ex-libris perhaps indicates the relative unimportance of His Majesty's library at Buckingham Palace by comparison with the Royal Library at Windsor and the one at his beloved Sandringham; though he came to love Buckingham Palace after he had cleared it of the clutter of Queen Victoria's reign. The library there was on the ground floor in the Council Room (now called the Bow Room) and the two rooms on either side, on the garden front. An illustration of the Council Room as it was indicates that books featured in it rather than predominated.

Queen Victoria's bookplate for the library at Buckingham Palace is (147). The book stamp used at Osborne House on the Isle of Wight in King Edward VII's reign, when it had ceased to be a Royal residence, is shown with (134).

58

E (Prince Edward, later Prince of Wales, King Edward VIII, and Duke of Windsor)

Signed 'INV W P B(arrett) 1904', and thus commissioned from Messrs J. & E. Bumpus, of London, but engraved by J. A. C. Harrison, at the same time that a bookplate was made for his younger brother, Prince Albert (99). Initial within a decorative oval incorporating roses, thistles and shamrock; coronet above. There are three varieties:

a)   A rejected engraving, of which only three prints are known. The initial is larger than its successors, and on a partly shaded ground. The coronet is incorrect, being the one appropriate to the children of the sovereign: four crosses patée and four fleurs de lys. Winterburn Coll.29.

b)   The initial is smaller and on an unshaded ground, but the coronet is still incorrect. Author's coll.

c)   Prince Edward's grandfather, King Edward VII, still being on the throne, the coronet was amended to the one for the children of the heir apparent: two strawberry leaves, two crosses patée and four fleurs de lys. Author's coll.

All the versions appear to be from the same copper, for the border is identical; and all bear the same signature. This ex-libris was engraved when Prince Edward was only ten years of age (see p. 9).

His Royal Highness Prince Edward Albert Christian George Andrew Patrick David was born at White Lodge, Richmond Park, Surrey, on 23 June 1894, the eldest son of the future King George V (88–96) and Queen Mary (124–129). He became Duke of Cornwall and Duke of Rothesay on his father's accession in 1910, and within a month was created Prince of Wales. His investiture at Caernarvon was the first there for six hundred years (and the invitation card to it was etched by George W. Eve, who made the series of bookplates in three sizes for the Royal Library at Windsor for Queen Victoria, King Edward VII and King George V). Popular with the public, as Prince of Wales he travelled throughout the Empire, and was of a very sociable disposition. He succeeded his father as King on 20 January 1936, but his determination to marry Mrs Wallis Simpson, who was twice divorced, led to a constitutional crisis. He abdicated the throne on 10 December 1936, and the following year was created Duke of Windsor with the qualification of Royal Highness for himself but not his wife. He married at the Château de Candé in 1937 (Bessie) Wallis Warfield, former wife of Ernest Aldrich Simpson and Edward Winfield Spencer, Jr. She was the only child of Teackle Wallis Warfield, of Baltimore, USA, by his wife Alice, the daughter of William Montague, of Virginia. There were no children of the marriage. The Duke of Windsor was Governor and Commander-in-Chief of the Bahamas 1940–45, and he and his wife subsequently settled in France. He was the author of *A King's Story*, 1951, and *A Family Album*. The Duke died at Paris on 28 May 1972; his lying-in-state was at St George's Chapel, Windsor, and he was buried at Frogmore.

For a note on John Augustus Charles Harrison see (15).

59

E (Edward, Prince of Wales, later King Edward VIII, and Duke of Windsor)

Signed 'P T(ilden) MCMXXI'. Pictorial: within a library a desk with a volume open to pages bearing an 'E' and the Prince of Wales's feathers; window beyond, open at centre to reveal a sailing ship. This bookplate was designed by the architect Philip Armstrong Tilden, who for several years from 1918, having time on his hands, essayed making ex-libris. In his *True Remembrances*, Country Life Ltd, 1954, Tilden recalls his first meeting with the Prince. Having recently met Dudley Ward and his wife at Lympne, Tilden called on them, and Ward greeted him with, 'Come in, there's nobody here but the Prince of Wales'. He and the Prince took to each other, and Tilden visited St James's Palace several times to discuss the composition of the bookplate the Prince had asked him to make. He writes:

> For some reason or other, I was obsessed with the wildness of nature at the time. . . I had always seen and appreciated the beauty of the three Prince of Wales's feathers, and I made several sketches of them, not trimly and stiffly formal, but in

one case floppy all on one side, in another case [as shown overleaf] against a gigantic if desultory sky. The Prince put his head on one side and said of the latter, "I like it – but I don't think it quite suitable – we haven't come to that yet". Then I decided to have a great ship in full sail leaving harbour, seen through a window, with an open book on the sill, where a man might sit and watch the slow-moving greatness of the world. This was the bookplate that he eventually had, and when he had received a great batch of them he said, "Now I want a nice comfortable illness, so I can sit up in bed and stick them in".

The bookplate as used was etched, it is not known by whom. Royal Library Coll., Windsor. Tilden also designed a bookplate for Princess Mary, later the Princess Royal (see (130)), but it apparently was never used.

Philip Armstrong Tilden (1887–1956), the only son of Sir William Augustus Tilden, married in 1914 Caroline Brodin. He practised alone as an architect, built many country houses, and worked at Port Lympne, Easton Lodge, Churt, Chartwell, Long Crendon Manor, etc., as recorded in his memoirs, which make pleasant reading. He exhibited at the Royal Academy for some years, was a governor of the Old Vic Theatre, and was a fellow of the Devon and Cornwall Architectural Society. His home was in Hill Road, St John's Wood.

Rejected design by Tilden (see above).

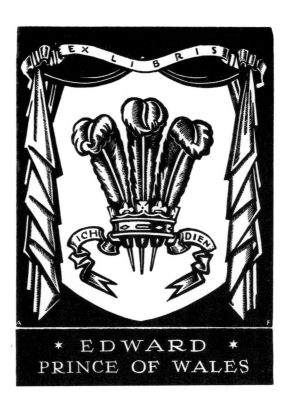

60

EDWARD PRINCE OF WALES (later King Edward VIII, and Duke of Windsor)

Signed 'A(drian) F(eint)' and cut on wood, 1934. The Prince of Wales's feathers with coronet and motto within drapery forming a shield shape; 'EX LIBRIS' above, name below. It occurs printed in blue and in black, and in two varieties:

a) With 'H.R.H' in the inscription on the lower block. Only the prints in the Pincott Collection have been seen, and these – the full bookplate and two examples of the inscription block on one sheet of paper – suggest trials of an inscription which was decided against and discarded.

b) As illustrated above. Author's coll.

As stated earlier (17) interest in bookplates in Australia was sufficiently strong for the Australian Ex Libris Society to be formed in 1923. The author of most books published on the subject in that country was Percy Neville Barnett. In his *Australian Book-plates and book-plates of interest to Australia*, 1950, a print of (b) above is tipped-in at p. 113. As Barnett explains in his chapter on Royal bookplates, this plate was offered by the Society and accepted on behalf of the Prince of Wales by King George V. Similar

presentations were made to the Duke and Duchess of York (100 and 65) when they visited Australia in 1927 – also the work of Feint. A lino-cut bookplate by G. D. Perrottet was given in 1934 for Princess Elizabeth's use in the little Welsh Cottage in the grounds of Royal Lodge; an armorial by Gayfield Shaw was presented to the Royal Library at Windsor (171); and an armorial cut on wood by Feint was presented to the Duke of Gloucester (110) in 1934 on his first visit to Australia, eleven years before he became Governor-General.

Adrian Feint (1894–1971), born at Narrandera, New South Wales, was a student of Julian Ashton at Sydney Art School, but served in the First World War in France and Flanders before completing his studies. Noted for his book illustrations and decorative pen work, his ex-libris were acclaimed, and the first of over 220 was made in 1922. Almost all were woodcuts, etchings or pen and ink drawings reproduced by line block; and the influence of Rockwell Kent is discernible in his work. A fastidious artist who mixed his own inks and did his own printing, he was one of the foremost Australian designers of his time.

61

E R ROYAL LIBRARY WINDSOR CASTLE (King Edward VIII, later Duke of Windsor)

Unsigned, but engraved by Stephen Gooden in 1936. Pictorial: St George and the Dragon above an inscriptional tablet, within an oval formed by the Garter ribbon; cypher and Royal crown above. There is an earlier, unfinished state, with a dark but broken and cloudy sky. There are also third and fourth states: the former with the cypher changed to 'G R VI', the latter with the cypher removed (see (103)). Gooden's beautiful and large preliminary wash drawing for this bookplate is in the Royal Library at Windsor. Only fifty proofs were printed of the above version. An undated press cutting in the author's possession indicates that King George VI subsequently made a gift of some signed proofs of Royal ex-libris to be sold at Christie's in a sale for the benefit of the Lord Mayor's Red Cross Fund, and that it included one of the King Edward VIII proofs. Royal Library Coll., Windsor.

Stephen Gooden (1892–1955) was the son of a picture dealer. He studied at the Slade, served in the First World War, and from the 1920s engaged in book illustration, notably for the Nonsuch Press. He also engraved forty-three bookplates, a number of them for the Royal family. The above was the first, but by the time it was completed King Edward VIII had abdicated. The cypher was then changed as indicated above, and has been removed for prints used in books since 1952. There are three plates in the Royal Library series for the reign of King George VI (102–104). Gooden also made ex-libris for Queen Elizabeth, now the Queen Mother (66–67), and for Princess Elizabeth (now Queen Elizabeth II) and Princess Margaret, but the latter lie beyond the scope of this study. The George and the Dragon design of the above bookplate was adapted by Paul Kruger Gray for the George Medal (established 1940), and in recognition of this the C.B.E. was conferred on Stephen Gooden in 1942.

NB   Prints of the Gooden Royal bookplates found in collections come almost entirely from friends to whom the artist had given them, the Samuels Collection, and Elkin Mathews Ltd, booksellers at Takeley, Bishops Stort-ford, the firm which published Campbell Dodgson's *Iconography of the Engravings of Stephen Gooden*, 1944. The last acquired the entire contents of his studio, and produced a catalogue [No. 159], half of which was devoted to Gooden's work. Item 459 is a proof of the above ex-libris, inscribed to friends for Christmas 1937, and a pencil sketch of part of the design is at Item 456(2).

62

Elizabeth. (Princess, later Landgravine of Hesse-Homburg)

Unsigned. Lozenge armorial with the Royal supporters, coronet above. In 1789 Princess Elizabeth was granted the Royal arms, without an inescutcheon in the Hanoverian quarter, over all a label of three points argent, the centre charged with a cross and the others with a rose gules; but her arms as depicted on this bookplate – used before her marriage – are the Royal arms as used 1801–37 and lack the label. It was, therefore, engraved between 1801 and 1818. The coronet is also incorrect on the evidence of later authorities, being appropriate to a Princess Royal. For a brief outline of this matter see p. 13. Very rare. Winterburn Coll.67. Author's coll.

Her Royal Highness Princess Elizabeth was born at The Queen's House, St James's Park on 22 May 1770, the third daughter and seventh child of King George III (75–77) and Queen Charlotte (35–36). She showed artistic talent from an early age, and was called 'The Muse'. A number of her pictures were engraved, the first of them a series designed in 1795 and called 'The Birth and Triumph of Cupid', engraved by Peltro William Tomkins and published at the King's expense. The Princess lived sometime at The Cottage, Old Windsor, and was a patroness of literature. She married at The Queen's House in 1818 Friedrich VI, Landgrave of Hesse-Homburg from 1820. After her husband's death in 1829 the Landgravine lived in Hanover in a palace provided by King William IV (169–170). She died without issue at Frankfurt am Main on 10 January 1840 and was buried in the mausoleum of the landgraves of Hesse-Homburg. A note on her library follows with her other probable bookplate, which depicts a correct rendering of her arms. Neither ex-libris is in the Franks Collection, but one there ascribed to her (No.33211) is here ascribed to Prince Edward, Duke of Kent (47). It shows the initial 'E' on a shaded ground in a decorative frame, and incorporates the Garter – which excludes Her Royal Highness as its owner.

This Book, which formed part of the Library of
H.R.H. The Princess Elizabeth,
Landgravine of Hesse Homburg,
Daughter of H.M. George the Third, was purchased
at the Sale of the said Library by Sotheby and
Wilkinson, April, 1863.—John Owen Smith.

63

Princess Elizabeth

Unsigned. Armorial: the Royal arms, without an inescutcheon in the Hanoverian quarter, over all a label of three points argent, the centre charged with a cross and the others with a rose gules (granted 1789). The coronet above differs from the one on the preceding plate and is as designated for the children of the sovereign (see p. 13). The supporters are the Royal supporters charged on the shoulders with a label as in the arms. Exceedingly rare, like the label below. Author's coll.

This armorial was almost certainly engraved for another purpose, and it is not proven that it was actually an ex-libris, but it occurred pasted to the label below in the Strong Collection, which suggests that the two were removed together from a book. The label in question was evidently printed for John Owen Smith's purchases at the sale of Princess Elizabeth's books by Sotheby and Wilkinson in April 1863. The identity of Smith has yet to be traced. The catalogue of the sale indicates that the Princess's library comprised works of English, French and German literature, theology, history, biography, archaeology, geography, voyages and travels, belles-lettres, natural history, heraldry, dictionaries and grammars, with some fine illustrated books and a few illuminated manuscripts. No mention is made in it of her own bookplate(s), but the majority of the works bore her signature, and some had an 'E' stamped in gold on the boards. There were 1,606 lots and they raised £915.12.6d. One of the most curious items – and a mark of the interest she had in Sir Joseph Banks' travels – is her transcript of an unpublished manuscript of Banks' private journal of his voyage round the world with Captain Cook, 1768–71, in three volumes. This was entirely written out by the Princess herself and occupied upwards of 2,000 pages.

64

ELIZABETH DUCHESS OF YORK (later Queen Elizabeth, Consort of King George VI, and since his death the Queen Mother)

Signed 'W P B (arrett) 1925', and therefore commissioned from Messrs J. & E. Bumpus; but engraved by Robert Osmond. Armorial: Two shields accolé: dexter, the Royal arms as borne by King George VI from 1912 as Prince and Duke of York, with over all a label of three points argent charged on the centre point with an anchor azure, within the ribbon of the Garter; sinister, quarterly, 1st and 4th, Argent, a lion rampant azure armed and langued gules, within a double tressure flory counterflory (shown here azure, but should be) of the second (Lyon); 2nd and 3rd, Ermine, three bows, stringed palewise proper (Bowes); within a ribbon bearing the Bowes-Lyon motto. The armorials are surmounted by a coronet, with rose and thistle above, with mantling to the arms, and below is the name and style on a ribbon with another rose and thistle. The design extends beyond the rectangular border on all sides. Winterburn Coll.37.

Her Royal Highness Elizabeth, Duchess of York, formerly Lady Elizabeth Angela Marguerite Bowes-Lyon, was born on 4 August 1900 at St Paul's Walden Bury, Hertfordshire, the fourth and youngest daughter of Claude George

Bowes-Lyon, 14th Earl of Strathmore and Kinghorne, and Nina Cecilia (181), daughter of the Revd Charles William Frederick Cavendish-Bentinck. She married at Westminster Abbey in 1923 His Royal Highness Prince Albert Frederick Arthur George, Duke of York (99–106). There were two children of the marriage: Her Majesty Queen Elizabeth II and Her Royal Highness Princess Margaret. On her husband's accession to the throne as King George VI in 1936, after the abdication of King Edward VIII, Queen Elizabeth gave her husband great support, and she has throughout the subsequent fifty-five years been a most dearly loved and admired Queen and Queen Mother. Since His Majesty's death in 1952 the Queen Mother has many times served as a Counsellor of State, and was sometime Chancellor of London and Dundee Universities. The celebrations for her ninetieth birthday in 1990 were without any parallel or precedent in the history of our Royal family, an indication of the place Her Majesty holds in the hearts of the people she has served so well for so long.

Robert Osmond (1874–1959) was born at Islington, the

youngest son of Robert Osmond, a painter and grainer. On his fourteenth birthday he was apprenticed to William E. Corks, engraver, of Northampton Square, Clerkenwell, and in his early twenties he took over Corks' West End business at Carnaby Street. Osmond built up a good connection with the West End gold and silversmiths, was from 1908 employed by Messrs J. & E. Bumpus for their bookplate work (see (15)), and for them and independently he engraved over 500 ex-libris of high quality on copper. Five are included here.

65

ELIZABETH, DUCHESS OF YORK (later Queen)

Signed 'A(drian) F(eint)'. A floral composition, which has been described as a still life, depicting the protected flowers of Australia, and therefore emblematic of that country. It was cut on wood and printed in black with coloured flowers and leaves. The colours are green, red, orange, yellow and pink. Uncoloured prints have also been seen. This bookplate was presented to Her Royal Highness on her visit to Australia in 1927 (see (60)), but was probably little used, if at all. A print of it in colour was tipped-in to all three (de luxe, special and standard) editions of Percy Neville Barnett's *Australian Book-plates and book-plates of interest to Australia*, 1950. This work has a chapter on Royal ex-libris (pp. 100–125). Any prints encountered will either have been removed from the above book or have been provided by the artist.

For a note on Adrian Feint see (60).

66

ELIZABETH R (Queen)

Unsigned, but engraved by Stephen Gooden in 1942. Armorial: Within the ribbon of the Garter the Royal arms impaling, quarterly, 1st and 4th, Argent, a lion rampant azure armed and langued gules within a double tressure flory counterflory of the second (Lyon); 2nd and 3rd, Ermine, three bows, stringed palewise proper (Bowes); but the engraver has eschewed use of tinctures in order to achieve a sculptured effect. Similarly adapted, the supporters are, Dexter, A lion guardant or Imperially crowned proper; sinister, A lion per fess or and gules (Earl of Strathmore and Kinghorne, father of Her Majesty). The design is on a shaped panel, with a Royal crown and festoons or ribands, roses and leaves on top, and the name tablet with a garland of thistles and shamrock below. A bookplate for larger-sized books. Royal Library Coll., Windsor.

There are six states of this plate in progress, recorded in full in Campbell Dodgson's *Iconography* (see (61)). In an abbreviated form, as seems appropriate here (our concern being with bookplates as used), they are as follows:

a) The plate is 6 × 4in, the large panel is virtually finished, the arms are complete in outline, but the background is not shaded, etc.
b) The crown, Garter, etc., are engraved, but the supporters remain white.
c) The supporters are engraved, but the arms are not shaded; some letters of the Queen's name and the 'R' are almost white, etc.
d) The arms are lightly shaded, but shading elsewhere, e.g. upper thistles, is incomplete.
e) The shading is complete, and the thistle nearest to 'H' is definitely darkened.
f) The plate is cut on all four sides.

Elkin Mathews Ltd, who purchased Gooden's studio contents, in their catalogue 159, as Item 465, offered two original drawings, white on black, of the Royal lion, a similar drawing, which is described as the Royal 'unicorn', but is surely the other lion supporter, and a completely finished drawing of a variant design in pencil and grey wash. The last of these drawings is now in America. The handsome completed sketch for this ex-libris is in the Royal Library at Windor.

For details of Stephen Gooden and Elkin Mathews' connection with him see (61).

67

ELIZABETH R. (Queen)

Unsigned, but engraved by Stephen Gooden in 1942. The Royal lion with a Royal crown, a book on which are interlaced 'E's' and a crown held in his paws, and a ribbon inscribed 'EX LIBRIS' hovering above; the name is on a ribbon at base, around the steps on which the lion rests. Only one state of this bookplate (C.D.184) is recorded, and it was for Her Majesty's smaller books. Royal Library Coll., Windsor.

Elkin Mathews Ltd, who purchased the contents of Gooden's studio, offered in their catalogue 159, as Item 466, a pen drawing of a lion, uncrowned, holding a shield with the Royal crown and the letter 'E' in reverse. The lion is seated on a plinth with three steps, and at the foot is a crown and the words 'Elizabeth R'. With it was a second drawing, of an abandoned design, depicting St George and the dragon above a cartouche with the crown and 'Elizabeth R'. There was also a proof of the bookplate. Item 467 was also relevant, being a copy of V. Wheeler-Howham's *Boutell's Manual of Heraldry. Revised and Illustrated*, with 32 plates in colour and illustrations in the text. The entry indicates that Gooden used the book in executing the various Royal commissions entrusted to him; and he inserted as a bookplate in this copy a proof of this particular ex-libris.

For a note on Stephen Gooden and Elkin Mathews' connection with him see (61).

OW.Sherborn R.E. fecit 1896

68

F T (Prince Francis, Duke of Teck)

Signed: 'C. W. Sherborn R. E. fecit 1896'. Initials on a pounced ground within a cartouche, surrounded by the collar and pendant badge of the Order of the Bath; palm wreath below, continental crown above. He used a similar arrangement of initials on personal items like hairbrushes; and, probably as a seal for envelopes or otherwise for personal correspondence, a tiny 'F T' monogram with coronet in a line border, 16mm high, which occurs embossed on gummed paper printed in gold, green, blue, red or mauve, and in gold on black paper. Uncommon. Winterburn Coll.47.

Francis Paul Charles Louis Alexander was born at Vienna on 27 August 1837, the only son of Duke Alexander of Württemberg and his morganatic wife, Claudine (created Countess von Hohenstein 1835), daughter of Laszlo, Count Rhédey de Kis-Rhéde. He married at St Anne's Church, Kew, Surrey, in 1866 Princess Mary Adelaide (123), younger daughter of Prince Adolphus Frederick, Duke of Cambridge. Though he was known in early life as Count Hohenstein, he was made a Serene Highness in 1863 and given the title of Prince of Teck; and he was created Duke of Teck in 1871 and granted the style of

Highness by Queen Victoria in 1887. Their eldest child and only daughter was the future Queen Mary (124–129), and they had three sons: Adolphus, 2nd Duke of Teck (later 1st Marquess of Cambridge), Francis and Alexander George (10) who became Earl of Athlone. The family lived at Kensington Place and from 1870 at White Lodge, Richmond Park – for a summary history of which see (123). The Duke of Teck died at White Lodge on 20 January 1900 and was buried at St George's Chapel, Windsor.

Charles William Sherborn (1831–1912) was the finest exponent of copper-engraved bookplates in the Victorian era and largely inspired the revival of armorial ex-libris design in this country. He is recorded in *A Sketch of the Life and Work of Charles William Sherborn*, 1912, by his son Charles Davies Sherborn. It includes a checklist by G. H. Viner of his ex-libris, numbering more than 400, to which he largely devoted over thirty years. He engraved, however, only three Royal bookplates, all for the Tecks. The other two were for Princess Mary Adelaide (123) and Princess May as Duchess of York (124).

69

D Y (Prince Frederick, Duke of York and Albany)

Unsigned. Crest plate: the Royal crest within the ribbon of the Garter, coronet above, in a single line rectangular border. It occurs on a map recording a battle retreat (Franks Coll.33198), and there are prints in the E. E. Spencer and author's colls., but it is rare.

His Royal Highness Prince Frederick was born at The Queen's House, St James's Park, London, on 16 August 1763, the second son of King George III (75–77) and Queen Charlotte (35–36). He was made Bishop of Osnabrugh at the age of seven months (see (78)) and studied as a boy with his elder brother, the future King George IV. Two ex-libris were engraved to mark their school-books (78 and 79). In 1784 he was created Duke of York and Albany. He married in Berlin and in London in 1791 Princess Frederica Charlotte Ulrica Catherine (1767–1820), eldest daughter of Friedrich Wilhelm II, King of Prussia. There was no issue of the marriage, and he kept several mistresses, including the notorious Mary Anne Clarke. A Field Marshal, he was sometime Colonel-in-Chief of the 60th Regiment of Foot and of the Forces in Great Britain, etc. Warden and Keeper of the New Forest, Keeper and Lieutenant of Windsor Forest and High Steward of New Windsor, 1811, he died at Rutland House, Arlington Street, London on 5 January 1827 and was buried at St George's Chapel, Windsor. Prince Frederick and his wife had after their marriage settled at Oatlands Park, near Weybridge, where he built a house after the old one had burnt down; and here – at least for a time – his library would have been. He spent little time there, however, and subsequently had a number of residences, one of them in South Audley Street; and it was from there that his books were taken to Sothebys for sale in May 1827. The sale occupied twenty-two days and realized £4,703. His maps, charts, etc., were sold by the same auctioneers in July of that year, over four days, and realized £1,014. Prince Frederick was not, however, a collector of antiquarian books, for most of his volumes were modern, and he was not exactly a scholar. His qualities were his affectionate character and enthusiasm, but he was a wretched husband and he needed supervision as a military leader.

70

Anonymous (Prince Frederick)

Unsigned. Armorial: the Royal arms as borne 1714–1800, with over all a label of three points argent charged on the centre point with a cross gules, with coronet and supporters, the latter with Royal coronets and charged on the shoulders with a label as in the arms. The armorial is within the ribbon of the Garter in the collar of the Order of the Bath, from which its badge depends. This print is No. 96 in the Winterburn Collection, and although it is most unlikely that the armorial was created as an ex-libris the shelf-mark at lower centre suggests that it was so used.

There are, inevitably, 'grey' areas in bookplate research and documentation, as elsewhere. The crest plate illustrated is in the Viner collection. Its coronet, appropriate to the sons and daughters of the monarch, seems on stylistic grounds to belong to the decades around 1800. The Royal crest is equally suggestive of probable Royal usage, but the Garter would seem to limit the field to a son of King George III. A print in the E. E. Spencer Coll. is pasted to a piece of paper which has an inscription in ink:

'Purchased at the late Duke of York's sale by Chas. Chaplin (?) 1827'. The character of the lettering of the inscription being probably contemporary, one would like to think (and it may be the case) that this was yet another bookplate used sometime by Frederick, Duke of York and Albany. The doubt which still exists is on account of there being a smaller version of the crest plate. It exists without any lettering (Franks Coll.33217); but there are also prints in two other varieties. One has the inscription 'E.D.K.' and the other 'E.D.C'. The former was in a copy of Thomas Pennant's *History and Antiquities of London*, new edition (ed. Jeffery, 1814), one of 175 quarto copies of this printing, in full crimson morocco (offered for sale by Toby English, of Lamb Arcade, Wallingford, Oxfordshire in 1988). The 'E.D.C.' variety occurs in a book in the Library of the University of Constance (R74/51–1). Usage as a bookplate is thus proven. The larger was illustrated amongst ex-libris for identification in *The Ex Libris Journal*, Vol. 5, 1895, on p. 217. It was suggested in reply that this was probably the bookplate of a regimental library, this being the badge of the Life Guards and Blues.

71

GEORGIUS D.G. MAG. BR. FR. ET HIB. REX F.D. MUNIFICENTIA REGIA 1715 [George by the Grace of God King of Great Britain, France and Ireland, Defender of the Faith] (King George I)

Signed 'J. Pine sculp.'. Pictorial-armorial: the arms of Cambridge University within a Chippendale frame surmounted by a classical head; the armorial rests upon a Jacobean tablet, with books beside it, and fronting it is an inscribed seal of the King's head and the inscription continued on a ribbon, all within a single line rectangular border. Franks Coll.33252 (33253 is a late print from the worn copper).

This is the smallest of four ex-libris engraved for books given by King George I to Cambridge University Library. In total he gave 28,965 volumes and 1,790 manuscripts, the library of John Moore (1646–1714), Bishop of Ely, purchased after his death by the King. Charles, 2nd Viscount Townshend, Secretary of State, suggested the gift to acknowledge the University's loyalty to the Crown – Oxford being Jacobite in its sympathies. His Majesty's munificence, and his sending soon afterwards a troop of horse into Oxford, gave rise to two well-known epigrams. Dr Joseph Trapp of Oxford wrote:

> King George, observing with judicious eyes,
> The state of both his Universities,
> To one he sends a regiment – For why?
> That *learned* body wanted *loyalty*;
> To th'other books he gave, as well discerning
> How much that *loyal* body wanted *learning*.

To this Sir William Browne of Cambridge replied:

> The King to Oxford sent his troop of horse,
> For Tories own no *argument* but *force*:
> With equal care, to Cambridge books he sent,
> For Whigs allow no *force* but *argument*.

Received in 1715, the books were housed in rooms prepared for them in 1734, and the bookplates for them in four sizes were not made until after the King's death. They were apparently commissioned by John Taylor, Librarian of St John's College 1731–34. A letter from Pine (at Aldersgate Street, London) of 29 August 1736 to the Vice-Chancellor, Dr John Adams, offers to make the King's face 'more like'. The receipted bill for the ex-libris of 8 July 1737, indicates the printings and prices:

	£	s.	d.
Largest size cost of engraving	5	5	0
cost of printing 2,200 copies	4	8	0
Second size cost of printing	3	13	6
cost of printing 6,000 copies	7	10	0
Third size cost of engraving	2	2	0
cost of printing 7,000 copies	5	5	0
Fourth size cost of engraving	1	11	6
cost of printing 13,000 copies	8	2	6

The total cost of engraving was thus £12.12.0, and of printing 28,200 bookplates £25.5.6, a grand total of £37.17.6. The reason for the 'short fall' of ex-libris – there being 765 more volumes than plates – is not clear. Perhaps books were lost, or some were sold as duplicates. The larger plates differ from the smallest in composition, its size not offering scope for full-blown allegory. They are, however, all of identical design, depicting Minerva and Apollo etc., beneath a pyramid or masonry corner, with the sun's rays and with clouds. The arms of Cambridge University are: Gules, a cross ermine charged at the centre with a clasped book of the first; in each quarter, a lion passant guardant or. Winterburn Coll.3.

72

Inscription as on the smallest bookplate, but of composition as detailed above. 80mm high. Signed 'J.P. Sc.' like the following (a little curiously only the smallest and largest plates bear the engraver's surname). Late prints of this have the initials 'J.B', identified as the initials of John Baldrey in *The Ex Libris Journal*, Vol. 4, 1894, p. 30. Redgrave gave him as John K. Baldrey, but he was Joshua Kirby Baldrey (1754–1828) who is recorded in the *Dictionary of National Biography*. Baldrey improved and partly re-cut the original coppers when, due to rebinding, there was need of further prints. It seems impressive, incidentally, that the original supply of bookplates was – on the evidence of prints examined – so generally satisfactory in view of the softness of copper (they were made, of course, before 'steeling' enabled mass printing without wear). Winterburn Coll. 4 and 5.

Joshua Kirby Baldrey (1754–1828) was an engraver and draughtsman in both Cambridge and London. Many of his works were in colour, the chief of these being the east window of King's College Chapel, Cambridge. For his various London addresses see Ian Maxted's *The London Book Trades 1775–1800*, Dawson, 1977. Baldrey's only other bookplate work recorded was a Chippendale armorial for George Mercer.

73

As the foregoing, but 125mm high. Signed 'J.P. Sc.' or 'J.B. SC.' on late prints after recutting. Winterburn Coll.6.

This and 74 evidence how much more satisfactory so grandiose a composition is when engraved large.

74

As the foregoing, but the largest plate, 208mm high. Signed 'J. Pine sculp.' Very rare. Winterburn Coll.7 and author's coll. (Illustrated overleaf.)

John Pine (1690–1756) was a noted engraver in his time. He kept a print-shop in St Martin's Lane, and was a close friend of William Hogarth, in whose 'Calais Gate' he

appears as a friar. His best works include engravings from the House of Lords' tapestry of the 'Destruction of the Spanish Armada', and his engraved text and illustrations for an edition of Horace. From 1743 until his death he was Bluemantle Pursuivant at the College of Arms. Pine engraved several other bookplates, including a fine one for Gray's Inn.

J. Pine sculp.

75

The Gift of his Royal Highness George Prince of Wales, 1757.
(later King George III)

Signed 'J. Kirk Fecit'. Armorial: within the Garter ribbon the Royal arms as borne 1714–1800, but with the inescutcheon of the fourth (Hanoverian) quarter blank, with over all a label of three points argent; Prince of Wales's coronet, Royal crest and supporters charged on the shoulder with a label as on the arms; the Prince of Wales's motto and an inscriptional tablet below. Franks Coll.33181.

NB. An armorial plate with a trophy below for 'His Royal Highness GEORGE Prince of Wales', unsigned by its engraver but dated 1756, sometimes found in bookplate collections, was almost certainly cut from a book and is not known to have been used as an ex-libris.

His Royal Highness Prince George William Frederick was born at Norfolk House, St James's Square on 4 June 1738, the eldest son of Prince Frederick Louis, Prince of Wales (I) and Princess Augusta, youngest daughter of Friedrich II, Duke of Saxe-Gotha and Altenburg. On the death of his father in 1751 he became heir to the throne and was created Prince of Wales. Whatever gift of books six years later the above ex-libris marked is not evident. He succeeded his grandfather, King George II (J) in 1760, and the

following year married at St James's Palace Princess Sophia Charlotte (35–36), youngest daughter of Karl Ludwig Friedrich, Duke of Mecklenburg-Strelitz. There were fifteen children of the marriage. A happy family man, his brothers' romantic exploits caused him to introduce the Royal Marriages Act in 1772, which survives to this day. The American colonies were lost during his reign, but the Indian empire was gained. After some years of unstable mental health he lost his reason finally in 1811 (as a result of the metabolic disorder porphyria), and his eldest son became Prince Regent (78–86). George III died at Windsor Castle on 29 January 1820 and was buried at St George's Chapel.

John Kirk (1724?–78?) was a medallist and engraver on the north side of St Paul's Churchyard. His Chippendale trade card indicates that he engraved 'Stone Steel and Silver Seals: Also Dies for Tickets Watch-Hooks, Chain pieces, Keys', etc. Fincham gives Kirk's Christian name as James, on the evidence of the signatures of several ex-libris, and has clearly confused the work of two engravers, though probably of the same family and firm.

76

G R III (King George III)

Unsigned. Armorial: on a mantle and within the ribbon of the Garter and the collars of the Orders of the Thistle and the Bath (Civil), the Royal arms as borne 1714–1800, with Royal crown above; the George and the badges of the aforementioned Orders are below, with motto, rose and thistle, etc. For large books. Franks Coll.33182. A heraldic book-stamp of rather similar composition (but without the mantle) on a copy of Petavius, *De Nithardo breve Syntagma*, Paris, 1613, is one of eight for King George III illustrated in Cyril Davenport's *English Heraldic Book-Stamps*, 1909.

King George III, the first of our monarchs known to have had ex-libris engraved for pasting into his books, understandably opted to have them in two sizes. When he ascended the throne in 1760 bookplates were of course in popular use, and the reason for his adoption of them is not hard to discover. The 'Old' Royal Library, dating from 1485 onwards, spent most of the first half of the eighteenth century in obscurity.* When in 1757 King George II presented its printed books and manuscripts to the recently-founded British Museum, they were languishing in some confusion in the Old Dormitory of Westminster School. As has been indicated (see p. 2) bookbindings or book-stamps had traditionally adorned Royal books, and use of ex-libris was not significantly established in Britain until *c.* 1700. Queen Anne, King George I and King George II were not sufficiently 'bookish' to desire bookplates; King George III was so thoroughly a bibliophile that a mark of ownership would commend itself. The bookplate also befitted his lack of ostentation, and that of his consort (see 35–36).

* For a discerning and fascinating introduction to the 'Old' Royal Library see T. A. Birrell's *English monarchs and their books: from Henry VII to Charles II* (the text of the Panizzi Lectures 1986, with preface and introduction), The British Library, London, 1987.

77

G R III (King George III)

Unsigned. Armorial: on a mantle and within the ribbon of the Garter, the Royal arms as borne 1714 to 1800, with Royal crown above. For smaller books. Winterburn Coll. 60. Scarce.

The print in the author's collection is accompanied by an inscription on a separate sheet of paper:

> From a book formerly in the possession of Sir F. A. Barnard for 57 years Librarian to George III . . . & who was the Collector of George IIIrds Library now in the British Museum. The book from which this plate was taken was sold by Auction at Cross Deep Twickenham Nov 16 1893.

The rest of the inscription states erroneously that he was also librarian to George IV, William IV and Queen Victoria. Barnard, who had charge of George III's collection from its commencement to the time when it was acquired by the nation, according to W.Y. Fletcher, in his *English Book Collectors*, 1902, died on 27 January 1830, aged 87. Fletcher and others also state that Sir Frederick Augusta Barnard was the King's illegitimate half-brother. A catalogue of the library was his work. It was Barnard who engineered a meeting between the King and Dr Johnson, during one of the latter's visits to peruse the books at The Queen's House, as Buckingham Palace was then called; and James Northcote, the friend and biographer of Sir Joshua Reynolds, observed that the King was 'more afraid of this interview than Dr. Johnson was, and went to it as a schoolboy to his task'. John Brooke, in his *King George III*, 1972, gives useful detail on the King's collecting of and expenditure on books, and makes the point that The Queen's House Library in four rooms (the Great Library, the Octagon, the South Library, and the East Library) was intended as the nucleus of a national library (which it became), and that the King's personal library was kept at Windsor.

NB   Fincham's *Artists and Engravers of British and American Book Plates*, 1897, records an armorial bookplate, *c.* 1790, for King George III by Barak Longmate (1739–93), a London engraver in Portland Street, Soho and then Noel Street. This has not been seen, but was most likely wrongly described as an ex-libris, for Longmate was a noted heraldic engraver.

78

PRINCE OF WALES and the BISHOP OF OSNABRUGH. 3d. MAY 1771 (the Princes George and Frederick, later King George IV and Duke of York and Albany)

Signed 'J. Kirk sculpt. Bedford Str. Covt. Garden'. The Prince of Wales's feathers and the Royal crest differenced by a coronet and a label of three points argent charged at the centre point with a cross gules – surrounded by a label tied at centre, on a shaded ground within a rectangle. Franks Coll. 33188. Winterburn Coll. 64.

His Royal Highness Prince George, Prince of Wales and His Royal Highness Prince Frederick, for biographical notes on whom see (79) and (69), were the eldest sons of King George III (75–77) and Queen Charlotte (35–36). The Princes' rather curious joint bookplate is of especial interest in two respects. In the first place it is precisely dated, and in the second the princes were so young, being then eight and seven years old respectively. This ex-libris was evidently created to dignify their schoolbooks, for in May 1771 they were promoted from the schoolroom to begin their joint studies under Dr William Markham, Bishop of Chester and afterwards Archbishop of York. A separate household for them at The Queen's House (now Buckingham Palace) was established; and in the *Annual Register* for 1771 it is recorded, under 2nd May: 'The gentlemen of His Royal Highness the Prince of Wales's newly appointed household met at the Queen's Palace for the first time. A separate table was kept on the occasion.' When aged 11 and 10 their studies were transferred to the

Dutch House at Kew, under the supervision of Robert D'Arcy, 4th Earl of Holdernesse, Leonard Smelt and Dr Markham, who was dismissed in 1776. Here they worked from early morning until eight at night, and their studies included the classics, French, German and Italian, larded with much moral guidance. The Prince of Wales's spelling nevertheless remained disparate – and verged on the desperate until the end of his life. The bookplate is also of particular interest in the title 'the Bishop of Osnabrugh', which requires explanation. One suspects that Prince Frederick must have been unique in having been created a bishop at the age of seven months! The explanation is, however, not hard to discern. The See of Osnabrugh in Hanover was, alternately with the Emperor, in the gift of the King of England as Elector of Hanover. In 1764 the right of appointment fell to King George III, and – as considerable revenues accrued from it – he wanted to keep it in the family. The baby Prince Frederick was consequently made a Right Reverend Father in God, and until he was created Duke of York and Albany in 1784 he was known as the Bishop of Osnabrugh. Indeed, his very first set of china, provided by the famed Josiah Wedgwood, bore his mitre. Osnabrugh is elsewhere referred to as Osnaburg, and is today spelt Osnabrück.

For a note on John Kirk see (75).

79

Anonymous (George, Prince of Wales, and Prince Frederick, Duke of York and Albany)

Unsigned. Within a beribboned spade shield the crests of the Princes (as on the foregoing) within coronet-topped garters, and ornamented with wreaths; all within a shaded rectangular border. The blank space below the wreath may be for a shelf-mark, but no print has been seen in a book. Very rare. Franks Coll. 33195.

This was presumably an ex-libris for later schoolbooks used by the Princes during their studies at Kew. Though the spade shield occurs on bookplates from about 1770, the greater number appear after 1780; so, in view of the Princes' ages, this is an early example. Prince Frederick was abroad for over six years from 1781. By the time he returned the Prince of Wales was established at Carlton House, the ex-libris for which follow.

His Royal Highness Prince George Augustus Frederick was born at St James's Palace on 12 August 1762, the eldest son of King George III (75–77) and Queen Charlotte Sophia (35–36). His schooldays have already been commented upon, but they were excessively strict, and he was soon to kick over the traces. From the age of 16 he engaged in amorous intrigues and unwarranted expenditure, and by the time he was 23 his debts amounted to £160,000. In 1785, in contravention of the Royal Marriages Act, he secretly married a Roman Catholic widow, Mrs Maria Anne FitzHerbert, formerly wife of Edward Weld, and daughter of Walter Smythe (207). He married secondly at the Chapel Royal, St James's Palace, in 1795 his first cousin Princess Caroline Amelia Elizabeth, the second daughter of Karl II, Duke of Brunswick, and by her had one daughter, Princess Charlotte (37–38). It was a most unhappy alliance. When King George III lost his reason in 1811, the Prince of Wales became Prince Regent; and he succeeded to the throne in 1820. Through a period of nineteen years, therefore, he ruled England – and with marked splendour, even if he allowed his subjects little sight of him in his last years. A man of exquisite taste, and as a result a patron of the arts, the Windsor Castle we know today was his creation. Nor to be belittled is the architectural quality which – with John Nash – he brought to London. He died at Windsor Castle on 26 June 1830, and was buried at St George's Chapel.

CARLETON HOUSE LIBRARY

80

CARLETON HOUSE LIBRARY (George, Prince of Wales, later Prince Regent and King George IV)

Unsigned. Badge plate: the Prince of Wales's feathers and motto within the collar of the Order of the Garter, the George depending; Prince of Wales's coronet above. This rare bookplate was probably used by the Prince in his early years at Carlton House before he became Prince Regent, being then superseded by the three armorials which follow. Franks Coll. 33194.

Carlton (or Carleton) House, built at the beginning of the eighteenth century for Henry, Baron Carleton, was bought in 1732 for Frederick, Prince of Wales. His widow, Augusta, Princess of Wales, resided there until her death in 1772, and her son, the King, then gave the Prince of Wales use of the house. With the assistance of several great architects, he turned his official London residence into the most splendid palace London had seen. Its interior was more sumptuous than its outside, with columns of porphyry and yellow Siena marble, bronze and silver capitals, and cascades of crystal chandeliers. When, sadly, he later became bored with it, thinking it not fine enough when he became King, he had it razed to the ground. As a result, only the Royal Pavilion at Brighton survives as evidence of the full flamboyance of his taste. The above and following bookplates of this Prince and King's maturity are impressive but somewhat mystifying to the researcher. King George IV was not, of course, the great lover of books his father had been and his brother, the Duke of Sussex, became; and until he gave his father's library to the nation he had, according to W.Y. Fletcher, in his *English Book Collectors*, 1902, regarded it as a 'costly burden'. The notable rarity of the above plate and those he used as King contrasts oddly with the remarkable frequency of prints of the Carleton House Library series which follows.

CARLETON HOUSE LIBRARY.

81

CARLETON HOUSE LIBRARY. (George, Prince of Wales, Prince Regent and King George IV)

Unsigned. Armorial: within the ribbon of the Garter, the Royal arms as borne 1801 to 1837 with over all a label of three points argent, the inescutcheon within the Hanoverian inescutcheon blank; with the Royal crest, Prince of Wales's feathers and the Royal supporters, charged on the shoulder with a label as on the arms, the Prince of Wales's motto below; all enclosed by a mantle with the Prince of Wales's coronet above. The largest of three sizes of this bookplate, it occurs in three varieties:

a) The end of the supporting lion's tail does not join the mantle. Franks Coll. 33189.
b) The foregoing, but without inscription. Franks Coll. 33190.
c) With inscription, but the lion's tail touching the mantle. Franks Coll. 33191.

This was the first series of British Royal bookplates to be engraved in three sizes to suit books of diverse format,

and it may well date from after 1811, when the Prince of Wales became Prince Regent, and in effect King. The similar series of handsome bookplates he had made for the Royal Library when he ascended the throne follow after the smaller varieties of the above. Excepting King William IV, all subsequent monarchs have commissioned bookplates in three sizes for the Royal Library at Windsor.

In view of the fact that the Viner Collection at the British Museum contains unfinished states of both the Carleton House ex-libris and the series of three the Prince used as King, it seems probable that the Carleton House plates were also the work of R. Silvester (for a note on whom see (84)). Progress proofs are rarely come by, and it seems unlikely that Viner obtained such an interesting series from two different sources (though his annotations are unhelpful on this point); nor does the manner of the engraving dispute such an assertion.

CARLETON HOUSE LIBRARY.

82

CARLETON HOUSE LIBRARY. (George, Prince of Wales, Prince Regent and King George IV)

Unsigned. Armorial: as the foregoing in its detail, but with the mantle ornamented on its outer edge by four bands. Doubtless made at the same time by the same engraver for books of medium size. Franks Coll. 33192.

CARLETON HOUSE LIBRARY.

83

CARLETON HOUSE LIBRARY. (as above)

Unsigned. Armorial: as the foregoing in its detail, but variation to the mantle. Also doubtless made at the same time by the same engraver for books of small size. Franks Coll. 33193.

Progress proofs of this and the preceding plate in the Viner Collection show only minor differences to the shading of the motto scrolls and Garter ribbon, etc. An earlier proof of the smaller, in the author's collection, lacks 'ICH DIEN', the Garter motto and 'CARLETON HOUSE LIBRARY'. Whilst, however, proofs are scarcely ever encountered, the Carlton House series of ex-libris compare with the bookplates of the Duke of Sussex and of Princess Sophia in being the most commonly encountered of Royal plates.

G. IV. R.

ROYAL LIBRARY.

84

G. IV. R. ROYAL LIBRARY. (King George IV)

Signed 'Silvester Sc. 27, Strand'. Armorial: within the ribbon and collar of the Garter, the Royal arms as borne 1816–37, with the George depending; helm, Royal crest, supporters and motto, all within a richly-ermined and be-tasselled mantle. For its size one of the most handsome of British Royal bookplates, it is finely engraved, and the advantage of showing the Royal and Garter mottoes white on black is evident. There is in the Viner Collection at the British Museum a proof before the engraver's signature and inscription below were added. Very rare.

King George IV presented his father's library to the nation in 1823. His own Carleton House Library was apparently moved in 1826, and books from it were stored at Cumberland Lodge (for mention of which see (108)); but some of the books were subsequently dispersed, and in consequence the Carleton House ex-libris are very frequently encountered, nearly all of them as loose prints showing evidence of their removal from books. W. Y. Fletcher, in *English Book Collectors*, 1902, makes a couple of points which may be of relevance. He writes: 'On his succession to the throne William IV., as he remarked, found himself the only sovereign in Europe not possessed of a library, and speedily took steps to acquire one.' He adds, of the Royal Library at Windsor, that 'the few books reserved by George IV give it importance as an anti-quarian collection.' These were from King George III's library, and were kept back when that went to the British Museum. A substantial portion of King George IV's Carleton House Library, and probably of what he added to it when King, is now in the present Royal Library which, as we know it today, has existed only since 1834. When, incidentally, space and bookshelves had been made ready at Windsor the books were given place there in no particular order, but simply as they fitted particular shelf sizes; and it took several decades of work to reorganize them logically. We have also to bear in mind the life and character of King George IV. At the time he came to the throne he was 57; he reigned but ten years, in the latter part of which he was scarcely seen by his subjects; and the ambition, flamboyance and energy of his earlier years had by then been largely dissipated. Never a thorough bibliophile, and having now other preoccupations, the three Royal Library ex-libris probably indicate an intention scarcely carried out. At any rate, prints and proofs of these plates examined by the author have been unused.

R. Silvester, of 27 Strand, London, first appears in the London *Directory* in 1806, and Fincham — who lists over sixty bookplates signed by him — suggests that he was active until 1841. There are, however, as many plates again bearing his signature unknown to Fincham; so he was clearly a significant bookplate engraver.

G. IV. R.

ROYAL LIBRARY.

G. IV. R.

ROYAL LIBRARY.

85

G. IV. R. ROYAL LIBRARY. (King George IV)

Signed as the foregoing. Armorial: as the last, but a bookplate for medium-sized books. The Viner Collection contains, as of the above, a progress proof lacking the inscription below and the engraver's signature. Very rare.

86

G. IV. R. ROYAL LIBRARY. (King George IV)

Signed as the two bookplates above. Armorial: as the foregoing, but for small-sized books. The Viner Collection contains a progress proof before the lettering of the motto and Garter ribbon were engraved, lacking also the engraver's signature and the inscription below. Very rare.

NB   An uninscribed and unsigned armorial in the E.E.

Spencer Collection, in size almost comparable to (84) but broader, may well be Silvester's work. It differs in several respects from the above: the lettering is black on white; the bars of the helm are less elaborate; the armorial is circular; and the collar of the Garter and the George are not included. Only the one print has been seen, and its use or commissioning as a bookplate is unproven.

87

George, Prince of Cambridge. (later 2nd Duke of Cambridge)

Unsigned. Armorial: within the ribbon and collar of the Garter, from which the George depends, the Royal arms as borne 1801–37 but with no inescutcheon within the Hanoverian inescutcheon, and over all two labels: the upper is of three points argent, the centre point charged with a cross and each of the others with two hearts in pale gules; the lower is of three points argent. With Royal coronet, the Royal supporters with coronets and labels on the shoulders as on the arms. Franks Coll. 33208†, pasted into a volume entitled *Reflections on the Revolution in France*. Winterburn Coll. 75. As a young man Prince George used the simple book stamp shown here, with his initial and coronet in an oval.

Prince George William Frederick Charles was born at Hanover on 26 March 1819, the only son of Prince

Adolphus Frederick, Duke of Cambridge, and Princess Augusta Wilhelmina Louisa, third daughter of Friedrich II, Landgrave of Hesse Cassel. He married at St John's Church, Clerkenwell, in 1847 (in contravention of the Royal Marriages Act of 1772) the actress Sarah – known as Louisa – Fairbrother, the daughter of Robert Fairbrother (198). She was called Mrs FitzGeorge, and bore him three sons, the second of whom was Sir Adolphus FitzGeorge (199). Prince George succeeded as 2nd Duke of Cambridge in 1850. His homes were St James's Palace from 1840 to 1859 and thereafter Gloucester House, Park Lane, and Kew Cottage. A Field Marshal in the Army from 1862, he was Commander-in-Chief of British Forces 1856–95. The Duke died at Gloucester House, Park Lane, on 17 March 1904 and was buried at Kensal Green Cemetery.

88

The Duke of York's Library. (later King George V)

Unsigned. Armorial: within the ribbon of the Garter, the Royal arms with over all an inescutcheon of Saxony and a label argent charged at the centre point with an anchor azure; with the coronet of a son of the heir apparent, the Royal crest, the badge of York, and the Royal supporters charged on the shoulders with a label as on the arms. It dates from 1892–1901. Uncommon. Royal Library Coll., Windsor.

His Royal Highness Prince George Frederick Ernest Albert was born at Marlborough House, London on 3 June 1865, the second son of King Edward VII (48–57) and Queen Alexandra (13–15). He was educated privately and in 1892 was created Duke of York; and he was created Prince of Wales in 1901. On the death of his elder brother, Prince Albert Victor, Duke of Clarence, in 1892, he became second in line to the throne, and he married at the Chapel Royal, St James's Palace, in 1893 Princess Victoria Mary Augusta Louisa Olga Pauline Claudine Agnes (known as Princess May) (124–129), the only daughter of Francis, Prince and 1st Duke of Teck (68) and Princess Mary Adelaide (123). Though he served in the Royal Navy in his youth, Royal responsibilities precluded his following this career, and he toured the Empire in 1901

and India in 1905–6. He succeeded to the throne as King George V in 1910, and in 1917 changed the family name from Saxe-Coburg and Gotha to Windsor. There were five sons and a daughter of the marriage, and two of his sons subsequently succeeded to the throne: King Edward VIII and King George VI. King George V was the only monarch to visit India as King-Emperor, which he did with Queen Mary in 1911–12, the culmination of their visit being the splendid Delhi Durbar. In character notably straightforward and frank, with a good heart, his qualities made him a thoroughly good King and Emperor, and recognition of the public's awareness of this in the 1935 Silver Jubilee celebrations was touching to him. He died at Sandringham on 20 January 1936, and was buried at St George's Chapel, Windsor.

NB A modest printed label, within a border of tiny ornaments, reading 'GRV PRIVATE PROPERTY', with an Imperial crown above the cypher, was used by him as King for items other than books, probably including pictures and suchlike. There is no evidence of it ever having served as a bookplate. The rectangular frame measures 45 × 70mm, and it was probably printed at the same time as the one for Queen Mary (see (129)).

89

EX LIBRIS. GEORGE & MARY. (the Duke and Duchess of York, later King George V and Queen Mary)

Unsigned, but designed by John Leighton. Armorial: within two heart-shaped shields accolé, at left a fanciful rendering of the Royal arms with a label, in the ribbon of the Garter, and on the right, enclosed by a wreath of may, the arms of Württemberg impaling Swabia with over all an inescutcheon of Teck. For proper rendering of these arms see (88) and (125). Roses contain the initials of the bridal couple, and the design includes helm, Royal crest, the Royal supporters, differenced by a label on the shoulders, all embraced by an over-elaborate ornamental surround. Three varieties in black, a fourth incorporating yellow, rose and white, and the original drawing for the bookplate are in the Winterburn Collection (Nos. 24–28). The armorial was never used, however, and its varieties

do not deserve separate detailing in the light of the information which follows. Author's coll.

This gift ex-libris, a present on the occasion of the Duke of York's marriage to Princess May of Teck in 1893, occasioned a furore in the Ex Libris Society. Illustrated in *The Graphic* on 15 July of that year, it was described as 'The Book-plate presented by the Ex Libris Society. Designed by Mr. John Leighton, President'. He was not, however, President, but a Vice-President, and the Society knew nothing of the gift. A letter of 17 July 1893 from J. G. Bradford, published in *The Ex Libris Journal*, deplores the gift and comments upon its inaccurate heraldry; and the Editor found it necessary to advise that 'the Society as

a body will not recognise, or be held responsible for the works, artistic or literary, of individual members.' Leighton was sufficiently thick-skinned to continue to be a Vice-President, and seems to have been unmoved by his reprimand, for in his own *The Book-plate Annual & Armorial Year Book*, 1895, he illustrates the design for the second year running and offers prints on Japanese paper at 2/6d. He does there, however, take personal responsibility for the gift. His subsequent incorporation into the design – on the ribbon below the Duchess's arms – of 'Exhib. at the Imperial Inst[itute] London Jul & Aug AD 1893' is a further piece of impertinence, and it is seen on the larger variety shown.

John Leighton (1822–1912) was born in London and studied under Henry Howard R.A. He became an artist, illustrator, book decorator and designer of ex-libris. Of the last he made a sizeable number, as well as some imaginary bookplates; but they are quite unsought today, for they largely display the less attractive qualities of late nineteenth century graphic art. Leighton wrote extensively under the name 'Luke Limner', he edited *The Bookplate Annual & Armorial Year Book*, 1894–97, referred to above, and was a founder proprietor of *The Graphic* in 1869.

The above ex-libris, which strictly have greater right perhaps to be in the book's final section, are included here partly on account of their occurrence in bookplate collections, but also because of the questions they raise. If a bookplate is created for presentation and then accepted, it could be argued that it is a genuine ex-libris. In general, however, the crux of the matter is whether or not it was ever used in books. Amongst such gifts the series of bookplates presented by the Australian Ex Libris Society to members of the Royal family are perhaps an especial case. Though few if any of them (see (60)) were in a marked measure used they were presentations of an official nature. The Australian bookplate for the Royal Library at Windsor (171) was sent to Queen Mary via Lady Gowrie, and the artist, Gayfield Shaw, was sent Her Majesty's photograph in reciprocation. In the days of Empire such loyal tokens from the Crown's antipodean subjects were not to be ignored. It is a totally different

matter when individual artists — including Leighton — choose to make Royal presentations. In the century's early years especially, and intermittently ever since, such gifts have been made, though more often to European than to British Royalty. Royal courtesy generally ensures their acceptance, but it should be understood that this does not imply usage. With bookplate societies now almost worldwide, many of them offering publications incorporating checklists of artists' works, one is obliged to admit that the inclusion of ex-libris for Royal personages (or, indeed, to a lesser extent famous people) adds greatly to the kudos of the individual concerned. Though there are of course exceptions, this practice is generally to be deplored, being no more than an exercise in self-aggrandisement.

90

THE LIBRARY OF GEORGE FREDERICK ERNEST ALBERT PRINCE OF WALES (later King George V)

Signed 'INV W P B(arrett) 1904', and thus commissioned from Messrs J. & E. Bumpus of London, but engraved by J. A. C. Harrison. Armorial: within the ribbon of the Garter, the Royal arms as on (88), though the label – since he had become Prince of Wales – is of three points argent; with helm, the Prince of Wales's coronet, badge and motto, the Royal crest and dragon of Wales, the Rose of York in the top corners, and the Royal supporters with Royal coronets, charged on the shoulder with a label as on the arms. The anchors ornamenting the inscriptional tablet were suggested by the Prince himself. Of three varieties only two were used as ex-libris:

a) As the illustration, described above. Winterburn Coll. 22.

b) A version of the above, inscribed at base, 'Photogravure from original by Allen & Co.'. It occurs as illustration in *The Ex Libris Journal*, Vol. 15, 1905 as frontispiece to the July–August issue, with a note: 'H.R.H. The Prince of Wales has most graciously accorded permission to Messrs. Bumpus to have a photogravure reproduction made from the plate for insertion.' It is, therefore, not an ex-libris, though a note in the journal confusingly offers 'Extra copies of this number, with the new book-plate of H.R.H. the Prince of Wales', price 2/6*d*.

c) A process reproduction, about half the size of the original, made for use in books. Rare.

For a note on J. A. C. Harrison see (15). This is one of his finest ex-libris, and in the early 1950s Harrison presented to Liverpool Public Library the original sketch for this bookplate together with a unique set of eleven progress proofs which show the composition gradually taking shape. In view of their singular interest illustrations of these follow.

Preliminary drawing

State I

State II

State III

State IV

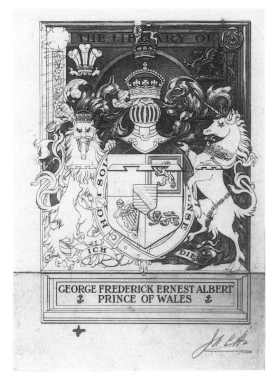

State V

State VI

State VII

State VIII

State IX

State X

XIth and final state

91

EX BIBLIOTHECA REGIA IN CASTEL. DE WINDESOR G R V (King George V)

Signed 'G W E(ve) 1911'. Armorial: within the ribbon of the Garter, with the middle of the collar and George below, the Royal arms with Royal crowns, crest and supporters, motto below; in a shaded rectangle with ornamental border. It was etched for folio books. Rare. Royal Library Coll., Windsor.

His Majesty King George V decided to have a completely new set of three bookplates for the Royal Library at Windsor, and these, together with the three simple cypher plates which follow, were completed in 1911. George W. Eve was the obvious choice for this commission. He had provided similar series of bookplates for Queen Victoria (156–158) and King Edward VII (52–54), with other Royal commissions. The decidedly 'modern' character of his 1911 work by comparison with its forerunners is impressive, and collectors will be interested by the frequency or rarity of his Royal ex-libris. Excepting a handful of proofs in colour or on vellum, and the fifty sets of proofs with remarque of the King Edward VII series (sold in aid of King Edward's Hospital Fund), Eve's earlier series of Windsor bookplates are frequently encountered. By contrast, all three of King George V's Royal Library bookplates are notably rare, probably on account of His Majesty having been inundated with requests for prints. His eminently fair view on the subject is made clear in the letter quoted on p. 1.

For a note on George W. Eve see (53).

92

EX BIBLIOTHECA REG. IN CASTEL. WINDESOR G R V (King George V)

Signed 'G W E(ve) 1911'. Arnorial: within the ribbon of Garter, the Royal arms, with Royal crown and cypher above, ornamented at base with roses, thistles and shamrock. It has, like other plates in this series, a Celtic frieze above; but the inscription at base has been simplified in order to retain focus on the bookplate's size. For quarto books. Rare. Winterburn Coll.21.

93

EX BIBLIOTHECA REG. IN CASTEL. WINDESOR G R V (King George V)

Signed 'G W E(ve) 1911'. The Royal crest only, flanked with the cypher, in a similar rectangular reeded frame as the foregoing, with Celtic ornament above. Its nobility is achieved by the delineation of the lion and the elegant lines of the crown. For octavo books. Rare. Royal Library Coll., Windsor.

Unlike his predecessors, King George V had – in addition to the by then traditional set of Royal Library Windsor ex-libris in three sizes – three simple cypher bookplates. These were cut on wood by H.S. Ulrich, after George W. Eve's pen drawings, having taken advice from the Hon. John Fortescue, Librarian to the King. A letter from Fortescue to Campbell Dodgson, Keeper of Prints and Drawings at the British Museum, reads:

The woodblock bookplates were executed only for King George; Queen Victoria & King Edward having nothing of the kind. One of them is the King's private bookplate; all the others we use in the Library . . . one crown that I copied from them as a bookstamp is far and away the most beautiful to be found in the Library. Eve stole it from Henry VII's privy seal.

The three woodcut ex-libris are as follows:

94

G R V (King George V)

The Royal cypher surmounted by a Royal crown on a heavily pounced background. This variety was used in the Royal Library at Windsor. Eve's original drawing for it is in the Viner Collection at the British Museum. Uncommon. Royal Library Coll., Windsor.

95

G R V (as above)

The Royal cypher in open letters with a line indicating relief running down the centre of each. No background. This variety was used in the Royal Library at Windsor. Rare. Royal Library Coll., Windsor.

96

G R V (as above)

The Royal cypher in solid black letters. The simplest of the designs, used by the King as his personal bookplate. His son, King George VI, adapted the same design (101). Rare. Author's coll.

Heinrich Sigismund Ulrich (b. 1846) was a German-born wood engraver working chiefly from Chelsfield in Kent. He contributed work to *The Graphic* and other journals; was an exponent of the 'tonal' school of engraving in the 1880s; exhibited portrait engravings at the Royal Academy from 1889; and worked until at least 1913, when a vignette by him accompanied an article in *The Imprint*.

97

GEORGE EARL OF MEDINA ROYAL NAVY (Mountbatten)

Unsigned, but designed by his father, Prince Louis, and etched by Alfred Sparkes. Armorial: within an oval bearing the inscription and flanked by flags (the White Ensign at left, the Union Jack at right), Quarterly, 1st and 4th, Azure, a lion rampant double-queued barry (should be) of ten argent and gules, within a bordure componée of the second and third (Hesse modified); 2nd and 3rd, Argent, two pallets sable (Battenberg); the whole charged at the honour point with an inescutcheon of the Royal arms with a label of three points argent (which should correctly be charged as on the following bookplate); an earl's coronet above, a label reading 'Mountbatten' and the crest of Hesse modified, all within a lightly-toned rectangular ground. Etched 1917–21, and printed in brown. Rare. Winterburn Coll.55.

His Serene Highness Prince George Louis Victor Henry Serge of Battenberg was born at Darmstadt on 6 November 1892, the elder son of Prince Louis of Battenberg (113–114) and Princess Victoria of Hesse (162). He entered the Royal Navy as a cadet in 1905 and rose to the rank of Captain in 1937, in the First World War being present at the Battles of Heligoland, Dogger Bank and Jutland. He married in London in 1916 Nadejda (Nada),

the youngest daughter of the Grand Duke Mikhail Mikhailovitch of Russia and his morganatic wife, Sophie, Countess de Torby (both of whom, incidentally, used ex-libris engraved by J. A. C. Harrison). There was one son and one daughter of the marriage. In 1917, along with other members of his family, he renounced his title of Prince of Battenberg and the qualification of Serene Highness and assumed the surname of Mountbatten, being known as Earl of Medina — his father's second title. In 1921 he succeeded his father as 2nd Marquess of Milford Haven. His residence was Lynden Manor, Holyport, Maidenhead, Berkshire. The 2nd Marquess of Milford Haven died in London on 8 April 1938.

Alfred Sparkes, 'copper plate engraver', was at 51 Milton Street, London, EC, in 1899, and in 1902 had premises at 21 Farringdon Avenue. By 1907 he had moved to No. 15, where he remained until 1926, when his address became 29 Knightrider Street, EC4. In 1930 he was at 10 Godliman Street, EC4; but from 1933 only Alfred James Sparkes is recorded, at 1 Fleur-de-lis Court, Carter Lane, and at 1 Carter Court in Carter Lane in 1940. The business went under the name of Alfred Sparkes again from 1942 until 1950.

98

GEORGE 2D MARQUESS OF MILFORD HAVEN ROYAL NAVY

Signed 'A BATCHELOR F LONDON 1927'. Armorial: within the ribbon of the Royal Victorian Order, from which the badge depends, quarterly arms as on the fore-going bookplate, but with the lion rampant of the 1st and 4th quarters crowned or, and the Royal arms at the honour point charged (correctly) with a label of three points argent, the centre point charged with a rose gules and each of the others with an ermine spot sable (as had been granted to his maternal grandmother, Princess Alice (19), Grand Duchess of Hesse); a marquess's coronet above, and crests of Hesse modified and Battenberg (see p. 15), with, as supporters, Two lions double-queued and crowned all or, with motto and name cartouche beneath, the composition all within a rectangular frame upon a cross-hatched ground. Though larger, this armorial is based upon the 1923 ex-libris of his younger brother, Lord Louis Mountbatten (115–116). Rare. Winterburn Coll.54.

Acheson Batchelor (1870?–1952) was educated at the Bluecoat School, and became an engraver, heraldic sta-tioner and designer of buttons, etc., for regiments. He started his working life with the seal engraver, Allan Wyon, who also produced ex-libris, but subsequently had his own premises at 25 Margaret Street from 1908 to 1941. A far more prolific bookplate engraver than has generally been recognized, his ex-libris for Lord Beaver-brook is well-known; but he seems also to have made a speciality of ecclesiastical ex-libris. He lived at 35 Cedar Road, Cricklewood.

99

A (Prince Albert, later King George VI)

Signed 'W P B(arrett) 1904', and thus commissioned from Messrs J & E. Bumpus, of London, but engraved by J. A. C. Harrison, at the same time that a bookplate was made for his elder brother, Prince Edward (58). Initial within a decorative oval incorporating roses, thistles and shamrock; coronet above. There are two states:

a) The coronet is the one appropriate to the children of the sovereign: four crosses patée and four fleurs de lys.
b) Prince Albert's grandfather, King Edward VII, still being on the throne, the coronet was amended to the one for children of sons of the sovereign: two strawberry leaves, two crosses patée and four fleurs de lys.

This ex-libris was engraved when Prince Albert was only nine years of age (see p. 9). Author's coll. (both states).

His Royal Highness Prince Albert Frederick Arthur George was born at York Cottage, Sandringham, on 14 December 1895, the second son of the future King George V (88–96) and Queen Mary (124–129), the eldest child and only daughter of Prince Francis, Duke of Teck, and Princess Mary Adelaide. He served in the Royal Navy, was present at the Battle of Jutland, and was created Duke of York in 1920. In 1923 he married at Westminster Abbey Lady Elizabeth Angela Marguerite Bowes-Lyon, the youngest daughter of the 14th Earl of Strathmore and Kinghorne. The two daughters of the marriage were Queen Elizabeth II and the Princess Margaret. On the abdication of his elder brother, King Edward VIII, in December 1936, he ascended the throne as King George VI; but he relinquished the title of Emperor of India in 1948. A gentle and totally dedicated monarch, his remarkable personal qualities and lack of ostentation endeared him to his people, with whom he shared to the full the rigours of life in the Second World War. Ever at heart a family man, he was blessed with a wife who gave him immeasurable support when the duties of kingship were thrust upon him; and he enjoyed the pursuits of country life, especially at Sandringham. He died there on 6 February 1952 and was buried in the King George VI Memorial Chapel at St George's Chapel, Windsor.

For a note on J. A. C. Harrison see (15).

100

ALBERT FREDERICK ARTHUR GEORGE DUKE OF YORK (later King George VI)

Signed 'Adrian Feint'. Pictorial: the Parliament House in Canberra, within a decorative rectangular border; the inscription in a compartment below. An etched bookplate, rarely ever encountered in collections, it is the only one of the Australian series not Royal in its subject. In 1927 the Duke and Duchess of York made a tour of New Zealand and Australia, the highlight of which was the opening of the first meeting of Parliament at Canberra on 9 May. The Parliament had earlier met at Melbourne, and the building depicted was intended to be temporary, but has continued to serve. The bookplate was a gift to His Royal Highness from the Australian Ex Libris Society (see (60)), but it is unlikely that it was ever used. A print was reproduced in the Society's Annual Report for 1927. The floral bookplate given at the same time to the Duchess of York is (65). Percy Neville Barnett, in his *Australian Book-plates and book-plates of interest to Australia*, 1950, made several interesting observations about the gifts, on p. 191. He indicates that permission to present them had been sought in advance; that most of them appeared in the Society's publications either as originals or reproductions; and that they served the purposes of expressing loyalty to the Crown, of bringing notable plates into being, and of popularizing ex-libris.

For a note on Adrian Feint see (60).

101

G R VI (King George VI)

Unsigned, but designed by George W. Eve and originally cut on wood by H. S. Ulrich (see (96)). When King George came to the throne in 1936 he had the simple cypher bookplate his father had used for personal books adapted for himself, having the 'V' changed to 'VI'. Very rare. Author's coll.

102

ROYAL LIBRARY WINDSOR CASTLE G R VI (King George VI)

Unsigned, but engraved in 1937 by Stephen Gooden. Lion's head crowned, with inscription around in a shaded oval. The large and magnificent finished sketch for this (bearing King Edward VIII's cypher but dated in pencil 1937) is in the Royal Library at Windsor. Uncommon. Royal Library Coll., Windsor.

During the brief reign of King Edward VIII, King George VI's elder brother, Stephen Gooden had been commissioned to engrave a new series of ex-libris for the Royal Library at Windsor, but only the medium-sized 'St. George and the Dragon' plate (61) was completed before his abdication in December 1936. As a result, the cypher of that was re-engraved, and the other two bookplates were completed for King George VI. This, the smallest plate, occurs in two states:

a) The plate is 4 inches high, and one inch from its foot a line is ruled across it.

b) The plate cut to 2 9/10 inches. Winterburn Coll.35.

Elkin Mathews Ltd, who purchased the contents of Gooden's studio and offered them for sale in its Catalogue 159, included as Items 456 and 458 prints of the second state of this plate, together with two photographs of discarded designs. The first of these has the cypher of King Edward VIII, and the second has no cypher but the lion's mouth is open. Item 457 is described as the small plate but 'an undescribed and unused design', the lion's head and crown much larger and the mouth open; but this was probably a print of the new engraving which Gooden made when Queen Elizabeth II came to the throne — which lies beyond the scope of this book.

For a note on Stephen Gooden see (61).

103

G R VI ROYAL LIBRARY WINDSOR CASTLE (King George VI)

Unsigned, but engraved by Stephen Gooden in 1936–37. Pictorial: St George and the Dragon above an inscriptional tablet, within an oval formed by the Garter ribbon; cypher and Royal crown above. The large and magnificent finished sketch for this is in the Royal Library at Windsor. Uncommon.

This was the medium-sized bookplate for the Royal Library, and was, apart from the cypher, completed during the reign of King Edward VIII, for whom this series of ex-libris was commissioned. There are four states:

a) The plate measures 6½ × 4¼ inches. The background depicts a dark but broken and cloudy sky.
b) The plate cut, and the background now black. The cypher is that of King Edward VIII. See (61) for illustration and fuller details.
c) The cypher of King George VI substituted. Winterburn Coll.33.
d) Without cypher, as amended after 1952.

A print of the third state of the bookplate was offered in Elkin Mathews Ltd's Catalogue 159, together with a sketch of part of the design in pencil. This handsome composition was adapted by Paul Kruger Gray for the George Medal, and in recognition of this the C.B.E. was conferred on Stephen Gooden in 1942.

For a note on Stephen Gooden see (61).

104

G R VI ROYAL LIBRARY WINDSOR CASTLE (King George VI)

Unsigned, but engraved by Stephen Gooden in 1937. Armorial: within the ribbon of the Garter the Royal arms, with Royal crest, supporters and motto, the last ornamented with roses, thistles and shamrock; all in a decorative frame with the appearance of carved wood. The large and magnificent sketch for it is in the Royal Library at Windsor. Uncommon.

The largest of the series of three ex-libris for the Royal Library in King George VI's reign, it occurs in six states:

a) In outline, but with the lettering at the foot engraved.
b) Background shaded, crown and crest complete, but the supporters still white.
c) The upper part of the lion shaded.
d) Shading darkened but not extended.
e) Completed, but before 'VI' within the letter 'G'.
f) The numeral 'VI' added. Winterburn Coll.34.

A print of the penultimate state of this bookplate was offered in Elkin Mathews Ltd's Catalogue 159 together with a photograph of the completed sketch with the cypher of King Edward VIII, in which form no engraving was made. Included also was an original drawing on tracing paper of a heraldic lion, a group of five Windsor Castle heraldic bookplates provided for Gooden's guidance, and impressions of heraldic book stamps on books at Windsor.

For a note on Stephen Gooden see (61).

This Book
forms part of the library
presented at Christmas 1942
by
THE KING & THE QUEEN
to the
BRITISH PRISONERS OF WAR
with THEIR MAJESTIES'
best wishes

✺

105

**This Book forms part of the library presented at Christmas 1942 by THE KING
& THE QUEEN to the BRITISH PRISONERS OF WAR with THEIR MAJESTIES'
best wishes**

Printed book label, with no border but a single ornament at base. Rare. Royal Library Coll., Windsor.

1942 was the second of four years in the Second World War in which King George VI and Queen Elizabeth sent presents of books at Christmas to our prisoners-of-war in Germany. The idea originated in the autumn of 1941, and the gifts were sent via the Prisoners of War Department of the War Organisation of the British Red Cross Society and the Order of St John of Jerusalem. Owen (later Sir Owen) Morshead, the Royal Librarian at Windsor, was asked to organize the gifts, and it was he who proposed the printing of the book labels to mark them. Since they were not for Royal personal use they are allotted only one number in this catalogue; but examples dated 1941, 1943 and 1944 may also be encountered. They are modest reminders of the heartfelt concern of the King and Queen for their people who served and suffered in dark days. Their own example was inspiring. Buckingham Palace itself was hit by enemy bombs nine times during the war. The Princesses Elizabeth and Margaret would not leave their parents for safety, and the Queen saw her place at her husband's side as he shared the dangers of war with his subjects in the capital. At one point the Chapel at Buckingham Palace suffered a direct hit, and the Queen's comment that they could now look the East End of London in the face was a token of their insistence to seek no privilege but that of endurance alongside their own people.

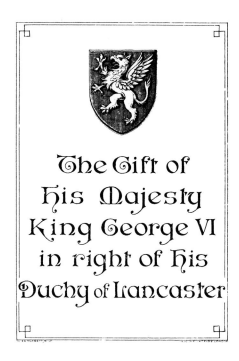

106

The Gift of His Majesty King George VI in right of His Duchy of Lancaster

Signed 'W. & A. MUSSETT fecit LINCOLN'S INN FIELDS LONDON'. Engraved label bearing the arms of Gray's Inn (Sable, a griffin segreant or), inscription below, all within a rectangular double line border. Rare. Author's coll.

The Honourable Society of Gray's Inn was, like the other three Inns of Court, founded in the thirteenth century on the command of King Edward I to his judges to bring attorneys and their apprentices into London and settle them in places where they could live together and study and practise law. The label commemorates a handsome gift from King George VI of a complete set (of 133 volumes) of the Statutes at Large from Magna Carta to 1944. It was the library's first gift after the Holker Library, of *c.* 30,000 volumes, was destroyed in May 1941 by enemy action. The Duchy of Lancaster has a close association with Gray's Inn, for its offices were there until just before 1788, situated between the Hall and the Chapel (see (45) and (46)). Amongst the Inn's Royal associations, the Hall screen is, by tradition, claimed to be of wood from a captured Spanish Armada galleon of 1588 and the gift of Queen Elizabeth I, then the Inn's Patron Lady; and

it has a contemporary portrait of her, aged 26, by an unknown artist. Members of the Royal family have been or are Honorary Benchers of the Inns of Court: the late Duke of Gloucester and Prince Charles, Prince of Wales, of Gray's Inn; King George VI and the present Queen of the Inner Temple; Princess Margaret of Lincoln's Inn; and Queen Elizabeth the Queen Mother of the Middle Temple.

W. & A. Mussett's Lincoln's Inn Heraldic Office was at 9 Great Turnstile, London WC1, until the site was demolished in 1951, then at 24 Red Lion Street, Holborn, surviving until the end of the 1970s. Papers back to 1727 refer to the old premises, which by December 1844 were occupied by Henry Salt's Heraldic Office. Pugh Brothers then ran the business, but by June 1888 William Mussett and his son A. A. Mussett Sr had taken over. A. A. Mussett Jr joined and then ran the firm until he was over 90. Hundred of bookplates, for many of which they employed freelance engravers, were amongst their diverse work, extending to hatchments, illuminated title-pages, monumental brasses, stained glass windows, etc.

107

HELENA (Princess, later Princess Christian of Schleswig-Holstein)

Unsigned. Pictorial: sprigs of rose, thistle and shamrock bound by a Royal coronet, the name on a ribbon below, within a double line lozenge border. It occurs in black, and on tinted paper in red, mauve and blue, generally cut close to the lozenge. Though different in composition, it was probably inspired by the ex-libris of her elder sister, Princess Alice (19). Uncommon. Author's coll.

Her Royal Highness Princess Helena Augusta Victoria was born at Buckingham Palace on 25 May 1846, the third daughter of Queen Victoria (144–158) and Prince Albert of Saxe-Coburg and Gotha (2–9). She married at the Private Chapel, Windsor Castle in 1866 Prince Frederick Christian Charles Augustus of Schleswig-Holstein-Sonderburg-Augustenburg (39–41), the third son of Christian, Duke of the same, and Luise Sophie, daughter of Christian Konrad Sophus, Count of Danneskjold-Samsoe. There were three sons and two daughters of the marriage. Longest-lived of them were Her Highness Princess Helena Victoria (164–165) and Her Highness Princess Marie Louise, the only one to marry. She died at Schomberg House, Pall Mall on 9 June 1923 and was buried at Frogmore. Princess Helena founded the Princess Christian Nursing Home at Windsor in 1894, and was the author of *Alice, Grand Duchess of Hesse: Letters to H.M. the Queen*, 1885, a record of her sister, mother of Alexandra Feodorovna, the last Empress of Russia. Princess Marie Louise, in *My Memories of Six Reigns*, 1956, commented that her mother was

> very lovely, with wavy brown hair, a beautiful little straight nose, and lovely amber coloured eyes. She was very talented: played the piano exquisitely, had a distinct gift for drawing and painting in water-colours, and she had a very clear, though not very strong, soprano voice. Her outstanding gift was her loyalty to her friends . . . she was brilliantly clever, had a wonderful head for business, and, indeed, she was truly a daughter of Queen Victoria.

The family lived at Cumberland Lodge (see the following).

NB An anonymous lozenge armorial with Princess Helena's arms as a widow has found place in bookplate collections, but there is as yet no evidence it was ever used as an ex-libris. The arms are: dexter, as (39) for Prince Christian; sinister, the Royal arms with over all a label of three points argent, charged on the centre point with a cross and on the others with a rose gules; Royal coronet above, the supporters charged on the shoulder with a label as on the arms. Engraved 1917–23, it is shown on p. 252 of Pinches' *The Royal Heraldry of England*, 1974.

108

HELENA (Princess Christian of Schleswig-Holstein)

Signed 'INV F G H(ouse)' and thus commissioned from Messrs Truslove & Hanson, but engraved by J. A. C. Harrison in 1905. Pictorial: a view of Cumberland Lodge, in a decorative rectangle enclosing name and coronet in an oval, national emblems, books, and a piano with score, etc. It occurs printed in black and in brown. Harrison's original sketch is shown alongside, the view of Cumberland Lodge being an original photograph, no doubt supplied by the Princess. It evidences how beautifully finished his preparatory designs were. Winterburn Coll.50.

For a biographical note on Princess Helena, which indicates the aptness of this bookplate's composition, see the foregoing. Cumberland Lodge, built as a hunting-lodge for the Stuarts, is described by Princess Helena's daughter Princess Marie Louise in *My Memories of Six Reigns*, 1956:

> The house was a warm red brick, covered with virginia creeper and honeysuckle. There was a large lake, and legend says that Cromwell had this lake dug by troops whilst they were trying to catch Charles the First. The great Duke of Marlborough lived (and died) there, and his Duchess was Ranger of Windsor Park ... She planted a beautiful lime

avenue leading up to the house, and whilst I am sitting here I feel I can still smell the perfume of the limes and hear the hum of the bees ... In the Duke of Marlborough's day Cumberland Lodge was called the Great Lodge. Shortly before his death, the Bishop – I think of Oxford – came to the Great Lodge to offer his services and religious ministrations to the dying Duke. This enraged Sarah – why, I do not know – and tradition relates that she pulled off his Bishop's wig, slapped his face, and bundled him down the stairs.

Prince and Princess Christian moved to Cumberland Lodge just before Princess Marie Louise was born in 1872. When dry rot was discovered in 1912 passages under the house were revealed leading to Royal Lodge and Windsor Castle.

For a note on J. A. C. Harrison see (15).

Frank George House's initials appear on over 130 ex-libris commissioned from Truslove & Hanson, Ltd, of Sloane Street, London, SW1. House was responsible for their bookplate orders, but a number of freelance engravers were employed.

GLOUCESTER

109

H GLOUCESTER (Prince Henry, Duke of Gloucester)

Unsigned, but engraved by Robert Osmond. Initial 'H' within the ribbon of the Garter, coronet above. Early proofs and prints (which may occur in bookplate collections since Osmond's archive was dispersed) differ in the lettering of the name, having a bowed 'U' and an upward curling tail to the 'R'. Winterburn Coll.38.

His Royal Highness Prince Henry William Frederick Albert was born at York Cottage, Sandringham, on 31 March 1900, the third son of the future King George V (88–96) and Queen Mary (124–129). He was educated at Eton – the first son of an English king to go to a public school – and Trinity College, Cambridge, then at the Royal Military College, before serving in the 10th Royal Hussars. Created Knight of the Garter in 1921 and Duke of Gloucester in 1928, he married at Buckingham Palace in 1935 the Lady Alice Christabel Montagu-Douglas-Scott

(21), third daughter of the 7th Duke of Buccleuch and (9th Duke of) Queensberry. She bore him two sons: Prince William, who was killed in an air crash in 1972, and Prince Richard, the present Duke of Gloucester. A Field Marshal and Marshal of the Royal Air Force, Prince Henry was Governor-General of Australia 1945–47 (see the following bookplate). He was President of Wellington College (see (8) and (9)), and became Great Master of the Order of the Bath in 1942. The homes of the Duke and Duchess of Gloucester were Barnwell Manor, Northamptonshire, and York House, St James's Palace. The Duke devoted himself unstintingly for almost half a century to the service of the Crown and the country, and died at Barnwell Manor on 10 June 1974. He was buried at Frogmore.

For a note on Robert Osmond see (64).

110

HENRY DUKE OF GLOUCESTER

Signed 'A F(eint)' and cut on wood, 1934. Armorial: the Royal arms with over all a label of three points argent charged on the centre point with a lion passant guardant and on each of the others with a cross gules; with helm, Royal crest, and supporters with coronets of his rank, charged on the shoulder with a label as on the arms. Uncommon. Author's coll.

This bookplate was presented to Prince Henry, Duke of Gloucester, by the Australian Ex Libris Society on his first visit to the country in 1934, and is one of a series of bookplates presented by it to members of the Royal family (see 60). It is doubtful, however, that it was ever used. Eleven years later His Royal Highness became Governor-General of Australia, and was in fact the last Englishman to hold the post. Two chapters of Percy Neville Barnett's *Australian Book-plates and book-plates of interest to Australia*, 1950, are devoted to vice-regal ex-libris, and an original print of this plate is tipped-in to the book. The Duke and Duchess of Gloucester were warmly welcomed in Australia, first because of the honour which King George VI brought to them in appointing his own brother as Governor-General, and then for the modesty, friendliness and clear dedication to duty which they brought to their years there. Indeed, the warmth of the Duke's feeling for Australia is evidenced by the determination with which he made sure its people were not let down when, in very failing health, he last visited it. His wife's *The Memoirs of Princess Alice Duchess of Gloucester*, 1983, provides fascinating insights into their sojourn in Australia.

For a note on Adrian Feint see (60).

H.R.H. Prince Leopold, K.G.

111

H.R.H. Prince Leopold, K.G.

Unsigned. Armorial: within the ribbon of the Garter, the Royal arms with over all an inescutcheon of Saxony and a label of three points argent charged on the centre point with a cross and on each of the others with a heart gules; with coronet, the Royal crest and crests of Saxony and Thuringia (see (6)), and the Royal supporters with coronets of his rank, charged on the shoulders with a label as on the arms. There are two varieties:

a)   Inscribed as above. Uncommon. Franks Coll.33228. Winterburn Coll.92.
b)   Inscribed 'H.R.H. The Duke of Albany. K.G', and therefore not earlier than 1881. Most prints of this variety show the copper to be significantly worn. Author's coll.

His Royal Highness Prince Leopold George Duncan Albert was born at Buckingham Palace on 7 April 1853, the fourth son of Queen Victoria (144–158) and Prince Albert of Saxe-Coburg and Gotha (2–9). He was ever delicate, having epilepsy and haemophilia, and was thus very over-protected; but he was fortunately very intelli-gent, artistic and bookish, and studied first with tutors and then at Christ Church, Oxford. He was created Duke of Albany in 1881, and married in 1882 at St George's Chapel, Windsor Princess Helen, the third daughter of Georg Viktor, Prince of Waldeck and Pyrmont and Helene, daughter of Wilhelm, Duke of Nassau. There were two children of the marriage: Princess Alice (20), later Countess of Athlone, and Prince Charles Edward, 2nd Duke of Albany, who was born after his father's death and became Duke of Saxe-Coburg and Gotha (34). The Duke and Duchess lived at Claremont, near Esher (see p. 4ff and (112)). After a fall down a staircase, Prince Leopold died suddenly at Cannes on 28 March 1884 and was buried in the Albert Memorial Chapel at Windsor.

NB   The Duchess of Albany continued to use her husband's ex-libris in her books for at least fourteen years after his death. Her daughter, Princess Alice, Countess of Athlone, was of the opinion that her mother had a book-plate made for her own use, *c.* 1896. No print of it has, however, been seen.

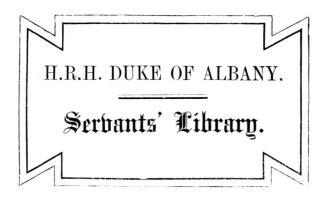

112

H.R.H. DUKE OF ALBANY. Servants' Library. (Prince Leopold)

Printed label with plain double line border angled at the corners. Only one print seen. Author's coll.

In view of the fact that Prince Leopold was created Duke of Albany less than a year before his marriage, it is to be assumed that this label marked books in the servants' library at Claremont, near Esher, where the Duke and Duchess of Albany made their home. Only two other instances of similar libraries for servants of Royalty are recorded. The one which was established by Queen Victoria and Prince Albert at Balmoral in 1859 (A.1) was for the wider use of tenants, servants and cottagers. The 'Royal Gardens, Windsor. Book Society' (A.2 & 3) probably fulfilled a similar function. It is not surprising that these libraries were set up. Queen Victoria and Prince Albert had a thorough concern for the all-round welfare of their staff and retainers, and at Balmoral could mix with and care for humble local people with a familiarity impossible elsewhere. Of all the Royal children, Leopold was probably the one who most truly loved books, and in view of his character and disposition a wish to share literary pleasures was to be expected. An illustrated article on Claremont, with pictures of the Duchess of Albany and her children, in the *Strand Magazine* for January–June, 1895 (see pp. 5–6), naturally features the family's apartments; and the servants, of which there must have been many in so sizeable a residence, are of course unvisited and unheard. With the hindsight of a hundred years it is sad to recollect that the servants' library there has been dispersed without record. Apart from its indicating something of Prince Leopold's taste, what insights into both Victorian attitudes towards education and their acceptance of what was 'improving' or 'allowable' such a library would have given. It would in a measure still be possible at Balmoral, where at least part of the library established in 1859 survives.

113

LUDWIG ALEXANDER PRINZ VON BATTENBERG (Prince Louis of Battenberg)

Unsigned, but perhaps by A. & C. Downey, *c.* 1885. Seal armorial: Quarterly, 1st and 4th, Azure, a lion rampant double-queued barry of ten argent and gules (should be crowned or), within a bordure componée of the second and third (Hesse modified); 2nd and 3rd, Argent, two pallets sable (Battenberg); with the crests of Hesse and Battenberg and the supporters of Hesse (but uncrowned), a continental coronet above, and motto below; the Order of the Golden Lion of Hesse-Cassel draped across the arms; inscription around. Rare. Author's coll.

His Serene Highness Prince Louis Alexander was born at Graz on 24 May 1854, the eldest son of Prince Alexander of Hesse and Julie Therese von Hauke (who in 1858 was created Princess of Battenberg), the daughter of Johann Moritz, Count von Hauke, and Sophie Lafontaine. He became a naturalized British subject in 1868, when he entered the Royal Navy. Prince Louis married at Darmstadt in 1884 his first cousin once removed, Princess Victoria of Hesse (162), the eldest daughter of Ludwig IV, Grand Duke of Hesse and by Rhine, and Princess Alice, the second daughter of Queen Victoria and Prince Albert. There were two sons and two daughters of the marriage: George, 2nd Marquess of Milford Haven (97–98), Earl Mountbatten of Burma (115–116), Princess Alice – the mother of Prince Philip, Duke of Edinburgh – and Queen Louise of Sweden. Prince Louis's career in the Royal Navy was very distinguished, and he was Commander-in-Chief of the Atlantic Fleet 1908 (in which year he became Vice-Admiral) to 1910. He was appointed First Sea Lord in 1912, but had to resign two years later due to anti-German feeling. It was a tragic situation, for his loyalty was absolute and his experience immensely desirable. In 1917, along with others of his family, he renounced the title of Prince of Battenberg and the qualification of Serene Highness, assumed the surname of Mountbatten, and was created Marquess of Milford Haven. He died in London on 11 September 1921.

Prince Louis showed signs of artistic talent from early childhood, and his parents positively encouraged a love of the arts in their children. When as a young man he accompanied the Prince of Wales on his Indian tour of 1875–76, he once had opportunity to use his talent commercially: *The Illustrated London News'* artist was ordered to China from Bombay, and Prince Louis agreed to help out. He depicted for them the final scenes before the Royal departure, and a pictorial record of the animals the Prince had been given. He later designed at least eight Royal bookplates (see p. 9), and possibly more.

See also (28), where there is a note on A. & C. Downey.

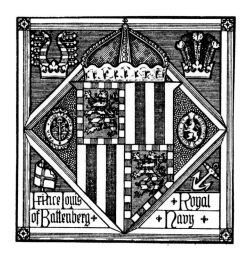

114

Prince Louis of Battenberg. Royal Navy

Unsigned, but designed by the Prince for his own use (see p. 9). Armorial: Quarterly, as the foregoing, with the arches of the continental coronet above the arms forming the apex of a lozenge in which are incorporated the badges of the Order of the Bath and the Order of the Golden Lion of Hesse-Cassel; the upper corners between the lozenge and rectangular border contain the crests of Hesse and Battenberg, the latter having five feathers instead of the customary four; in the lower corners are a flag, anchor and the inscription. Almost certainly reproduced by process, though it has an etched appearance, it is printed in brown. The plate must date from between 1887, when Prince Louis was made a Knight Grand Cross of the Order of the Bath (Civil), and 1901, when he became a Knight Grand Cross of the Royal Victorian Order – for had it been designed later that Order's badge would surely have been also included. Rare. Winterburn Coll.95.

Though artistically this is not the finest of Prince Louis's ex-libris designs, it must have meant much to him perso-nally, for he was so proud to belong to the Royal Navy, which indeed he served with distinction (see (113)). His passion for the sea had been stirred by the tales and uniform of Prince Alfred (16–18), and Princess Alice (19) effectively used her influence to get him into the navy as a British subject at the age of fourteen. At first his fellows gave him a difficult time, but he persevered. Prince Louis served in the Royal Yacht *Victoria and Albert* (see (138)), and was promoted to Commander in 1885, serving 1902–05 as Director of Naval Intelligence, and reaching the rank of Vice-Admiral in 1904. He became Commander-in-Chief of the Atlantic Fleet in 1908, Commander of the 3rd and 4th Divisions of the Home Fleet in 1911, and First Sea Lord the following year; but he had to resign in 1914 due to anti-German feeling. No doubt as token of such misplaced public suspicion, and in an effort to set the record straight on so loyal and distinguished a career, Prince Louis was specially promoted to Admiral of the Fleet on the retired list and was made Knight Grand Cross of the Military Divison of the Order of the Bath.

115

LORD LOUIS MOUNTBATTEN ROYAL NAVY

Signed 'A. BATCHELOR, F. LONDON 1923'. Armorial: within the ribbon of the Royal Victorian Order, from which the badge depends, Quarterly, 1st and 4th, Azure, a lion rampant double-queued barry of ten argent and gules crowned or, within a bordure componée of the second and third (Hesse modified); 2nd and 3rd, Argent, two pallets sable (Battenberg); the whole charged at the honour point with an inescutcheon of the Royal arms with a label of three points argent, the centre point charged with a rose gules and each of the others with an ermine spot sable (Princess Alice (98)); helms and crests of Hesse modified and Battenberg (see p. 15); supporters, Two lions double-queued and crowned all or, with motto and name cartouche beneath; all within a rectangular frame upon a cross-hatched ground. The 1927 ex-libris of his brother, George, 2nd Marquess of Milford Haven (98), was based on this design. Winterburn Coll.56.

His Serene Highness Prince Louis Francis Albert Victor Nicholas was born at Windsor Castle on 25 June 1900, the second son of Prince Louis of Battenberg, later 1st Marquess of Milford Haven (113–114) and Princess Victoria (162), the eldest daughter of Ludwig IV, Grand Duke of Hesse and by Rhine. He entered the Royal Navy in 1913, and in 1917, with others in his family, renounced the title of Prince of Battenberg and the qualification of Serene Highness. Lord Louis married at St Margaret's Church, Westminster in 1922 the Honourable Edwina Cynthia Annette Ashley, elder daughter of the 1st and last Baron Mount Temple. There were two daughters of the marriage: Lady Patricia, now Countess Mountbatten of Burma, and Lady Pamela Hicks. A.D.C. to the Prince of Wales on his Australian and Indian tours 1920–22, he served in both World Wars, and in the latter commanded *HMS Kelly* and *HMS Illustrious*; and he was Supreme Allied Commander in South-east Asia from 1943, receiving the surrender of the Japanese at Singapore in 1945. Further details of his life are given with his second bookplate, which follows.

For a note on Acheson Batchelor see (98).

116

MOUNTBATTEN OF BURMA

Unsigned, but engraved by George Taylor Friend. Armorial: the arms, crests, supporters and motto as in the foregoing bookplate, but the ribbon encircling the arms is now that of the Garter, and there is an earl's coronet above. The bookplate was commissioned from a Bond Street stationer, probably soon after 1947. Author's coll.

Lord Louis Mountbatten (for earlier details of whom see the foregoing) was created Viscount in 1946 and Earl Mountbatten of Burma in 1947. He became an Admiral of the Fleet in 1956, and from 1955 to 1959 was First Sea Lord, after which he was Chief of the United Kingdom Defence Staff until 1965. Earl Mountbatten, who lacked the disadvantage of diffidence, had a great interest in his family's genealogy; he was an excellent raconteur, as his television appearances evidenced, and his diverse interests and affiliations made him widely known. He lived at Broadlands in Hampshire, had a London house and Classiebawn Castle in County Sligo, Ireland. It was whilst on

holiday at the last of these that he and several others on his boat were murdered by the IRA on 27 August 1979. He was buried at Romsey Abbey, Hampshire.

George Taylor Friend (1881–1969), the son of Robert and Mary Friend, was apprenticed at the age of fourteen to James F. Barnard of Holborn, from whom he learnt engraving on gold and silver. He became a distinguished teacher at the Central School of Arts and Crafts in London, and in 1912 set up his own workshop in Holborn, where he carried on an engraving business for half a century. He engraved the Stalingrad sword, made over 500 ex-libris of high quality (continuing the Sherborn and Bumpus tradition), and was in 1954 awarded the O.B.E. for services to the teaching of engraving. This is the only British Royal bookplate he engraved, but he made several others for Indian princes, including the Nawab of Bahawalpur and the Maharajah of Jaipur.

117

L (Princess Louise, Marchioness of Lorne, late Duchess of Argyll)

Unsigned. Entwined ornate and shaded 'L's bound by a marquess's coronet, Royal coronet above. Engraved before 1900, when she became Duchess of Argyll. Royal Library Coll., Windsor.

Her Royal Highness Princess Louise Caroline Alberta was born at Buckingham Palace on 18 March 1848, the fourth daughter of Queen Victoria (144–158) and Prince Albert of Saxe-Coburg and Gotha (2–9). Beautiful and intelligent, she was a favourite of her father, and her artistic gifts were early apparent. She married at St George's Chapel, Windsor, in 1871 John Douglas Sutherland Campbell, Marquess of Lorne, and later 9th Duke of Argyll, son of the 8th Duke (182). It was the first marriage sanctioned by the sovereign of a princess with a man not of a reigning house since Henry VIII's sister Mary married Charles Brandon, Duke of Suffolk; but as the Marquess commented to the Queen when Berlin disapproved the engagement: 'Ma'am, my ancestors were Kings when the Hohenzollerns were parvenus.' There were no children of the marriage. They spent five years in Canada, where the Marquess was Governor-General. Both were artistic and bookish, and the Princess was a fine sculptress. Her best-known work is the statue of Queen Victoria in Kensington Gardens, but the monument to Prince Henry of Battenberg at Whippingham Church is also fine. An Honorary Fellow of the Royal Society of Painters in Water Colour, the Princess wrote as a journalist under the name 'Myra Fontenoy'. Not fond of Royal functions, and relishing privacy, their home at Kensington Palace became a centre for artists; and she was a firm supporter of education for women. Princess Louise died in her ninety-second year at Kensington Palace on 3 December 1939. She was cremated at Golders Green, and her ashes were buried at Frogmore.

An armorial in the Garraway Rice Collection of bookplates at the Society of Antiquaries shows their arms accolé as Marquess and Marchioness of Lorne. Princess Louise's label, there depicted, was of three points argent charged on the centre point with a rose and on each of the others with a canton gules. Since two months after his marriage the Marquess was created a Knight of the Thistle, which is not represented on the armorial, and since the present Duke of Argyll has only ever seen the ex-libris with crossed 'L's, it appears that the armorial served another purpose.

Harrison's preliminary sketches for the bookplate (reduced).

118

L M (Princess Louise Margaret of Prussia, Duchess of Connaught)

Signed 'INV W P B(arrett) 1905', and thus from Messrs J. & E. Bumpus of London but engraved by J. A. C. Harrison. Pictorial: in a festooned decorative rectangle, the initials in an oval cartouche, with wreath etc., coronet above. Though Barrett, responsible for Bumpus's bookplate commissions, in this period put 'INV' in inscriptions, he did not actually design ex-libris, as evidenced by Harrison's two variant preparatory designs. Winterburn Coll.45 and 46 (proof).

Her Royal Highness Princess Louise Margaret Alexandra Victoria Agnes was born at the Marmorpalais, Potsdam, on 25 June 1860, the fourth daughter of Prince Friedrich Karl of Prussia and Princess Maria Anna, youngest daughter of Leopold IV, Duke of Anhalt. She married at St George's Chapel, Windsor, in 1879 Prince Arthur, Duke of Connaught and Strathearn (22), the third son of Queen Victoria and Prince Albert of Saxe-Coburg and Gotha. They had one son, Prince Arthur of Connaught, and two daughters, Margaret, Crown Princess of Sweden, and Lady Patricia Ramsay (135). The family lived at Bagshot Park, Surrey and until the death of Queen Victoria in London at Buckingham Palace and thereafter at Clarence House. The Duchess died at Clarence House, St James's, on 14 March 1917 and was buried at Frogmore. (For a note on J. A. C. Harrison see (15)).

193

119

L (Princess Louise, Duchess of Fife and Princess Royal)

Unsigned. Crossed 'L's with coronet above, but no border. The form of the coronet indicates that the bookplate was made after her father became King in 1901. Uncommon. Author's coll.

Her Royal Highness Princess Louise Victoria Alexandra Dagmar was born at Marlborough House, London, on 20 February 1867, the eldest daughter of the future King Edward VII (48–57) and Queen Alexandra (13–15). She married at Buckingham Palace in 1889 Alexander William George Duff, 1st Duke of Fife (183), who was, incidentally, a great-grandson of King William IV on the distaff side, his maternal grandmother being Elizabeth FitzClarence. There were two daughters of the marriage: Alexandra, later Duchess of Fife, and Lady Maud Carnegie, later Countess of Southesk (both of them were given the title of Princess and the qualification of Highness in 1905). In 1905 Princess Louise was declared Princess Royal of Great Britain. She was Colonel-in-Chief of the 4th/7th Dragoon Guards. A lover of the outdoors, of salmon-fishing, and of privacy, the family's Scottish homes at Mar Lodge and Duff House were ideal for her; and she had a residence in Portman Square, London. Princess Louise died on 4 January 1931 and was buried at St George's Chapel, Windsor, but her remains were later transferred to Scotland.

In an auction sale at Sothebys, 4–6 February 1963, lot 594 comprised seventy-four miscellaneous books, mostly pocket editions, bound in limp leather, calf or morocco. Many of them contained a book label with the inscription, 'From the library of Her late Royal Highness Princess Royal'. This was evidently Princess Louise, and indicates that use of her ex-libris was by no means universal in her library; but no print of the label has been seen by the writer. Such labels are not uncommonly inserted into the books of well-known personages as a note of provenance after their deaths, but most often in the case of famous writers.

The title of Princess Royal has on occasion been conferred upon the eldest daughter of the monarch, but in three and a half centuries only seven princesses have been accorded this style. They were King Charles I's daughter Princess Mary, King George II's daughter Princess Anne, King George III's daughter Princess Charlotte, Queen Victoria's daughter Princess Victoria (159–61), King Edward VII's daughter Princess Louise, King George V's daughter Princess Mary (130), and Queen Elizabeth II's daughter Princess Anne. See the note on Royal coronets, p. 13.

Maria Countess Waldegrave

120

Maria Countess Waldegrave (later Duchess of Gloucester)

Unsigned. Armorial: within the ribbon of the Garter, Per pale argent and gules (Waldegrave), impaling Or, on a fess between two chevrons sable three crosses crosslet of the first (Walpole); with supporters, motto and earl's coronet. Franks Coll.30540. See the following.

HER ROYAL HIGHNESS

M A R I A

DUCHESS OF GLOUCESTER.

121

HER ROYAL HIGHNESS MARIA DUCHESS OF GLOUCESTER

Printed label without ornament. It probably belonged to the 1st Duchess (120), rather than her daughter-in-law, Princess Mary, fourth daughter of King George III who married her son William Frederick, the 2nd Duke. Viner Coll. Very rare.

Maria, born probably in 1736 (see below), second natural daughter of the Hon. Sir Edward Walpole by Dorothy Clements, married in 1759 James, 2nd Earl Waldegrave, lord of the bedchamber and most intimate friend and adviser of King George II. Said at one time to be the handsomest woman in England, with a wit to match, Reynolds painted her no fewer than seven times. Though Waldegrave was twice her age, and died after four years, she bore him three daughters. In 1766 she secretly married at her house in Pall Mall, London, Prince William Henry, Duke of Gloucester (see (167)), younger brother of King George III. On the Royal Marriages Act being passed in 1772, the Duke confessed to the King and was banished from court. The marriage was investigated and allowed, and in 1780 he was restored to favour. They had three children: William Frederick, 2nd Duke of Gloucester (167–168), Princess Sophia Matilda, who never married, and a daughter who died in infancy. Maria, Duchess of Gloucester, died at Brompton on 23 August 1807 and was buried at St George's Chapel, Windsor.

Authorities differ on her year of birth. Violet Biddulph, *The Three Ladies Waldegrave,* 1938, follows Horace Walpole in saying 1735; *The Complete Peerage* gives, under Waldegrave 'bapt. 10 July 1736', and under Gloucester 'b. 10 July 1736'; *Gentlemen's Magazine,* 1807, p. 790, says died 'in her 72nd year'; but the same, p. 885, 'corrects' to 'born 3 July 1739', though her coffin plate is there cited as reading 'aetatis suae 71'. Her younger sister was born 1738, and the evidence seems to favour July 1736.

122

M (Princess Marina, Duchess of Kent)

Unsigned. Initial with coronet above; a smaller and shaded version was used by the Princess on her note-paper. Although this bookplate does not appear to have been used, evidence indicates that it was made as an ex-libris. Viner Coll.

Her Royal Highness Princess Marina was born in Athens on 13 December 1906, the third daughter of Prince Nicholas of Greece and Denmark and Helena, only daughter of the Grand Duke Vladimir Alexandrovitch of Russia. Although she saw the splendour of the Russian Imperial Court as a child, the Princess's upbringing under her English nanny, Miss Fox, was strict; but it was also very loving, and English was her first language. In 1917 her family were exiled for four years, spent mostly in Switzerland. They returned to Greece, but soon had to leave again, and settled in Paris. She married at Westminster Abbey in 1934 Prince George, Duke of Kent, the fourth son of King George V (88–96) and Queen Mary (124–129), who shared her interest in the arts. There were three children of the marriage: Prince Edward, now Duke of Kent, Princess Alexandra, and Prince Michael. Their homes were 3 Belgrave Square, Coppins, near Iver, Bucks., and Kensington Palace. Princess Marina, a great beauty

and one of the best-dressed women of her time, knew great family sorrows, and lost her husband in a flying accident in the Second World War, in 1942. Though somewhat shy and diffident she undertook Royal engagements, including overseas tours; and her patronage extended to the Lawn Tennis Association, of which she was a devoted President for many years. Princess Marina died at Kensington Palace on 27 August 1968, and was buried at Frogmore.

A photograph of a drawing for an armorial bookplate inscribed 'H.R.H. THE DUKE OF KENT K.G' in the author's collection bore a note that the design was by F.G. House (see (108)). Over the arms is his label of three points argent each charged with an anchor azure, with which the supporters are also charged on the shoulders. It could not be earlier than 1934, when Prince George was created Duke of Kent, but was probably designed then, for he was made a Knight of the Thistle the following year (and the composition includes no reference to this). No print has been seen, so perhaps it was never engraved; but it is evidence that the Duke made moves to acquire a personal ex-libris.

123

M A (Princess Mary Adelaide, Duchess of Teck)

Signed 'C. W. Sherborn ft. 1890'. Entwined initials within an oval cartouche ornamented with branches of palm, with coronet above. A print of this bookplate, from the original copper, appears as illustration in Norna Labouchere's *Ladies' Book-plates*, 1895. Franks Coll.33233. Winterburn Coll.49. It also occurs as a process reproduction.

Her Royal Highness Princess Mary Adelaide Wilhelmina Elizabeth was born at Hanover on 22 November 1833, the second daughter of Prince Adolphus Frederick, Duke of Cambridge and seventh son of King George III (75–77), and Princess Auguste Wilhelmine Louise, the third daughter of Friedrich II, Landgrave of Hesse-Cassel. She married at St Anne's Church at Kew, Surrey in 1866 Francis Paul Charles Louis Alexander, Prince and 1st Duke of Teck (68). Their eldest child and only daughter was the future Queen Mary (124–129), and they had three sons: Adolphus, 2nd Duke of Teck, Francis and Alexander George (10), who became Earl of Athlone. The family lived at Kensington Palace and from 1870 at White Lodge, Richmond Park – a note on which follows. Princess Mary Adelaide, a lady of very ample proportions, was immensely popular with the British public; but she was notoriously bad at managing financially, and friends and relations often had to come to her aid. She died at White Lodge on 27 October 1897 and was buried at St George's Chapel, Windsor.

White Lodge in Richmond Park, built as a hunting-box by King George I, was enlarged by King George II and was much used by his wife, Queen Caroline. Lord Bute was its next occupant, then Addington, followed by Princess Mary, Duchess of Gloucester, daughter of King George III. It was loaned by Queen Victoria to Lady Phipps before becoming the residence of the Tecks. The Duke of Teck's study was also used as the library, but – as James Pope-Hennessy points out in his *Queen Mary*, 1959 – its bookshelves, in a pilastered alcove, would have held at most about 800 volumes. Since 1955 White Lodge has been the junior school of the Royal Ballet.

For a note on Charles William Sherborn see (68).

124

V M (Princess Victoria Mary, Duchess of York, later Queen Mary)

Signed 'C W. Sherborn Sc.'. Entwined initials on a stippled ground in an oval cartouche surrounded by may blossom; the form of the coronet above is incorrect (see p. 13). This bookplate is wrongly ascribed in the catalogue of Sherborn's work (see (68)) to the year 1890, for the white rose of York below the coronet, and the coronet itself, evidence that it was engraved after the Princess's marriage to the Duke of York in 1893. Franks Coll.33234. Winterburn Coll.48.

Her Serene Highness Princess Victoria Mary Augusta Louisa Olga Pauline Claudine Agnes (known as Princess May) was born at Kensington Palace on 26 May 1867, the only daughter of Prince Francis, Duke of Teck (68), and Princess Mary Adelaide (123). Engaged first to the Duke of Clarence, who died shortly afterwards, she married at the Chapel Royal, St James's Palace in 1893 his next brother, the future King George V (88–96). There were five sons and one daughter of the marriage. From 1901 she was Princess of Wales, and became Queen Consort on her husband's accession to the throne in 1910.

Light-hearted in early life, her strong sense of duty and dedication later made her a revered and immensely dignified Queen. She had a fine sense of history, was an enthusiastic collector of works of art, and was a very accomplished needlewoman. Widowed in 1936, in the brief reign of her eldest son, King Edward VIII (58–61), she showed a rock-like steadfastness which did much to maintain the stability of the Crown. Queen Mary broke with tradition in attending as Queen Dowager the coronation of her second son, King George VI (99–106). Thereafter, she continued her public service and her interest in the arts and the lives of her family. As James Pope-Hennessy observed, in his excellent biography, *Queen Mary*, 1959, 'By undeviating service to her own highest ideals, she . . . ended by becoming for millions, an ideal in herself.' Queen Mary died at Marlborough House on 24 March 1953 and was buried at St George's Chapel, Windsor.

For a note on Charles William Sherborn see (68).

The Duchess of York's Library

125

The Duchess of York's Library. (later Queen Mary)

Unsigned. Armorial: two shields accolé: dexter, within the ribbon of the Garter the Royal arms with over all an inescutcheon of Saxony and a label of three points argent charged at the centre point with an anchor azure (Prince George, Duke of York); sinister, Or three stags' attires fessways in pale points to the sinister sable (Württemburg), impaling Or, three lions passant in pale sable langued gules the dexter forepaws of the last (Swabia), and over all an inescutcheon paly bendy sinister sable and or (Teck); with coronet of the Duke's rank and Royal crest above, the Royal supporters charged on the shoulder with a label as on the arms and with coronets as above. It was engraved between 1893 and 1901 when her husband, the future King George V (88–96), became Prince of Wales. Rare. Royal Library Coll., Windsor.

Between the marriage of Princess Mary (May) of Teck and Prince George, Duke of York, in 1893 and the death of Queen Alexandra in 1925 they lived at York Cottage on the Sandringham estate and until 1901 at York House, St James's Palace, moving then to Marlborough House where they lived until 1910. The former had been given to the Duke by the Prince of Wales as a wedding present, but was far too small to be really convenient – and a little too close to their 'in-laws' at Sandringham for the sort of privacy for which a young married couple may hope. The Cottage had to be added to in an *ad hoc* way as their family increased. York House, by contrast, had seventy-five rooms, but was somewhat gloomy and sunless. One of the pleasures of their early days together was Prince George reading books aloud to his wife, as he had earlier been in the habit of doing as his mother had her hair dressed in the morning. James Pope-Hennessy, in his *Queen Mary*, 1959, records that one of the books was Greville's memoirs, which the Duchess thought amusing but spiteful. Books remained a life-long pleasure to Queen Mary, and she would often sit of an evening at her embroidery while a lady-in-waiting read to her; and even on the evening before her death, at the age of 85, she asked for a volume on India to be read. Three hundred and thirty-five books from Queen Mary's library were in 1962 presented to the University of the West Indies, of which her sister-in-law, Princess Alice, Countess of Athlone, was Chancellor; others were given to the London Library.

126

MARY (Queen)

Signed 'W. P. B(arrett)', and thus commissioned from Messrs J & E. Bumpus of London, but engraved by Robert Osmond, and dated '1910' below the name cartouche. Pictorial: within a panel with husked borders and winged cherub heads and roses in the corners, the name cartouche surmounted by a Royal crown supported by cherubs above an arrangement of roses, thistles and shamrock. Its design is based on a key-plate at Hampton Court. The original drawing is in the Royal Library at Windsor, with a number of progress proofs which show that it was engraved between August and 10 October 1910. Winterburn Coll.23.

127

M R I EX LIBRIS (Mary, Queen and Empress)

Unsigned, but commissioned from Messrs J. & E. Bumpus of London, and engraved by Robert Osmond in 1923. Cypher surmounted by a Royal crown. The size and year of engraving of this suggest that it was intended for Queen Mary's Dolls' House (see the following), and this purpose is indicated in Christine Price's *Catalogue of Royal Bookplates from the Louise E. Winterburn Collection*, 1944 (see p. 1), where the bookplate is No. 44. What is more significant is that there is a print of it in the bookplate collection at the Royal Library at Windsor. It is possible that Queen Mary, or a relative or friend, commissioned it only to find that another design had already been accepted for use in the books in the Dolls' House. On evidence available it does not seem to have been used there. Alternatively, Queen Mary may have had it made for other miniature books in her possession.

For a note on Robert Osmond see (64).

EX LIBRIS

128

M R EX LIBRIS (Queen Mary)

Signed 'E S' (Ernest Shepard). Within a rectangle a view of Windsor Castle, trees in the foreground, and the Royal cypher on a scroll above. A miniature bookplate, for Queen Mary's Dolls' House. Very rare.

The story of the creation of Queen Mary's Dolls' House — largely made in 1923 and completed in 1924 — is told in Princess Marie Louise's *My Memories of Six Reigns*, 1956. Finding her mother and sister one day collecting tiny *objets d'art* for Queen Mary, who was furnishing a dolls' house, the Princess had the idea of asking Sir Edwin Lutyens to design a dolls' house which could, as she put it, show 'how a King and Queen of England lived in the twentieth century, and what authors, artists, and craftsmen of note there were during the reign'. The Queen's approval was sought and given, and the Princess was appointed 'liaison officer'. With its Georgian facade, it was built on four floors, with mezzanine and basement; it housed a treasury of miniature objects, and its garden was designed and laid out by Gertrude Jekyll. Noted artists contributed a tiny picture; each piece of furniture was specially made; the King's red despatch boxes were purloined and copied; newspapers were made to scale and notepaper was exactly reproduced; and the King's motors

in the garage were faithful replicas. In the Library were 200 books, postage stamp size, written out by their authors. Kipling wrote out 'If', and added illustrations. The only author approached who replied rudely was George Bernard Shaw. Each volume was specially bound, with 'M' and a crown on the cover; and each had this tiny bookplate in it. The Dolls' House was on display in a small pavilion at the 1924 Wembley Exhibition, and may now be viewed at Windsor Castle.

Ernest Howard Shepard (1879–1976) was born in London, the son of an architect. He studied at Heatherleys and the R.A. Schools, and moved to Shamley Green, Guildford in 1904. Shepard drew for *Punch* from 1907 and became its chief cartoonist in 1945; but his best work related to childhood, and he was justly celebrated for his drawings for A. A. Milne's *Pooh* series, of which *Winnie-the-Pooh*, 1926, was the first. He exhibited at the Royal Academy for seventy-five years. His commissioning to make this bookplate, three years before *Pooh* brought him acclaim, indicates either that his *Punch* contributions were especially admired (he was elected to the *Punch* table in 1921) or that he was admired for his artistic works before he made his mark as a book illustrator.

EX LIBRIS

Enlargement of the above showing its detail.

129

MARY R (Queen Mary as Queen Dowager)

Signed 'H. J. F. Badeley 1946'. Armorial: within the ribbon of the Garter, the Royal arms impaling quarterly, 1st and 4th, the Royal arms as used 1801–37 with over all a label of three points argent charged on the centre point with a cross and on each of the others with two hearts in pale gules (Cambridge); 2nd and 3rd, Or, three stags' attires fessways in pale points to the sinister sable (Württemburg); impaling Or, three lions passant in pale sable langued gules the dexter forepaws of the last (Swabia); over all an inescutcheon paly bendy sinister sable and or (Teck); with Royal crown and mantling beneath the name cartouche; supporters, Dexter, a lion guardant or Imperially crowned proper; sinister, a stag proper; all within a rectangular frame broken at base with an ornamental leafy cartouche. Uncommon. Author's coll.

As Queen Dowager Buckingham Palace remained Queen Mary's home during the brief reign of her unmarried son, King Edward VIII, but she redecorated Marlborough House, into which she moved a couple of months before the King's abdication. Built for the 1st Duke of Marlbor-ough and his Duchess, Marlborough House had been the home of Prince Leopold as widower, before he became King of the Belgians; of the Dowager Queen Adelaide, and of King Edward VII and King George V and their wives as Princes and Princesses of Wales; so it was already a familiar home to Queen Mary. During the Second World War she moved for safety to Badminton, but thereafter she graced Marlborough House until her death; and it would have been there that this bookplate was used. Its engraver, Lord Badeley (for a note on whom see (11)), was a friend of Queen Mary, which no doubt accounted for his making this ex-libris for her and others for members of the Royal family (see p. 9).

NB   A modest printed label, within a border of tiny ornaments, reading 'M. PRIVATE PROPERTY', with a Royal crown above an ornamented letter 'M', was used as a mark of ownership for items other than books, probably including pictures and suchlike. There is no evidence it ever served as a bookplate. The rectangular frame measures 45 × 70mm.

130

M (Princess Mary, later Countess of Harewood and Princess Royal)

Signed 'W P B(arrett) 1909' and then '1910', and therefore commissioned from Messrs J. & E. Bumpus of London, but engraved by Robert Osmond. Initial in a decorative oval showing roses, thistles and shamrock, coronet above. When, in 1909, a bookplate was wanted for Princess Mary, the sister of Prince Edward and Prince Albert (58 and 99), Bumpus's were again called on. Since, however, J. A. C. Harrison, who engraved the Princes' ex-libris, had parted from Bumpus, the task was given to Robert Osmond. Though this bookplate is smaller, its composition is identical, so Osmond 'pirated' Harrison's design (he probably had no option). Three states of the plate have been seen:

a) Dated 1909, with the coronet of children of the heir apparent (two strawberry leaves, two crosses patée and four fleurs de lys).
b) As above, but the coronet changed to four crosses patée and four fleurs de lys, the date unchanged. These must have been 1910 intermediate proofs whilst changing the ex-libris to one appropriate to the sovereign's daughter.*
c) With the coronet of (b) above, but dated 1910. Princess Mary's father was now King George V. Author's coll.

All states of this plate are rare. Winterburn Coll.43.

Her Royal Highness Princess Victoria Alexandra Alice Mary was born at York Cottage, Sandringham on 25 April 1897, the third child but only daughter of the future King George V (88–96) and Queen Mary (124–129). She married at Westminster Abbey in 1922 Henry George Charles, Viscount Lascelles, who later became 6th Earl of Harewood (185–186), elder son of the 5th Earl of Harewood. There were two sons of the marriage. In 1932 Princess Mary was declared Princess Royal. Rather quiet and artistic, Princess Mary devoted much time to charitable work, and was a close companion to her mother in her widowhood. She died at Harewood House on 28 March 1965.

For a note on Robert Osmond see (64).

Philip Tilden (see (59)) records in his memoirs, *True Remembrances*, 1954, that *c.*1919 he made an ex-libris for Princess Mary, showing a basket of flowers and a great and glorified capital 'M'; but it seems never to have been used.

---

* The only reason why prints of this bookplate occur at all in collections is that the contents of Osmond's studio were sold by his family after his death to bookplate collectors.

131

M B (Mary, Duchess of Beaufort)

Unsigned. Monogram within a cartouche, originally a marquess's coronet above, and a tiny photographic reproduction of Badminton House, all framed by vases and formalized flowers at left and right and perhaps clouds above. The coronet was incorrect. At the time of their marriage her husband was still Marquess of Worcester; he succeeded his father as Duke in 1924. However, if the bookplate had been made before she became Duchess, the 'B' would have been wrong and the depiction of Badminton a little premature. Printed by process. Royal Library Coll., Windsor.

Her Serene Highness Princess Victoria Constance Mary was born at White Lodge, Richmond Park (see (123)) on 12 June 1897, the elder daughter of Prince Adolphus, 2nd Duke of Teck, and Lady Margaret Evelyn Grosvenor, fourth daughter of the 1st Duke of Westminster. Along with other members of her family she relinquished the qualification of Serene Highness in 1917 and took the name Cambridge. She married at St Margaret's, Westminster, in 1923 Henry Hugh Arthur FitzRoy Somerset, Marquess of Worcester and later 10th Duke of Beaufort.

There were no children of the marriage. Badminton House in Gloucestershire was their home, and the Dowager Duchess remained in residence there until her death. It was to Badminton that Queen Mary went to spend the war years, for it was at a distance from London and the Duchess was her niece. From the age of 11 — when his father gave him a pack of harriers — the Duke of Beaufort, who remained a great hunting man in the Beaufort tradition throughout his life, was known as 'Master'; and in 1936 he became Master of the Horse, one of the three senior positions in the Royal Household — an ancient dignity the title of which came into being in the lifetime of the Duke's ancestor, John of Gaunt. The Duke's memoirs were published by *Country Life* in 1981, and give a charmingly direct account of his life and service to the Crown, as well as of his ancestors. A chapter is devoted to Badminton. The stag seen in the foreground of the bookplate's photograph is no doubt one of the splendid two-hundred strong herd of red deer in the park there. The Dowager Duchess died at Badminton on 23 June 1987, and was buried there.

132

MAUD, QUEEN OF NORWAY (formerly Princess Maud, daughter of King Edward VII)

Signed 'INV W. P. B(arrett). 1907', and thus commissioned from Messrs J. & E. Bumpus of London, but engraved by J. A. C. Harrison. Pictorial: within a decorative rectangular frame with extended corners, a view of Byddoc Fiord with pine trees on a promontory, the scene moonlit; flags of Norway and Great Britain at left and right, with daffodils and (?) lilies; books and carnations at base, name cartouche above amid pansies and surmounted by a coronet. Though prints can in general be described as black, close examination shows subtle colour variations: black with a hint of brown, and black with a hint of blue. Winterburn Coll. 41.

Her Royal Highness Princess Maud Charlotte Mary Victoria was born at Marlborough House, London, on 26 November 1869, the third daughter of the future King Edward VII (48–57) and Queen Alexandra (13–15). She married at Buckingham Palace in 1896 her first cousin, Prince Christian Frederik Carl Georg Valdemar Axel of Denmark (later King Haakon VII of Norway), the second son of King Frederick VIII of Denmark, brother of Queen Alexandra. Their only son, who became King Olav V of Norway in 1957, was born at Appleton House, Sandringham, Norfolk – a home to which the Queen returned yearly throughout her life. Queen Maud attended the coronation of her nephew King George VI in 1937, and died rather suddenly in London on 20 November 1938. She was buried at Oslo. Known as 'Harry' in the family (for she had always wanted to be a boy), and the favourite sister-in-law of Queen Mary, the gentle and pretty – but somewhat delicate – Queen Maud of Norway loved art, music, country life and gardening.

For a note on J. A. C. Harrison see (15).

133

HENRY ABEL SMITH MAY HIS WIFE 1931

Unsigned. Armorial: Or, a chevron cotised sable, between three demi-griffins couped of the last, and two in chief respecting each other (Smith of Woodhall Park), impaling Quarterly, 1st and 4th, the Royal arms as borne 1801–37 with over all a label of three points argent charged on the centre point with a cross and on each of the others with two hearts in pale gules (Cambridge); 2nd and 3rd, Or, three stags' attires fessways in pale points to the sinister sable (Württemburg); impaling Or, three lions passant in pale sable langued gules the dexter forepaws of the last (Swabia); over all an inescutcheon paly bendy sinister sable or (Teck); with helm and the Smith crest and motto, the inscription on a tablet below, within a rectangular border. The rather unusual form of the inscription is based on that of Sir Henry Abel Smith's father's bookplate of 1885, which reads 'FRANCIS ABEL SMITH, MADELINE ST. MAUR, HIS WIFE'. Probably commissioned from the College of Arms, the bookplate occurs also in a smaller size, reduced by about half. Author's coll.

Her Serene Highness Princess May Helen Emma was born at Claremont, Esher, on 23 January 1906, the only daughter of Prince Alexander George of Teck (10) and Princess Alice (20), the only daughter of Prince Leopold, Duke of Albany. With her father (who became the Earl of Athlone) and her brother Rupert (who became Viscount Trematon, and died in 1928) she relinquished her German titles and the qualification of Serene Highness in 1917 and assumed the surname of Cambridge. She married in 1931 at Balcombe in Sussex Colonel Sir Henry Abel Smith, the elder surviving son of Francis Abel Smith of Wilford House, Nottinghamshire. There was one son and two daughters of the marriage. Sir Henry, who served in the Royal Horse Guards and was acting Colonel of the Corps of Household Cavalry, 1946, was Governor of Queensland 1958–66.

134

OSBORNE (Osborne House, Isle of Wight)

Unsigned. Name beneath a Royal crown in a scrolled circular cartouche. It occurs printed embossed in pale blue, medium blue, purple–brown, black and gold. Illustrated beneath it are two book-stamps used on volumes at Osborne, the earlier for Queen Victoria's domestic library. Some volumes bear both stamps, and it may be that the latter stamp was used for books given to the Naval College or Convalescent Home (see below). Rare. Author's coll.

The Italianate Osborne House, a mile outside East Cowes on the Isle of Wight, was a favourite residence of Queen Victoria (144–158) and Prince Albert (2–9). With an expanding family they wanted somewhere more comfortable than formal palaces where the Prince's personal taste and love of experiment could be applied. They heard of Osborne – a genteel residence with 200 acres of park, a farm and a wood – in 1843, when it belonged to Lady Isabella Blachford; they took the house for a year in 1844, bought it and then built a new house there, which was

finished in 1851. Prince Albert was largely responsible for its design, and he was assisted by Thomas Cubitt. The Royal family delighted in Osborne's informality, open air, opportunities for farming, and the sea at the end of the garden. The exotic Durbar Room, added in 1890, was – uniquely – dedicated to Queen Victoria's function as Empress of India. Its decoration was designed by Bhai Ram Singh, and Rudyard Kipling's father, John Lockwood Kipling, was consulted on its plans. After Queen Victoria's death at Osborne in 1901, King Edward VII found the future of the house a problem, for it was left to him but he did not wish to live there. His solution was to keep the central portion of the house closed and shrine-like, to give the stables and land around them for use as a new naval college, and to give the great wing as a convalescent home for officers. These were gifts to the nation, and they took effect from his coronation day. It may well be that books from the old Osborne Library were given for use within one or other of these institutions.

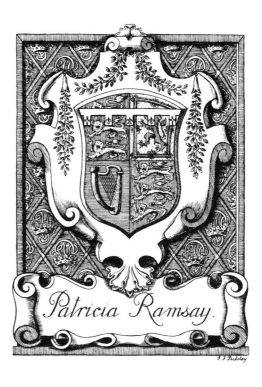

135

Patricia Ramsay. (formerly Princess Patricia of Connaught)

Signed 'J. F. Badeley'. Armorial: within a festooned cartouche the Royal arms with over all a label of five points argent charged on the two outer with a cross gules and on each of the others with a fleur de lys azure; on a latticed ground incorporating coronets and monograms, the name on a cartouche below, all within a rectangular border. It was engraved in 1919, and it is interesting to note that, having relinquished her title (see below), the coronet of her former rank is incorporated into the background of her ex-libris. Royal Library Coll., Windsor.

Her Royal Highness Princess Victoria Patricia Helena Elizabeth was born at Buckingham Palace on 17 March 1886, the second daughter of Prince Arthur, Duke of Connaught and Strathearn (22) and Princess Louise Margaret (118), third daughter of Prince Friedrich Karl of Prussia. Princess Patricia was Colonel-in-Chief of Princess Patricia's Canadian Light Infantry from 1914. She married at Westminster Abbey in 1919 Admiral the Hon. Sir Alexander Robert Maule Ramsey, third son of the 13th Earl of Dalhousie; and was authorized by Royal Warrant to relinquish the title of Princess and the qualification of Royal Highness and assume the title of Lady with precedence before the Marchionesses of England. There was one son of the marriage: Alexander Arthur Alfonso David Maule Ramsey of Mar. A dedicated painter, the Princess was taught by Archibald Standish Hartrick and became a member of the Royal Society of Painters in Water Colour. Sir Alexander was at the Royal Naval College, Dartmouth, and served in the Dardanelles 1914–15. Naval A.D.C. to King George V from 1931, he was Commodore of the Royal Naval Barracks at Portsmouth 1929–31, Commander-in-Chief East Indies 1936–38, Fifth Sea Lord and Chief of the Naval Air Service 1938–39 and was made Admiral in 1939. The Ramsays lived at Ribsden Holt, Windlesham, Surrey, and Lady Patricia died there on 12 January 1974. She was buried at Frogmore.

PRIVY PURSE LIBRARY,
BUCKINGHAM PALACE.

PRIVY PURSE LIBRARY,
BUCKINGHAM PALACE.

136

PRIVY PURSE LIBRARY, BUCKINGHAM PALACE

Unsigned. Armorial: within the ribbon of the Garter, the Royal arms, with helm, Royal crown and crest and supporters, motto below. It occurs printed in black, brown or gold, and the inscription is letterpress. The composition appears to be based on Reynolds Stone's design for the arms adopted by Queen Elizabeth II in 1953 issued with a press release in that year (Stone's design is illustrated on p. 273 of Charles Hasler's *The Royal Arms*, 1980); but see the following.

137

PRIVY PURSE LIBRARY, BUCKINGHAM PALACE

As the last in composition, with letterpress inscription, but the design is not oval and the motto lettering is black on white. The most significant difference is the coronet's shape. That of (136), often called an Imperial crown, was used from the time of Queen Victoria until 1954, when it was officially replaced by the St Edward's crown (though the latter understandably adorned 1953 coronation publications). It is likely, therefore, that (137) is the later of the two ex-libris.

Buckingham Palace, as well as being the London residence of the sovereign, houses many of the Royal Household's offices. The principal departments are those of the Lord Steward, the Lord Chamberlain and the Master of the Horse. The first – which is our concern here – cares for the running of the monarch's residences and deals with the Household's finances and other matters. In precedence next to the Lord Steward comes the Master of the Household (a salaried officer), who details staff, oversees the provision of victuals, presides over the Board of Green Cloth, etc., with the aid of clerks, housekeepers and assistants. The Keeper of the Privy Purse and Treasurer controls the sovereign's Civil List finances – the moneys voted to the King or Queen by Parliament to cover the cost of ceremonial and constitutional monarchy. This annual sum includes all salaries and the expense of public engagements, travel and entertaining. The Privy Purse is not concerned with the sovereign's personal wealth. The Royal Almonry is looked after by the Treasurer, and comes to public notice annually with the presentation of Maundy money. The Privy Purse originated in 1760 when King George III gave to Parliament the revenues from Crown Lands in exchange for a fixed sum.

138

EX LIBRIS THE ROYAL YACHT

Unsigned. Pictorial–armorial, showing the *Victoria and Albert II* off Osborne; below, flanked by dolphins, the Royal arms and Prince Albert's (see (2)) in oval shields accolé surmounted by Royal and continental crowns and embraced by a single Garter ribbon; the inscription on a ribbon above. Rare. Viner and author's colls.

There were more Royal yachts than is generally realized. Between 1660, when *Mary* (the first) was given to King Charles II by the Dutch, and 1877, when the *Royal Adelaide* of 1833 was broken up, there were over sixty Royal sailing yachts. The largest were the *Royal Caroline* of 1749, renamed *Royal Charlotte* 1761, dismantled in 1820 (232 tons); the *Royal Sovereign*, 1804–50 (278 tons); the *Royal George*, 1817–1905 (330 tons); and the *Prince Regent*, 1820, refitted 1836 and presented to the Imam of Muscat (282 tons). Of eight Royal steam yachts, the lesser were *Fairy*, 1844–68 (dismantled), tender to *Victoria and Albert*, as were *Elfin*, 1848–1901 (dismantled), and *Alberta*, 1863–1913 (broken up). *Osborne II*, of 1868, was sold in 1908, and *Alexandra*, of 1906, was sold to the Norwegian Shipping Company in 1925 and renamed *Prince Olaf*. Victoria as Queen first travelled with Prince Albert in 1842 in the *Royal George*. *Victoria and Albert I* was built in 1842, renamed *Osborne* in 1855, paid off in 1859 and broken up in 1868. *Victoria and Albert II* was completed in 1854. A paddle vessel of 2,470 tons, it was launched from Pembroke Dock, and was luxurious but unostentatious. The Royal apartments had red and black Brussels carpet in a coral pattern; and there was a pavilion, or breakfast room, the Queen's drawing room, measuring 26 × 18 feet, and a dining room hung with charts and portraits of former captains of the vessel. The first was Lord Adolphus Fitz-Clarence (191). As well as the Queen's bedroom and dressing room, there was the Princess Royal's room and a cabin for the Prince of Wales and Duke of Edinburgh adjoining their tutor's cabin. There is an article on this yacht in *The Strand Magazine*, January–June 1894. It was paid off in 1901 and broken up and burnt in 1904. *Victoria and Albert III*, launched in 1897, remained in service through much of the first half of this century. A vessel of 5,500 tons, it was bigger than either the Czar's *Standart*, of 4,344 tons, or the Kaiser's *Hohenzollern*, of 3,773 tons. See C. M. Gavin's *Royal Yachts*, Rich & Cowan Ltd, 1932, for fuller details of the Royal yachts.

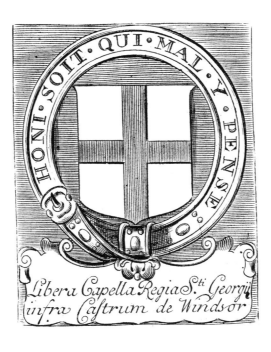

139

Libera Capella Regia Sti. Georgii infra Castrum de Windsor (St George's Chapel, Windsor)

Unsigned, but virtually certainly from William Jackson's workshop. Armorial: within the ribbon of the Garter, the cross of St George (Argent a cross gules), the inscription in a cartouche below; within a horizontally shaded rectangle. *c.*1700–10. There are three varieties:

a) As described above. Franks Coll. 33841.
b) From a different copper. The inscription's second line reads, 'infra Castrm sun de Windsor', and the circle within the Garter has cross-hatched shading. Very rare.
c) From the same copper as (b), but the inscription corrected to read 'Castrum suum'. Franks Coll. 33842.

St George's Chapel is a Royal Peculiar: extra-provincial and extra-diocesan, under the direct personal jurisdiction of the monarch. Founded in 1348 by King Edward III, the 'College of St George' offers Divine Service on behalf of the Sovereign, the Royal House and the Order of the Garter. The present chapel, last of a succession since the late eleventh century, is a superb example of perpendicular architecture, built 1477–1528, and restored in the 1920s. The choir contains the stalls of the Knights of the Garter, with contemporary banners and over 700 enamelled shields. Six kings and queens are buried in the Royal vaults, and the tombs of others are in the Chapel. Other Royal Peculiars are Westminster Abbey (166), the Royal Chapel of All Saints in Windsor Great Park, the Chapels Royal (including the Chapel Royal, St. James's and the Queen's Chapel, St James's, Hampton Court Palace Chapel, and St John the Evangelist and St Peter ad Vincula at the Tower of London), the Royal Memorial Chapel, Sandhurst, the Queen's Chapel of the Savoy (32), and the Royal Foundation of St Katharine in Ratcliffe in Stepney. See the following for a note on the Chapter Library at Windsor.

William Jackson (fl. 1696–1714), more than any other engraver, popularized bookplate use in his time, and was responsible for most of the early Oxford and Cambridge college ex-libris. He worked in London. A collection of 637 early bookplates bought by Lord de Tabley and later owned by Sir Augustus Franks, now in the British Museum, almost certainly comprises work from his engraving shop (see *The Bookplate Society Newsletter* for June 1974). Though the Windsor ex-libris are not represented there, they are in Jackson's style.

Litera Capella Regia Sti Georgii
infra Castrum de Windsor

140

Libera Capella Regia Sti Georgii infra Castrum de Windsor (St George's Chapel, Windsor)

Modern armorial, printed on white and somewhat shiny paper, showing only the Garter ribbon and arms, but evidently copied from (139); the inscription in letterpress below. A small number of prints are in books in the Chapter Library, which also, incidentally, has a modern and rather inferior process reproduction of (139) on cream gummed paper. The Chapter Library, which has housed the books of the Dean and Canons since 1694, is a stone building of 1415 near St George's Chapel. A decision to stop adding books to it, however, was made in 1949–50, and several thousand volumes published since 1715 were subsequently dispersed.

NB   There is an interesting and intriguing pictorial plate, signed 'Ottway Sculp. 27, Barbican', which may have served as a bookplate, though no tangible evidence of this has been found to date. It depicts, within the ribbon of the Garter, St George slaying the dragon on a ground defaced by bones and a couple of skulls (a concept intended no doubt to be fearsome and impressive, but charmingly ludicrous in execution). The Royal crown amid the sun's rays and between ribbons ornaments the top, and there are complementary ribbons below. It appears that this was originally engraved as an admission ticket, for its occurs inscribed, 'TICKET for the Installation in the. . . of St. George's Chapel WINDSOR. . .'. The only example seen, allowing admission to the Nave on 23 April 1805, was numbered '421', and was signed by two stewards. It is also known, however, with the inscription below altered to read, 'St. George's Chapel, Windsor'. This suggests usage as a bookplate, a view encouraged in the light of the Windsor source from whence a print derived. Since it is not known in the Chapter Library, one wonders if perhaps it was used for Chapel service books long since discarded. Sadly, it may be too late to prove or disprove the suggestion.

141

H R H Princess SOPHIA (daughter of King George III)

Unsigned. Inscription in a floral wreath, coronet above. This and ex-libris of the Duke of Sussex and the Prince Regent at Carleton House are the most commonly seen of Royal bookplates; but many prints of Princess Sophia's plate have clearly never served in books, and a stock of them must have come into the hands of a past bookseller or collector. For a note on the coronet see p. 13. Franks Coll. 33210. Winterburn Coll. 74.

142

Sophia (Princess)

Facsimile signature within a very simply decorated oval; printed on buff or pink paper. Only two prints seen. E. E. Spencer and author's colls.

Her Royal Highness Princess Sophia was born at The Queen's House, St James's Park on 3 November 1777, the fifth daughter and twelfth child of King George III (75–77) and Queen Charlotte Sophia (35–36). Always delicate, she never married, and is little recorded but for an indiscretion. She lived with her sisters, closely supervised, in the Lower Lodge at Windsor. On once becoming unwell, however, she was moved to the Upper Lodge, where a General Garth lived, whilst the King and Queen went to London. Nine months later she bore a child – though it was kept from the King. Her offspring was Captain Garth. Malicious tongues suggested her brother, Ernest Augustus, Duke of Cumberland, was the father, but it was not so, even if he had been a little forward towards her. Decades later the Duchesse de Dino noted in her memoirs, on 13 May 1834, 'I spent an hour or so with the Princess Sophia of England. She is well read, a good talker and very animated, and yet on the plea of bad health she lives a very retired life.' An extreme Tory, and favourite sister of the Duke of York (69–70) at the end of his life she would come and say prayers with him. She lived at Frogmore, and latterly at Vicarage Place, Kensington, where she died on 27 May 1848. She was buried at Kensal Green Cemetery.

143

VICTORIA. (Duchess of Kent, mother of Queen Victoria)

Unsigned. The name on a ribbon within a flowery wreath, tied at base, coronet above. Some prints seen are on cream paper and others on paper with a grey-blue tint. Uncommon. Royal Library Coll., Windsor.

Her Highness Princess Victoria Mary Louisa was born at Coburg on 17 August 1786, the fourth daughter of Franz Friedrich Anton, Duke of Saxe-Coburg-Saalfeld, and Auguste, eldest daughter of Heinrich XXIV, Count Reuss-Ebersdorf. She married first at Coburg in 1803, as his second wife, Emich Karl, 2nd Prince of Leiningen, who died in 1814. There was a son and a daughter of the marriage. She married secondly at Coburg and at Kew Palace in 1818 Prince Edward, Duke of Kent and Strathearn (47). Their only child, the future Queen Victoria (144–158) was born at Kensington Palace in 1819, and the Duke of Kent died the following year. The Duchess continued to live at Kensington Palace, and devoted herself overzealously to the education and training of her daughter. Queen Victoria herself recorded that 'I was extremely crushed and kept under and hardly dared say a word.' She never slept apart from her mother until her accession, and was not permitted to see anyone alone; she also seems to have had good reason to resent the influence of Sir John Conroy, her mother's Comptroller and friend. It must be realized that, having produced an heir to the throne at a critical time, during which others had failed, the Duchess of Kent was ambitious not only for her daughter but for acknowledgement of her own status in the scheme of things. King William IV, in retaliation, was anxious to survive long enough to prevent the Duchess of Kent becoming Regent. He succeeded in this by little short of a month. Thereafter the Duchess followed the Court's peregrinations; and Prince Albert did much to readjust the relationship between his wife and her mother. Princess Victoria died at Frogmore House, near Windsor, on 16 March 1861 and was buried at St George's Chapel, Windsor, but her remains were later transferred to a specially-built mausoleum at Frogmore.

Princess Victoria

144

Princess Victoria. (later Queen)

Unsigned. Engraved label without border. Uncommon.

145

VICTORIA. (Princess, later Queen)

Unsigned. Engraved label, the name on a ribbon. Uncommon. Winterburn Coll. 99.

Which of these is the earlier is impossible to say, but they were the ex-libris used by Queen Victoria as Princess, and one perhaps briefly served after her accession in 1837. Prints of both are in the Royal Library at Windsor.

Her Royal Highness Princess Alexandrina Victoria was born at Kensington Palace on 24 May 1819, the only child of Prince Edward, Duke of Kent and Strathearn (47) and Princess Victoria (143), widow of Emich Karl, 2nd Prince of Leiningen, and fourth daughter of Franz Friedrich Anton, Duke of Saxe-Coburg-Saalfeld. Her father died when the Princess was but eight months old, and she was thereafter brought up under the rigorous supervision of her personally ambitious and unpopular mother. Baroness Lehzen was Princess Victoria's governess, the Revd George Davys was her preceptor, and numerous tutors were called upon. She was not, however, told of her proximity to the throne until her twelfth year. In 1837 her uncle, King William IV, died and the Victorian era began. Queen Victoria married at the Chapel Royal, St James's Palace, in 1840 her first cousin Prince Albert of Saxe-Coburg and Gotha (2–9), and there were four sons and five daughters of the marriage. Balmoral and Osborne were added to the Royal residences, being ideal for the quiet family life they relished. Prince Albert planned the 1851 Great Exhibition, and in 1857 was created Prince Consort. After his untimely death in 1861 the Queen for many years largely eschewed public life but was meticulous in fulfilling her other duties as Queen – and in her reign the Empire grew from strength to strength. She was proclaimed Empress of India in 1877, and ten years later the celebration of her Golden Jubilee as Queen was a demonstration of the immense respect and love her subjects had for her. Indeed, it was eclipsed only by the 1897 Diamond Jubilee celebrations, but by then she seemed to her simpler subjects to have almost a divine aura. A woman of strong personal likes and dislikes, she was evidently much kindlier than some records of her life have suggested; and the account she herself left of her life in her *Letters* and her *Journal of our life in the Highlands*, 1868, is fascinating. She died – having lived longer than any other British sovereign – at Osborne House on the Isle of Wight on 22 January 1901 and was buried at the Royal Mausoleum at Frogmore.

146

V R (Queen Victoria)

Unsigned. Within the ribbon of the Garter the Royal cypher, a lover's knot entwining, with Royal crown above. This and the three ex-libris following are the earliest of the Queen's reign, and the design was clearly influenced by William IV's bookplate as King (170). Scarce. Royal Library Coll., Windsor.

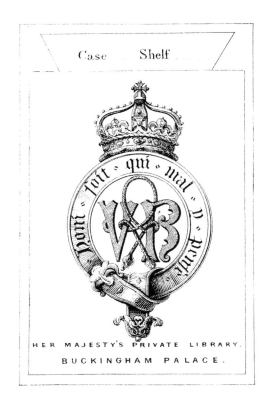

147

V R BUCKINGHAM PALACE. (Queen Victoria)

Unsigned. As the last in design, but smaller, and with a single line rectangular border. Rare.

148

V R HER MAJESTY'S PRIVATE LIBRARY. BUCKINGHAM PALACE. (Queen Victoria)

Unsigned. As the last in design, but with 'Case' and 'Shelf' above, altered inscription below, with extra border lines. Uncommon. Winterburn Coll. 12.

149

V R OSBORNE. (Queen Victoria)

As the foregoing for Buckingham Palace (147), with a single horizontal line above 'OSBORNE'. Very rare.

This was evidently the earliest bookplate for Osborne House on the Isle of Wight, a favourite residence of Queen Victoria and Prince Albert (see (134)).

No bookplate in this series for their other loved residence, Balmoral, has been seen, but one may well exist. Of the two recorded Balmoral ex-libris (excluding the 1859 book label for the lending library for servants etc. (A.1)), the earlier (154) dates probably from soon after their acquisition of the property in 1848, but was for the spines of books; and the later (155) was probably made near the century's end. It seems likely that Victoria's earliest bookplate as Queen (146) was made fairly soon after her accession. It was then clearly adapted for use in specific libraries. The above may date from soon after the completion of the building of Osborne House in 1851. No bookplate in this style has been seen for the Royal Library at Windsor, but it was twenty-three years after the Queen's accession before James West was asked to design a series of ex-libris in three sizes for it (151–153). The Royal Library, however, took many years to put in order, books originally being housed simply to suit shelf size – and that may account for the delay in acquiring bookplates for it.

150

THE QUEEN TO HER ARMY XMAS 1855 (Queen Victoria)

Unsigned. Engraved label, the lettering richly ornamented and with roses, thistles and shamrock framing the central ribbon; with wreath, tied and inscribed ribbon below, and Royal crown amid the sun's rays above. Uncommon. Franks Coll. 33221. Winterburn Coll. 84.

The Crimean War, 1854–56, greatly disturbed the Queen and Prince Albert. Beginning with a difference of opinion over the custody of the Holy Places in Jerusalem, hostilities began in 1853 when Russia invaded the Balkans and the Turkish fleet was sunk at Sinope. Britain and France declared war on Russia the following year, and in the course of the War lost 19,600 men, 15,700 of them by disease. It was this disgraceful state of affairs which led to

Florence Nightingale's organization of the military nursing services. The Royal anxiety for our suffering men is evident everywhere, in their discussions and meetings, and in the small ways in which they set out to help. The Queen, for instance, watched the departure of her troops in person, made woollen comforters and mittens for the men, sent them books (of which the above ex-libris is a tangible reminder), and even complained to Lord Raglan that the men were given green and unroasted coffee. Prince Albert was rightly concerned on hearing that wounded soldiers were returned to the line before they were fully recovered. Peace came finally in March 1856; and it was in that year that the first Victoria Crosses were awarded to soldiers for valour on the field of battle.

151

V R EX BIBLIOTHEC REG IN CASTEL WINDESOR (Queen Victoria)

Signed 'J WEST MARY BYFIELD Sc'. Armorial engraved on wood in two blocks, printed in black with the background in red: in the ribbon of the Garter the Royal arms as borne since 1837 with Royal crown and 'V R' above, and rose, thistle and shamrock below, in a decorative rectangular border incorporating the inscription. It was illustrated as frontispiece to the 1892 edition of Egerton Castle's *English Book-plates*, and facing p. 181 of the second edition and its reprintings. These are sometimes mistaken for original prints, but their paper and printing betray them. Rare. Franks Coll. 33218.

This bookplate is the largest of a series of three ordered by the Royal Library from James West on 3 December 1860, at the same time that he was asked to supply an embossing stamp. The original order survives, loose in an album mostly of West's drawings, purchased in 1953 for the Royal Library by Sir Owen Morshead, then Librarian.

West obviously used the services of several engravers, for the smaller versions of the above (which follow) were engraved by Ferrier. This was the first such series specifically for the Royal Library at Windsor. The tradition was continued with ex-libris by George W. Eve for Queen Victoria, King Edward VII and King George V, and by Stephen Gooden for King George VI and the present reign. King George IV first used similar series for Carlton House and then the Royal Library as King, but that was before the establishment of the Royal Library at Windsor as we know it today.

For a note on Mary Byfield see (2).

The only other ex-libris designed by James West recorded were for Princess Alice (19) and J. L. F. A. Carrick, both printed in red and black. West himself remains elusive.

152

V R EX BIBLIOTHEC REG IN CASTEL WINDESOR. (Queen Victoria)

Signed 'J WEST C A FERRIER Sc'. Armorial as the foregoing, and remarkably closely copied though it is by another
hand. For medium-sized books. Franks Coll. 33219.

153

V R EX BIBLIOTHEC REG IN CASTEL WINDESOR (Queen Victoria)

Signed as the above, and very similar in design. For small
books. Uncommon. Franks Coll. 33220.

For a word on James West see (151).

Charles Anderson Ferrier, a London wood-engraver, first
appears in the *Post Office London Directory* (Trades) in
1858. He was then at Wine Office Court, Fleet Street, but
briefly, for by the next year he had moved to 23 Bouverie
Street, Fleet Street. He remained there until 1865, when he
transferred to 11 Gough Square, but moved on to 9 Red
Lion Court, Fleet Street in 1868. His next premises were in
Fleet Street, at 73 from 1877, at 64 from 1880 and at 71
from 1888. Finally he went to 53 Paternoster Row, where
he remained until 1898. Only one other ex-libris signed
by him is recorded (19).

154

BALMORAL LIBRARY (Queen Victoria)

Unsigned. Inscription in a garter, with Royal crown above. Used on the base of the spines of books, it was probably made at the same time as the one for Prince Albert's library (4), most likely soon after Balmoral became a Royal residence. It occurs in two sizes – the smaller shown here, the larger 38mm high – and in a variety of colours. The crown, garter and inscriptions are in gold, and though only brown, green, pink and two shades of red paper have been seen in bookplate collections, there is no doubt that a range of colours was used to indicate classification in precisely the same pattern as for Prince Albert's library. The Balmoral library is predominantly Victorian, and a large proportion of the books show evidence of the removal of such labels from the spines, in some cases fading of the spine revealing clearly the shape of these ex-libris. They were probably removed near the end of the century when the lozenge-shaped Balmoral bookplate (155) came into use, possibly at the time a new classification system was introduced. In 1901 a catalogue using this was privately printed. Several of these bookplates have evaded the fate of their fellows at Balmoral, but they are not necessary as evidence of the colour-coding system, for proof of this exists in the form of a list of the library categories with the colours written beside them, in German. Whether the handwriting is

Prince Albert's has not been ascertained, but the system was certainly of his devising. This modest bookplate was perhaps made by Andrew Gibb of Aberdeen, for a note on whom see Prince Albert's similar bookplate. Exceedingly rare.

It was in 1848 that Queen Victoria and Prince Albert settled on Balmoral as their Scottish home, having three times previously stayed in Scotland and been entranced by the character of the Scottish people and the great beauty of the landscape. Sir James Clark, the Queen's physician, recommended its cold, clear and bracing air as ideal 'for the peculiar constitution of the Queen and Prince'. A simple and unofficial life was possible here – as it was from a little earlier on at Osborne (134) – and, as Greville described the Queen at Balmoral: 'She is running in and out of the house all day long, and often goes about alone, walks into the cottages and chats with the old women.' It was an enchanting contrast to the formality of court life; and in the Queen's widowhood it was loved for its memories and as the embodiment of a lifestyle dear both to her and her beloved Albert. Its popularity has, moreover, never diminished, for the Royal family still always spend a portion of the year there.

155

V R I BALMORAL (Queen Victoria)

Unsigned. Cypher and 'BALMORAL' with a Royal crown above in a lozenge with linear and dotted border; printed in red and black. It could not be earlier than 1877 (see below), but was probably commissioned near the century's end (see (154)). Extremely rare. Royal Libary Coll., Windsor.

Queen Victoria was, at Disraeli's urging, proclaimed Empress of India in 1877, and every subsequent monarch was Emperor until King George VI relinquished the title in 1948. The Queen's concern and love for India were very marked, and the Durbar Room at Osborne (134), her Indian attendants and portraits, etc., were tangible evidences of this. Her later Royal library bookplates by Eve

(156–158) have, like the above, 'I' for 'Imperatrix' in the cypher, but none of her successors used it on their ex-libris. This is particularly surprising in the case of King George V, our only monarch to visit India as Emperor. In 1911 he wore the specially-made Crown of India (it has never been worn since) at the third and most splendid of the Delhi Durbars. The King was immensely moved, and rather awestruck at the ceremonial amongst those millions of his subjects, and a new vision of his role as King–Emperor was borne in upon him. His Consort, Queen Mary accompanied him and shared the experience; and it is interesting to note that the only other Royal bookplate bearing 'R I' was the tiny one (127) which seems to have been designed for Queen Mary's Dolls' House.

156

V R I ex bibliotheca regia in castel de windesor (Queen Victoria)

Signed 'G W E(ve) 1898' at lower right. Armorial: the Royal arms within the Garter ribbon, Royal crown and crest above, with supporters, motto, and at upper left and right the badges of St George, Patron Saint of the Order of the Garter, and the Tudor rose of Henry VII over the 'sun-burst' badge of Edward III, its founder (see (54)); at base is a band of oak and laurel leaves placed alternately, with a Tudor rose at the centre. A few proofs were printed in sepia. For folio volumes. Winterburn Coll. 11.

In 1897 George W. Eve was commissioned to etch three bookplates for the Royal Library at Windsor, to replace the series by West, Byfield and Ferrier (151–153) that had served for thirty-seven years. They were, like their predecessors, to be made appropriate for folio, quarto and octavo volumes; and the resultant plates were so satisfactory that King Edward VII had them adapted for use throughout his reign (52–54). Eve etched, however, a completely new series for the Royal Library at the beginning of the reign of King George V (91–93). Of the Windsor ex-libris made for Queen Victoria only the one for quarto volumes was completed in 1897, the folio and octavo bookplates being completed in 1898. Prints of all three occur on several different papers.

For a note on George W. Eve see (53).

157

V R I ROYAL LIBRARY WINDSOR CASTLE (Queen Victoria)

Signed 'G W E(ve) '97' at the left and right between the Garter and the border at its narrowest point. Armorial: the Royal arms within the Garter ribbon, with Royal crown and 'V R I' above; roses, thistles and shamrock surround the Garter in the lower angles, and the inscription is on panels at top and bottom within a rectangular border. For quarto books. Winterburn Coll.10.

For a note on George W. Eve see (53).

158

V R I ROYAL LIBRARY WINDSOR CASTLE (Queen Victoria)

Signed 'G W E(ve)' at lower right, but not dated. Crest plate: the Royal crest flanked by 'V' on one side and 'R I' on the other, the inscription on a scroll below, all within a rectangular border. Some proofs and prints lack the etcher's monogram. For octavo volumes. Winterburn Coll.9.

For a note on George W. Eve see (53).

159

V Princess Royal (Princess Victoria, later the Empress Frederick of Germany)

Unsigned. Initial within a circular ribbon, tied at base, inscribed with her title; coronet above. It occurs in two varieties:

a) The circle enclosing 'V' is darkly shaded etc. Franks Coll.33230.

b) The circle enclosing 'V' is lightly shaded, and there are numerous other differences in the engraved lines. Either from a different copper, or much recut. Franks Coll. 33229.

Two hand-impressed book-stamps used when she was Crown Princess of Prussia are shown below.

Her Royal Highness Princess Victoria Adelaide Mary Louisa was born at Buckingham Palace on 21 November 1840, the eldest child of Queen Victoria (144–158) and Prince Albert of Saxe-Coburg and Gotha (2–9). She was granted the style of Princess Royal of Great Britain in 1841, and during her education very quickly revealed her remarkable intellectual, linguistic and artistic talents. Princess Victoria married at the Chapel Royal, St James's Palace in 1858 the future Emperor Friedrich III of Germany, the only son of Emperor Wilhelm I and the Empress Augusta, younger daughter of Karl Friedrich, Grand Duke of Saxe-Weimar-Eisenach. There were four sons and four daughters of the marriage. In 1888 Friedrich III became Emperor, but he reigned for only three months, and their eldest son, Kaiser Wilhelm II (180), had already aligned himself with the new militancy. The Dowager Empress settled at Cronberg, buying an estate in the Taunus mountains, and there she built Friedrichshof (see p. 4). She made many visits to England, and kept in touch with current affairs, but died after a long and painful illness on 5 August 1901 – having outlived her mother by only seven months. She was buried in the Friedenskirche at Potsdam. The ex-libris she used as Dowager Empress follow.

160

V F. VICTORIA A M L. IMPERATRIX REGINA (The Empress Frederick)

Signed 'S' for Josef Sattler (1897). Armorial: on a pounced ground, shields bearing the arms of the German Empire on the left, and, on the right, the Royal arms with over all an inescutcheon of Saxony and a label of three points argent charged on the centre point with a rose and on each of the others with a cross gules; with Imperial crown, rose, thistle, shamrock, etc., in a lined rectangular border. Reproduced by process. Rare. Winterburn Coll.85.

161

V F. VICTORIA A M L. IMPERATRIX REGINA (The Empress Frederick)

Identical to the above, but for smaller books. Author's coll.

Josef Sattler (1867–1931) was born at Schrobenhausen, and studied briefly at the Academy in Munich. He designed a monumental edition of the *Nibelungenlied*. Sattler was greatly influenced by Dürer and the early German masters, and his ex-libris – of which few are armorial – are archaic in style, very individual and show remarkable invention. His use of colour is nicely seen in *Art in Book-Plates. Forty Two original Ex-Libris designed by Joseph Sattler*, an album limited to 100 copies, published by H. Grevel & Co., London in 1895. Many of his bookplates were, however, undertaken as exercises, and thus never used. He died in Munich.

162

VICTORIA (Princess of Hesse and by Rhine, later Marchioness of Milford Haven)

Unsigned, but designed by her husband, Prince Louis of Battenberg. Armorial lozenge: Quarterly, 1st and 4th, quarterly, I and IV, Hesse modified, II and III, Battenberg; 2nd and 3rd, Hesse (see p. 15); continental crown above. Uncommon. Franks Coll.33235. Winterburn Coll.98.

Her Grand Ducal Highness Princess Victoria Alberta Elisabeth Matilda Marie* was born at Windsor Castle on 5 April 1863, the eldest daughter of Ludwig IV, Grand Duke of Hesse and by Rhine, and Princess Alice (19), the second daughter of Queen Victoria (144–158) and Prince Albert of Saxe-Coburg and Gotha (2–9). Fifteen when her mother died, she became the keystone of the young family – over which Queen Victoria watched with a maternal eye. She married in 1884 at Darmstadt her second cousin once removed, Louis, Prince of Battenberg (113–114), who in 1917 with others of the family renounced his title and the qualification of Serene Highness, taking the name Mountbatten and being created Marquess of Milford Haven. They had two sons and two daughters: George, 2nd Marquess of Milford Haven (97–98), Earl Mountbatten of Burma (115–116), Princess Alice, the mother of Prince Philip, Duke of Edinburgh, and Queen Louise of Sweden. Princess Victoria, always devoted to books, could never have enough of them even

as a young child. Her reading interests worried Queen Victoria, who wanted her to read serious and religious books, not materialistic and controversial ones – so dangerous, especially for the young. She kept little leather volumes entitled 'Books I have read', an asterisk by those read for the first time; and as late as May 1941 listed thirteen books of wide variety read in a month. A woman of formidable courage, the Marchioness suffered much sadness. Her husband, though supremely able, had to retire as First Sea Lord in 1914 due to anti-German feeling; her sisters – the Empress Alexandra Feodorovna (173) and the Grand Duchess Serge – were murdered in the Russian Revolution; and from early childhood she lost other close relatives tragically. She lived, however, to see her grandson Philip married to Princess Elizabeth, and the births of Prince Charles and Princess Anne. The Dowager Marchioness died at Kensington Palace on 24 September 1950, and was buried at Whippingham on the Isle of Wight.

For a note on Prince Louis's bookplate designs see p. 9 and (113).

---

* Though *The Complete Peerage* and *Burke's Peerage*, 1970, give her last Christian names as 'Marie Irene', her own evidence (in Duff, *Hessian Tapestry*, p. 101) verifies her names as above.

163

VICTORIA OF WALES (daughter of King Edward VII)

Signed 'INV W P B(arrett) 1900', and thus commissioned from Messrs J. & E. Bumpus of London, but engraved by John Edward Syson. Pictorial: in a rectangular frame decorated with sprigs of oak and laurel a moonlit coastal scene with a two-masted ship in the distance and a bird perched on a cross in the foreground; an open volume of *Lohengrin* beneath has an illustration depicting a swan on a reedy lake. It occurs printed in black or in green, and in two varieties:

a) As shown here with the inscription 'VICTORIA OF WALES'. A print of this from the copper was Plate I in *LV Book-plates engraved on copper from designs by W. P. Barrett*, Bumpus, 1900.

b) 'OF WALES' has been erased and oak leaves partly cover the blank lower ribbon. This amendment was probably made soon after the accession of her father as King Edward VII in 1901. Winterburn Coll. 42 and 57 (proof).

Her Royal Highness Princess Victoria Alexandra Olga Mary was born at Marlborough House, London on 6 July 1868, the second daughter of the future King Edward VII (48–57) and Queen Alexandra (13–15). Known throughout the family as 'Toria', she never married – the only man she had desired to marry being a commoner – and she lived a very retired life, mostly with her parents and often in poor health. After her father's death she became her mother's inseparable companion until Queen Alexandra died in 1925. Thereafter, Princess Victoria lived at Coppins, Iver, Buckinghamshire, finding pleasure in music and gardening and caring for animals. The favourite sister of King George V, she was staunch in her friendships and of a very generous disposition like her mother. Princess Victoria died at Coppins on 3 December 1935 and was buried at Frogmore.

For a note on John Edward Syson see (15).

164

Victoria (Princess Helena Victoria of Schleswig-Holstein)

Signed 'INV F G H(ouse)', and thus commissioned from Messrs Truslove & Hanson of Sloane Street, London, but engraved by J. A. C. Harrison, *c.*1906. Pictorial: name and continental crown within a laurel wreath. It occurs printed in black, brown or blue. Royal Library Coll., Windsor. Truslove & Hanson exhibited in 1906 at the Ex Libris Society her mother's bookplate (108) and another for her sister Princess Marie Louise. No print of the latter has, however, been seen, but it was probably similar and inscribed 'Louise'. It has been suggested, incidentally, that a Truslove & Hanson bookplate reading 'Marie Louise EX LIBRIS' was etched by G. W. Eve for the Princess, but it is most unlikely. It was used by the firm in a trade brochure, has no coronet, and was most likely a specimen bookplate. This plate is also erroneously attributed (Winterburn Coll. 154) to Marie Louise, the first wife of the future Czar Ferdinand of the Bulgarians.

Her Highness Princess Victoria Louise Sophia Augusta Amelia Helena was born at Frogmore House, near Windsor, on 3 May 1870, the elder daughter of Prince Christian of Schleswig-Holstein-Sonderburg-Augustenburg (39–41) and Princess Helena (41, 107 & 108), the third daughter of Queen Victoria and Prince Albert of Saxe-Coburg and Gotha. She lived as a child mostly at Cumberland Lodge, and her sister Princess Marie Louise gives an attractive picture of their life there in *My Memories of Six Reigns,* 1956. Princess Helena Victoria was an indefatigable worker for the Young Men's Christian Association, and in the First World War formed the Women's Auxiliary Force, in which she had almost 40,000 women working for her. Known as 'Thora' in the Royal family, she had a fine intelligence and was very kindly; but she suffered indifferent health in her latter years. She, her sister and her parents lived for a long time at Schomberg House in Pall Mall. This had been built for the 3rd Duke of Schomberg; was sometime the home of the artists Thomas Gainsborough and Richard Cosway; and in 1771 the Scottish doctor, James Graham, opened it as his 'Temple of Health and Hymen' (see Weinreb and Hibbert, *The London Encyclopaedia,* 1983, for a note on its £50 a night services). Prince Christian and his family enjoyed the house in more rational days; and leading musical artists performed there for them in the splendid salon stretching the whole depth of the house. Princess Helena Victoria died unmarried at FitzMaurice Place, Berkeley Square, London on 13 March 1948 and was buried at Frogmore.

For a note on J. A. C. Harrison see (15) and on F. G. House (108).

Victoria of Schleswig-Holstein.

165

Victoria of Schleswig-Holstein. (Princess)

Signed 'H J F B(adeley)', and engraved in 1911. Armorial within a lozenge: Quarterly, 1st and 4th, the Royal arms with over all an inescutcheon of Saxony and a label of three points argent charged at the centre point with a cross and on each of the others with a rose gules; 2nd and 3rd, Quarterly, I, Gules, a lion rampant crowned and holding with all four feet a long handled Danish axe or, the blade argent (Norway); II, Or, two lions passant azure (Schleswig); III, Gules, an inescutcheon per fess argent and of the field between three demi-nettle leaves and as many passion nails in pairle of the second (Holstein); IV, Gules, a swan, argent, beaked, membered and Royally gorged or (Stormarn); enté in point Gules, a knight in armour or on a horse and holding a sword argent and a shield azure charged with a cross patée of the second (Ditmarsken); over all an inescutcheon, quarterly, Or, two bars gules (Oldenburg) and Azure, a cross patée or (Delmenhorst). The arms are ornamented with mantling. There are three varieties:

a) As described and illustrated, with a continental crown above.

b) The inscription is the same, but a coronet (of four fleurs de lys and four strawberry leaves, appropriate to children of daughters of the sovereign) replaces the continental crown.

c) As the above, but inscribed 'Helena Victoria' and with the inescutcheon of Saxony erased. Winterburn Coll.91.

Artistically this is a rather unsatisfactory bookplate. The future Lord Badeley (see (11)) was a friend of Queen Mary, and as a result came to know other members of the Royal family. Princess Helena Victoria (for a biographical note on whom see the foregoing) was amongst them; but Badeley, who was but an amateur engraver, was incapable of depiction of such complex arms on so small a scale. It would have required someone of the ability of J. A. C. Harrison to do justice to such a composition.

ECCLESIAE S:PETRI
WESTMON:BIBLIOTHECA

166

ECCLESIAE S: PETRI WESTMON: BIBLIOTHECA (Westminster Abbey)

Signed 'J. F. Badeley 1934'. Armorial: Azure, a cross patonce between five martlets or; on a chief or France and England quarterly on a pale, between two roses gules, seeded and barbed proper; the arms, in a cartouche, are held by eagles, but only their heads are visible; also in the rectangular frame are smaller cartouches bearing arms (St Peter; another coat for the Abbey (Azure on a chief indented or, a crozier on the dexter and a mitre on the sinister both gules); and St Edward the Confessor) and a fourth for the inscription. Badeley in the same year engraved a label for the Abbey using a cartouche similar in spirit and with the same wording. The bookplate occurs printed in black or in sepia.

The Collegiate Church of St Peter in Westminster – or Westminster Abbey – is a Royal Peculiar, extra-provincial and extra-diocesan, under the personal jurisdiction of the sovereign; and even in these days its ceremonial occasions include the bearers of archaic offices such as 'the Queen's Almsmen' and the 'High Bailiff and Searcher of the Sanctuary'. St Peter's, by tradition said to have been founded by Sebert, King of the East Saxons in the early seventh

century, became a great Benedictine monastery; and since the dissolution in 1540 has become the central shrine of our national history and pageantry. Excepting King Edward V and King Edward VIII, all our sovereigns since William the Conqueror have been crowned there, and the Coronation Chair contains the Stone of Scone, on which the ancient Scottish kings were crowned. Fifteen monarchs were buried there between 1272 and 1760, and it is also the resting place of St Edward the Confessor. Interred there in 1066 in the church he had built, he was canonized in 1161, and two years later his body was re-enshrined by St Thomas of Canterbury; in 1269, in the rebuilt Abbey, it was moved to the present shrine. Great writers, poets, statesmen and leaders of Church and State are also interred or memorialized here, and yet it maintains a daily life of worship, and in the present century has seen a number of Royal weddings. The Abbey's ceaseless bombardment by the world's tourists has no power to diminish the deep awe the place inspires.

For a note on Lord Badeley see (11).

167

Anonymous (Prince William Henry, Duke and Gloucester, and/or Prince William Frederick, Duke of Gloucester)

Unsigned. Armorial: within the ribbon of the Garter the Royal Arms as borne 1801 to 1837, the Hanoverian coat – with here a blank inescutcheon – being in pretence, with over all a label of five points argent charged on the centre point with a fleur de lys azure and on each of the others with a cross gules; with coronet and Royal crest, the supporters with Royal coronets and charged on the shoulders with a label as on the arms. It occurs in two varieties:

a) In an octagonal frame, as illustrated. Some prints from the worn copper show signs of reworking, especially to the lower part of the lion's body. Franks Coll. 33200.
b) Without the octagonal frame. Franks Coll.33199. Winterburn Coll.70.

Not infrequently this bookplate, in the front of books, is accompanied by (168) at the back, Prince William Henry's son having inherited his books. The label relates to the former, who, on the arms' evidence, could only have used the bookplate in the last four years of his life. It is, however, believed that the plate occurs in some post-1805 volumes; so it is possible that Prince William Frederick had the bookplate made on acquisition of his father's library, thus posthumously recording their provenance.

Prince William Henry was born at Leicester House, London, on 14 November 1743, the third son of Prince Frederick Louis, Prince of Wales (I) and Princess Augusta, youngest daughter of Friedrich II, Duke of Saxe-Gotha and Altenburg. The favourite brother of the future King George III (75–77), he was created Duke of Gloucester and Edinburgh in 1764. A soldier, he rose to the rank of Field Marshal in 1793; and he was sometime also Ranger of Hampton Court, Ranger of Cranbourne Chace, Warden of the New Forest, and Chancellor of the University of Dublin. He married secretly at her house in Pall Mall, London, in 1766, Maria (120–121), widow of James Waldegrave, 2nd Earl Waldegrave, and second natural daughter of the Hon. Sir Edward Walpole. Though the court had its suspicions, he did not confess his marriage to the King until 1772, after the passing of the Royal Marriages Act. The marriage was allowed, but the Duke and Duchess were not restored to Royal favour until 1780. Part of the intervening period was spent abroad, notably in Italy. The Duke died at Gloucester House, London on 25 August 1805 and was buried at St George's Chapel, Windsor.

168

W F (Prince William Frederick, Duke of Gloucester)

Unsigned. Entwined initials within the ribbon of the Garter, surmounted by a Royal coronet. The coronet of both this and the foregoing are of four crosses patée and four fleurs de lys, appropriate to sons and daughters of the sovereign, which includes brothers and sisters of the sovereign. This, of course, was appropriate to William Frederick's father, Prince William Henry, 1st Duke of Gloucester and Edinburgh, brother of King George III. Prince William Frederick's entitlement, as son of the sovereign's brother, was to a coronet composed of four strawberry leaves and four crosses patée. There are two varieties of the bookplate:

a)   With a double line oval surround, as illustrated. Later prints evidence some reworking of the coronet and Garter circle. Franks Coll. 33201. Winterburn Coll.73.

b)   Without the oval surround. The shading of the coronet's velvet cap should be compared with prints of the above for evidence of reworking. Viner and author's colls.

This bookplate was not infrequently placed at the back of books which bore (167) at the front.

Prince William Frederick was born at the Teodoli Palace, Rome, on 15 January 1776, the only son of Prince William Henry, Duke of Gloucester and Edinburgh (167) and Maria (120–121), the widow of James Waldegrave, 2nd Earl Waldegrave, and second natural daughter of the Hon. Sir Edward Walpole. He studied at Trinity College, Cambridge, and in 1811 became Chancellor of the University; but he was destined for a military career, serving in Flanders and with gallantry in the expedition to the Helder in 1799. In 1816 he was raised to the rank of Field Marshal. He married at The Queen's House, St James's, in 1816 his first cousin Princess Mary, the fourth daughter of King George III (75–77) and Queen Charlotte Sophia (35–36), but there was no issue of the marriage. It was not, incidentally, until that year that he was allowed the style of Royal Highness, for he was only great-grandson to King George II. A charitable man, without self-importance, he was very happy in his marriage to Princess Mary, of whom he had been fond for years before their marriage. He died at Bagshot Park, Surrey, on 30 November 1834 and was buried at St George's Chapel, Windsor. His library was sold by Sotheby & Son in July–August 1835. The sale occupied eight days and realized £1,265. (See 167)

169

W H. (Prince William Henry, Duke of Clarence, later King William IV)

Unsigned. Initials within the ribbon of the Garter, with coronet above. Franks Coll. 33206. This often occurs with one of the two book labels (195–196) and/or the armorial bookplate (194) of his eldest illegitimate son by Mrs Jordan, George, Earl of Munster, pasted beneath. An instance is in the Broxbourne Library at the Bodleian Library, Oxford, where a volume of *The Prose and Poetical Works of the Rev. G. C. Smith*, 1824 (Broxbourne 41.24/2060) shows the Prince's ex-libris at centre, with the Earl of Munster's armorial above, and the 'Col. FitzClarence' label beneath.

His Royal Highness Prince William Henry was born at The Queen's House, St James's Park on 21 August 1765, the third son of King George III (75–77) and Queen Charlotte Sophia (35–36). At the age of thirteen (see p. 7) he went to sea, and in 1781 he was the first — and last — English prince to see New York whilst it had allegiance to the English Crown. He travelled in Germany for two years, and in 1789 was created Duke of Clarence and St Andrews and Earl of Munster. In 1791 he decided to live with the actress Dorothy Bland, Mrs Jordan, first at Petersham and then at Bushey Park (see p. 3–4). She bore him ten children, given the surname FitzClarence, including the Earl of Munster (194–196), Lord Frederick (193), Lord Adolphus (191) and Lord Augustus (192). By 1811, when King George III finally succumbed to porphyria and lost his reason, the Duke wanted a Royal marriage, and he parted company with Mrs Jordan. He married at Kew Palace in 1818 Princess Adelaide (1), the elder daughter of Georg I, Duke of Saxe-Meiningen; but though they had two daughters, they both died in infancy. In 1830 he came to the throne as King William IV, and his bluff, good-hearted but tactless manner made him — as did his modesty in financial matters — a total contrast to his late brother, King George IV (78–86). He died at Windsor Castle on 20 June 1837, and was buried at St George's Chapel, Windsor. The bookplate which he used as King follows.

Royal Library.

170

W R IIII (King William IV)

Unsigned. Initials within the ribbon of the Garter, Royal crown above. It occurs in two varieties, perhaps both printed at the same time:

a)   As above with 'Royal Library' at base. Franks Coll. 33208.
b)   Lacking 'Royal Library' at base, and perhaps intended for personal books. Franks Coll.33207. Winterburn Coll. 63.

The simplicity of this ex-libris contrasts sharply with the armorial splendour of the plates, especially the largest (84), for his brother, King George IV. Though this no doubt in part reflects the increasing simplicity of much bookplate design of the period, it also indicates his lack of fuss; and Queen Victoria's earliest ex-libris as Queen (146–149) were clearly based on this design.

On his accession to the throne, King William IV lamented that he was the only sovereign in Europe without a library (King George IV having given the Royal Library to the nation in 1823). He soon remedied this and, in July 1833, added a codicil to his will to the effect that,

Whereas His Majesty hath made considerable additions to the Royal Libraries in His Majesty's several Palaces, and may hereafter make further additions thereto, Now His Majesty doth give and bequeath all such additions, whether the same have been or may be made by and at the cost of His Majesty's Privy Purse or otherwise until and for the benefit of His Majesty's successors, in order that the said Royal Libraries may be transmitted entire.

In November 1834 he signed the document, and added an autograph note:

Approved and confirmed by me the King, and I further declare that all the books, drawings, and plans collected in all the palaces shall for ever continue Heirlooms to the Crown and on no pretence whatever be alienated from the Crown.

His books are, as a result, even now housed in rooms at Windsor. Nevertheless, a sale of books and prints of his, perhaps duplicates or superfluous, occupied a seven-days sale at Evans auction rooms in February 1837, months before his death. They realized £1,932. Personal books of his were, moreover, bequeathed by Queen Adelaide to Lord Frederick FitzClarence (193) and perhaps to other of his natural children.

171

1910 1935 EX BIBLIOTHECA REGIA IN CASTEL DE WINDESOR LIBER AD TERRAM AUSTRALEM PERTINENS

Signed 'Gayfield Shaw 14.10/35'. Armorial: within the Garter ribbon and a rectangular frame two coats of arms with supporters, helm, crowns, Royal crest and motto; the Royal arms above, the Royal arms impaling those borne by Queen Mary in her own right (see (129)) below. The composition is over-rich with mantling, upon which there is the cypher 'G V' at upper right and 'M' at lower left; and there is an outline of Australia with a boomerang below, perhaps intended as a remarque.

An Australian gift to commemorate the Silver Jubilee of King George V (88–96) in 1935, prints may exist in bookplate collections there, but the only ones seen in England were three proofs in the Royal Library at Windsor, where the copper also is. They seem to have been sent to Queen Mary from Gayfield Shaw via Lady Gowrie (whose husband was then Governor of New South Wales, and 1936–44 Governor-General of Australia), but the bookplate was almost certainly never used. For summary detailing of other Australian gift plates illustrated here see '(60).

Gerrard Gayfield Shaw was born in Adelaide in 1885. An ancestor, G. B. Shaw, was an engraver of portraits for Lockhart's *Life of Sir Walter Scott* etc., but Gayfield Shaw did not handle an engraving tool until he was past middle age. He started as a messenger in an Adelaide jewellery store, designed jewellery, went to Sydney as a journey-man printer, and studied at Adelaide School of Design and the J. S. Watkins School at Sydney. He ran the Gayfield Shaw Art Salon in Sydney, was in 1920 founder of the Australian Painter–Etchers Society, and became an etcher and engraver noted for his landscapes, street scenes and bookplates. His first ex-libris was made in 1930, and by 1939 he had created fifty. See the *1939 Year Book* of the American Society of Bookplate Collectors and Designers.

172

PRIVATE LIBRARY

Anonymous and as yet unidentified. Unsigned. Within the ribbon of the Garter the Royal arms as borne since 1837 within a linear border rounded at the corners. The only print of this seen is in the Royal Library Collection at Windsor Castle, and its usage as a Royal ex-libris may therefore be assumed, though it is not annotated at all. Absence of a label implies that it appertains to a monarch. Stylistically it suggests a twentieth-century date, and yet the crown is not of the Tudor style used by King Edward VII, King George V, King Edward VIII and King George VI. It remains, therefore, something of a puzzle.

ADDENDA

THIS WORK

BELONGS TO

THE BALMORAL LENDING LIBRARY,

ESTABLISHED BY

HER MAJESTY THE QUEEN,

AND

HIS ROYAL HIGHNESS THE PRINCE CONSORT,

IN

1859,

FOR THE USE OF

THE TENANTS, SERVANTS,

AND

COTTAGERS.

A.1

THIS WORK BELONGS TO THE BALMORAL LENDING LIBRARY, ESTABLISHED BY HER MAJESTY THE QUEEN, AND HIS ROYAL HIGHNESS THE PRINCE CONSORT, IN 1859, FOR THE USE OF THE TENANTS, SERVANTS, AND COTTAGERS

Unsigned. Book label with a double line rectangular border enclosing in the upper corners two armorials: at left, within the ribbon of the Garter and surmounted by a Royal crown the Royal arms as borne since 1837; at right, within the ribbon of the Garter and surmounted by a continental crown the Prince's quarterly arms as granted on his marriage to Queen Victoria in 1840 (for detailing

of which see (2)). The print illustrated is in a volume at Balmoral. No prints are recorded elsewhere.

The informality possible to Queen Victoria and Prince Albert at Balmoral (see (154)) is best understood by reference to the Queen's *Leaves from the journal of our life in the Highlands from 1848 to 1861*, London, 1868. As Arthur

Helps, its editor, comments: 'Perhaps... no person in these realms... takes a more deep and abiding interest in the welfare of the household committed to his charge than our gracious Queen does in hers, or... feels more keenly what are the reciprocal duties of masters and servants.'

The 1842 visit to Scotland was a revelation, the start of a life-long love affair with the country, whose people, free of obsequiousness or awe of majesty, they could meet on respectful and familiar terms.

A.2

Royal Gardens, WINDSOR. Book Society

Book label, the inscription in a decorative rectangular frame bowed at top and bottom with arabesque ornament. Extremely rare.

A.3

Royal Gardens, Windsor. Book Society

Book label, the inscription within a decorative frame having the character of antique penmanship. Extremely rare.

There are prints of both of the above in the Royal Library at Windsor, but only one or two of each have been seen elsewhere. It seems probable that the Book Society served the same function for staff at Windsor as the Lending Library at Balmoral, perhaps at the same time or a little later. Nothing, however, but these modest labels seems to survive as evidence of its existence.

Bookplates of
grandchildren of Queen Victoria
of, or married into, European Royal Houses

173

A F (Empress Alexandra Feodorovna of Russia, formerly Princess of Hesse and by Rhine)

Unsigned, but designed by Baron Armin Eugene von Fölkersam in 1914. Decorated initials (transliterated from the Russian) in monogram form, Russian Imperial crown above. It occurs in three varieties, differing probably only in size, the others 85 × 67mm and 65 × 53mm in paper size; and is a zincograph. See 'Knizhnye znaki b. Imperatorskoi Familii', *Trudy LOE*, IX (1927), pp. 49–52, at 51, item 39. The paper of the print illustrated here, in the Winterburn Collection (No. 170) is cut to a diamond shape. Very rare.

Her Grand Ducal Highness Princess Victoria Alix Helena Louise Beatrice was born at Darmstadt on 6 June 1872, the fourth daughter of Ludwig IV, Grand Duke of Hesse and by Rhine, and Princess Alice (19), the second daughter of Queen Victoria. Her mother died when Princess Alix was only 6, and Queen Victoria thereafter took a very particular interest in the lives and upbringing of Princess Alice's children. She married in 1894 at St Petersburg the Emperor Nicholas II of Russia, taking the name Alexandra Feodorovna on Orthodox baptism. She bore him one son and four daughters. Of a rather mystical and curiously fatalistic temperament, and prone to ill health, she was nevertheless a devoted wife and mother; but the anguish of her only son's haemophilia – and he heir to the throne of the Russia she had come to love – led to claims of Rasputin's influence over affairs beyond the healing of her son. After being held in captivity in several places during the Russian Revolution, the Emperor, the Empress and their children were murdered at Ekaterinburg on 16/17 July 1918.

Baron Armin Eugene von Fölkersam (1861–1917), of Berlin and St Petersburg, had property in the neighbourhood of Riga. His name is generally rendered as Fel-kerzam in Russian works on ex-libris, and he was an amateur bookplate artist of repute. The Retovskii Collection – the present whereabouts of which is unknown – contained about seventy ex-libris of his designing, excluding states and varieties of paper etc., and was probably virtually complete. Little is recorded of him, but his wife's name was Sophie, and they had four children. His other Imperial and Royal bookplates include armorials for the Empress Alexandra Feodorovna, Tsar Nicholas II (for the Winter, Livadi and Tsarskoe Selo palaces) and the Tsarevitch Alexei, as well as designs of 1911 for Ferdinand of Bulgaria. Several more modest ex-libris (like the above) for Tsar Nicholas II, his four daughters and several other members of the Imperial family are also ascribed to him. The Baron was a bookplate collector in a small way, having upwards of 1,500 examples in his collection.

174

E L (Ernst Ludwig, Grand Duke of Hesse and by Rhine)

Unsigned. The initials 'E L' entwined with perhaps 'P' in an oval surmounted by a continental coronet. This bookplate occurs in the library of Margaret, Princess of Hesse and by Rhine. Two other bookplates of the Grand Duke are recorded. One has the letters 'E' and 'L' conjoined and facing each other, angled hook-like at base, with a continental coronet atop the letters. The other, on blue paper, shows a continental coronet, printed in gold, above a decorative but blank rectangle, printed in black, with 'ERNST = LUDWIG BIBLIOTHEK' printed in gold below. On account of its colouring and paper it would not have reproduced well; but there are prints in the Royal Library Collection at The Hague (212/17) and the author's coll.

Prince Ernst Ludwig Karl Albrecht Wilhelm was born at Darmstadt on 25 November 1868, the elder son of Ludwig IV, Grand Duke of Hesse and by Rhine, and Princess Alice (19), the second daughter of Queen Victoria and Prince Albert of Saxe-Coburg and Gotha. His sisters included Victoria, Marchioness of Milford Haven (162), Irene, Princess Heinrich of Prussia (176), and the Empress Alexandra Feodorovna of Russia (173), who kept house for him as a young man. His mother died when he was ten, as a result of kissing him in his distress at his sister's death when he and others of the children had diphtheria. The shock of this time much affected his life, but Queen Victoria closely supervised his and his sisters' education, acting almost as a mother to them; and thereafter he embarked on a military career. He succeeded his father in 1892, and two years later he married at Coburg Princess Victoria Melita (179), the second daughter of Prince Alfred, Duke of Edinburgh and of Saxe-Coburg and Gotha, and Grand Duchess Marie Alexandrovna of Russia. There was a daughter (and a stillborn son) of the marriage, but it was not a happy relationship and they divorced in 1901. He married secondly, in 1905, Princess Eleonore Ernestine Marie, the daughter of Hermann, 5th Prince of Solms-Hohensolms-Lich, and his wife Countess Agnes of Stolberg-Wernigerode. There were two sons of this marriage, the elder of whom eventually succeeded his father as head of the Grand Ducal House. Grand Duke Ernst Ludwig was lively in personality, and intensely keen on music and art. He lost his throne on the proclamation of the Republic of Hesse in 1918, but always remained a popular figure, and greatly devoted himself to helping the war-wounded, giving them accommodation in the palace. He died at Schloss Wolfsgarten on 9 October 1937 and was buried at the Rosenhöhe.

175

PRINZ HEINRICH VON PREUSSEN (Prince Heinrich of Prussia)

Unsigned, but designed by Prince Louis of Battenberg, c.1896. Armorial in an architectural frame: the Prussian eagle displayed sable, langued gules, membered, treflé on the wings and crowned or, holding in the dexter claw a sceptre also or, surmounted by an eagle displayed sable, and in the sinister claw an orb azure, banded and surmounted by a cross or, charged on the breast with the cypher 'F R' or; within a Gothic quatrefoil, the name around the border. It occurs printed in black or in blue. Rare. Winterburn Coll.138.

His Royal Highness Prince Albert Wilhelm Heinrich was born at the Neues Palais, Potsdam, on 14 August 1862, the second son of the future Emperor Friedrich III of Germany, King of Prussia, and Princess Victoria (159–161), eldest daughter of Queen Victoria and Prince Albert of Saxe-Coburg and Gotha. He married at Charlottenburg in 1888 Princess Irene Maria Louise Anna (176), the third daughter of Ludwig IV, Grand Duke of Hesse and by Rhine, and Princess Alice, younger sister of his mother Princess Victoria. There were three sons of the marriage.

A Grand Admiral in the Imperial Navy, sometime in high command of the German Fleet, Prince Heinrich had in youth been little-read and fond of a good time; but he was immensely happy in his marriage, and the stability resulting from this made more tolerable the difficulties and tensions which his elder brother, Kaiser Wilhelm II (180), so lavishly bestowed on his life and activities. Fond of England and his relatives there – an affection which was reciprocated – he was amiable and apparently frank and straightforward, but by no means politically astute. He died at Herrenhaus Hemmelmark, near Eckernförde, Schleswig-Holstein, on 20 April 1929.

For a note on Prince Louis of Battenberg's bookplate designs see p. 9 and (113). Prince Louis designed a bookplate for Prince Heinrich's eldest son, Prince Waldemar (1889–1945). Inscribed 'WALDEMAR' on a ribbon, it is an armorial showing the Imperial black eagle with the badge suspended beneath; the design has a diamond-shaped ground with diaper, like the bookplate of his mother, Princess Irene, which follows.

176

IRENE (Princess Irene of Hesse and by Rhine, later Princess Heinrich of Prussia)

Unsigned, but designed by Prince Louis of Battenberg and engraved by P.C. Baker. Within a linear double-lined lozenge and on a diapered ground, the Prussian eagle and the Hessian lion supporting a continental crown, the name borne below on a ribbon. Inclusion of the Prussian eagle indicates that this bookplate was made after the Princess's marriage in 1888. Rare. Franks Coll.33236. Winterburn Coll.139.

Her Grand Ducal Highness Princess Irene Maria Louise Anna was born at Darmstadt on 11 July 1866, the third daughter of Ludwig IV, Grand Duke of Hesse and by Rhine, and Princess Alice (19), the second daughter of Queen Victoria and Prince Albert of Saxe-Coburg and Gotha. She married at Charlottenburg in 1888 Prince Albert Wilhelm Heinrich of Prussia (175), the second son of the Emperor Friedrich III of Germany and King of Prussia and the Empress Victoria, eldest daughter of Queen Victoria and formerly Princess Royal of Great Britain. They were thus first cousins. There were three sons of the marriage, but the youngest died of haemophilia as a child. Rather small and delicate in person, the Princess liked informality and was described at the Berlin Court as 'an amiable woman, of domestic habits'. She was very much attached to her three sisters, Princess Victoria (162), the Grand Duchess Elizabeth (Serge) of Russia, and the Empress Alexandra Feodorovna of Russia (173); and their finding themselves on opposing sides in the First World War was a great grief to her, as was the behaviour of her brother-in-law, Kaiser Wilhelm II. Prince Louis, who designed this bookplate, was also her brother-in-law, being married to her sister Princess Victoria. Prince and Princess Heinrich lived first at the Schloss at Kiel, and from 1896 at Hemmelmark by Eckernförde, near Kiel, which remained their home for life. There is a chapter on them in David Duff's *Hessian Tapestry*, 1967. Princess Irene died at Schloss Hemmelmark on 11 November 1953, the longest-lived of this family of two sons and five daughters – outliving her sister Alix, the last Empress of Russia, by thirty-five years.

For a note on Prince Louis of Battenberg see p. 9 and (113).

For a note on P.C. Baker see (30).

177

M (Princess Margarete, Landgravine of Hesse)

Unsigned. Continental crown within a frame which cleverly incorporates the initial 'M' four times in the round. It is printed in black, and is the smallest Royal ex-libris encountered; but see the bookplates for Queen Mary's Dolls' House (127 and 128), which are only fractionally larger. Prints occur in books in the library of the Landgrave of Hesse.

Her Royal Highness Princess Margarete (or Margarethe) Beatrice Feodora was born at Potsdam on 22 April 1872, the fourth daughter of the future Emperor Friedrich III of Germany, King of Prussia, and Princess Victoria (159–161), the eldest daughter of Queen Victoria and Prince Albert of Saxe-Coburg and Gotha. She married at Berlin in 1893 Friedrich Karl Ludwig Konstantin, Prince of Hesse, who in 1925 succeeded his brother as Landgrave, and died in 1940. There were six sons of the marriage, the third of whom, Prince Philipp, succeeded his father. Margarete, Landgravine of Hesse, was unique in Royal history in producing two pairs of twin boys. One of these sets of twins proved, incidentally, a minor comfort before birth to King Edward VII. On being asked to sit down thirteen to a table, the King was reassured by being told that – due to the presence of the expectant Princess – two unseen persons were also at the table. Landgravine Margarete died at Schönberg, near Kronberg, Taunus on 21 January 1954.

The House of Hesse (House of Brabant) derives its name from the *Hessi*, a Frankish tribe inhabiting the area from the first century AD. The House of Brabant is traceable to Giselbert, Count in the Maasgau in 841, who married a great-granddaughter of Charlemagne. In course of time Landgrave Philipp the Magnanimous (d.1567) was ancestor to all existing branches of the House. These were Hesse-Cassel (later the Electoral House of Hesse, into which Princess Margarete married), Hesse-Philippsthal, Hesse-Philippsthal-Barchfeld, and Hesse-Darmstadt, which became the Grand Ducal House of Hesse and by Rhine and was founded by Georg I (d.1597), the youngest son of Philipp the Magnanimous. Of these, the last features most in this book, on account of the marriages of Queen Victoria's daughters Princess Alice (19) and Princess Beatrice (29–31) into that family.

178

VICTORIA EUGENIA HISPANIARUM REGIN. (Queen Victoria Eugenie of Spain, formerly Princess of Battenberg)

Signed 'STERN GR. PARIS'. Pictorial—armorial: Quarterly, 1st and 4th, Gules, a castle or, masoned sable, port and fenestration azure (Castile); 2nd and 3rd, Argent, a lion rampant gules, armed, langued and crowned or (Leon); enté in point, Argent, a pomegranate gules, stalked and leaved vert (Granada); over all an inescutcheon Azure, three fleurs de lys or (Bourbon-Anjou); impaling the Royal arms with over all an inescutcheon of Battenberg. The arms, encircled by the inscriptional ribbon, rest on a mantle, the Spanish Royal crown above and books, inkwell and quill below. It is printed in sepia. Very rare.

Her Highness Princess Victoria Eugenie Julia Ena was born at Balmoral Castle on 24 October 1887, the second child and only daughter of Prince Henry of Battenberg (27–28) and Princess Beatrice (29–31), the youngest child of Queen Victoria and Prince Albert of Saxe-Coburg and Gotha. Lively, golden-haired and attractive, she and her family lived with Queen Victoria, and were a great joy to her. In 1906 she married at Madrid King Alfonso XIII of Spain, the posthumous son of Alfonso XII. As they were returning from the ceremony a bomb was thrown, which killed twenty people, though none of the Royal family or their guests was hurt. It was a tragic beginning to their partnership, but the Queen was to know much more unhappiness. One son was stillborn, another deaf and dumb, and two more sons suffered from haemophilia; but the fourth son and two daughters were healthy. Nor was the King constant. They had to flee the country in 1931, and ten years later – just before his death – King Alfonso abdicated in favour of his younger son. Queen Victoria Eugenie spent her last years at Lausanne in Switzerland, where she died on 15 April 1969. Her remains were returned to Spain in April 1985.

Stern of Paris was one of the most highly regarded of the French bookplate engravers in the decades around the turn of the century, but he refused to cooperate in bookplate documentation. He could be described as the Parisian equivalent of J. & E. Bumpus, though his work is less impressive than that of the Bumpus engravers. His ex-libris include examples for Queen Maria Cristina of Spain (mother-in-law of Queen Victoria Eugenie) and Luigi, Count of Aquila, sixth son of King Francesco I of the Kingdom of the Two Sicilies.

179

VICTORIA MELITA (Grand Duchess of Hesse and by Rhine, later Grand Duchess Cyril of Russia)

Unsigned, but perhaps by Peter Halm (see below). Armorial—pictorial: within a garter bearing the name, the arms accolé of Hesse (Azure, a lion rampant double-queued barry argent and gules crowned or holding in the dexter paw a sword argent, hilt and pommel or — here facing to the sinister) and Saxony (Barry of ten or and sable, a crown of rue in bend vert), continental crown above; the garter is framed by a cartouche with winged cherub heads in the top corners and a wreath below. Printed in colour, the border green, the garter grey, and the arms coloured as detailed above. There is a print in the Benkard Collection in the Austrian National Library at Vienna.

Princess Victoria Melita was born at the Palace of San Antonio, Malta, on 25 November 1876, the second daughter of Prince Alfred, Duke of Edinburgh (16–18), and the Grand Duchess Marie Alexandrovna, the second daughter of Emperor Alexander II of Russia. She spent her childhood at Clarence House, London, and married at Coburg in 1894 Ernst Ludwig, Grand Duke of Hesse and by Rhine (174), son of Grand Duke Ludwig IV. A stillborn son and a daughter who died aged 8 were born of the

marriage, which was not happy and ended in divorce in 1901. She married secondly at Tegernsee in 1905 the Grand Duke Kirill (Cyril) Vladimirovitch of Russia, eldest son of the Grand Duke Vladimir Alexandrovitch. There was one son and two daughters of the marriage. Following the murder of Emperor Nicholas II of Russia and his family in 1918, Grand Duke Kirill proclaimed himself Head of the Imperial House of Romanov and Curator of the Throne in 1922 and Emperor and Autocrat of all the Russias in 1924. Grand Duchess Victoria Melita died at Amorbach on 2 March 1936; Grand Duke Kirill died in 1938, and he was succeeded as Head of the Imperial House of Russia by his only son, Grand Duke Vladimir.

Grand Duchess Victoria Melita's bookplate by Peter Halm, 1895, is recorded on p. 455 of Leiningen-Westerburg's *German Book-plates*, London, 1901. The print illustrated is, however, ascribed in the Benkard Collection to Alexander von Frankenburg, though it compares in style and manner with other of Halm's ex-libris. Professor Peter Halm, of Munich, was well-known as an etcher, and quite a number of ex-libris by him are recorded. It is doubtful either bookplate was significantly used.

180

EX LIBRIS WILHELMI II IMPERATORIS REGIS (Kaiser Wilhelm II)

Signed 'E(mil) D(oepler).d.s.96'. Armorial–pictorial: Argent, an eagle displayed sable, langued, armed and membered gules, charged on the breast with an inescutcheon argent, thereon an eagle displayed sable, langued gules, armed, membered or, and charged on the breast with an inescutcheon Quarterly, argent and sable (Hohenzollern); the Royal crown of Prussia above, the inscription on an encircling ribbon, and around the arms the collar of the Order of the Black Eagle; the books beneath are arranged to form a letter 'W'. This is the smaller size of this ex-libris, the larger measuring 117 × 91mm. The Kaiser had another bookplate, also by Doepler and in two sizes, reading 'KAISER WILHELM BIBLIOTHEK POSEN'. Uncommon.

His Royal Highness Prince Friedrich Wilhelm Viktor Albert was born at Berlin on 27 January 1859, the eldest son of the future Emperor Friedrich III of Germany, King of Prussia, and Princess Victoria (159–161), eldest daughter of Queen Victoria and Prince Albert of Saxe-Coburg and Gotha. He married firstly at Berlin in 1881 Princess Auguste Viktoria, eldest daughter of Friedrich,

Duke of Schleswig-Holstein-Sonderburg-Augustenburg, by whom he had six sons and one daughter. An unpleasant and belligerent child, he managed excellently to develop these characteristics as he grew up, and – after the brief reign of his father – succeeded as German Emperor and King of Prussia in 1888. His interventions in foreign politics were constantly unfortunate, and he was too blundering to prevent the First World War in 1914. In 1918 he abdicated and fled to Doorn in Holland, where he spent the rest of his life in exile. He married secondly, at Haus Doorn in 1922, Princess Hermine, widow of Prince Johann Georg of Schoenaich-Carolath, the daughter of Prince Heinrich XXII Reuss (Elder line). He died at Haus Doorn on 4 June 1941.

Professor Emil Doepler, the younger, was born at Munich in 1855. He based his style in general as a bookplate artist on the old German masters, and made many ex-libris. Doepler taught at the Royal Industries School of Art, and became President of the German Exlibris-Verein. He died in Berlin in 1922.

Bookplates of related families

I
By marriage

181

CECILIA LADY GLAMIS (later Countess of Strathmore)

Signed 'R A(nning) B(ell) XXX' (1894). Pictorial: portrait in a cartouche, Baron's coronet above within a floral and leafy border, musical instruments, palette and brushes and a sheaf of arrows below. Reproduced by line block from a drawing. Very rare. Author's coll.

Cecilia Nina, the eldest daughter of the Revd Charles William Frederick Cavendish-Bentinck and his second wife, Caroline Louisa, eldest daughter of Edwyn Burnaby of Baggrave Hall, Leicestershire, was born on 11 September 1862. She married in 1881 Claude George Bowes-Lyon, Lord Glamis, eldest son of Claude, 13th Earl of Strathmore, and Frances Dora, daughter of Oswald Smith, of Blendon Hall, Kent. There were six sons and four daughters of the marriage. The youngest daughter, Lady Elizabeth Angela Marguerite Bowes-Lyon (64–67) married in 1923 Prince Albert, Duke of York, who ascended the throne in 1936 as King George VI (99–106) and died in 1952. Her Majesty is now the Queen Mother. The 14th Earl of Strathmore succeeded his father in 1904. The seat of the Strathmores is Glamis Castle. The Countess died on 23 June 1938.

Robert Anning Bell, R.A. (1863–1933), turned from architecture to art, and studied at the Royal Academy Schools and briefly in Paris. Like other artists of his time his range was wide: oil and tempera painting, drawing for book illustration, coloured relief, stained glass, mosaic, etc. His best-known mosaics are panels in the Houses of Parliament and the tympanum over the entrance to Westminster Cathedral. He made eighty-eight bookplates, and after several years took to numbering them; the above is number 30, but it is an untypical work. The *1980 Year Book* of the American Society of Bookplate Collectors and Designers is largely devoted to an article on Anning Bell by Keith Clark.

NB   A later bookplate used by the Countess of Strathmore is not shown here. Engraved on copper, it is signed 'W P B(arrett) 1910', and was thus commissioned from Messrs J. & E. Bumpus, but it was engraved by Robert Osmond (see (64)). The name 'CECILIA' imposed on a large 'S' is in a Chippendale cartouche bordered by a wreath, with coronet above.

182

GEORGE DOUGLAS DUKE OF ARGYLL K.G. K.T.

Signed 'GEO. W. EVE '93'. Seal armorial: Quarterly, 1st and 4th, Gyronny of eight or and sable (Campbell); 2nd and 3rd, Argent a lymphad sable, sails furled, flag and pennants flying, and oars in action proper (the lordship of Lorne); with ducal coronet, helm, motto and crest, a boar's head fesswise, erased or, armed argent, langued gules; behind the arms, two honourable badges borne in saltire, namely, first, A baton gules, powdered with thistles or, ensigned with an Imperial crown proper, thereon the crest of Scotland (for the office of Hereditary Great Master of the Household in Scotland). The other badge, A sword proper, hilt and pommel or, was borne for the office of Lord Justice General of Scotland, now no longer hereditary in the family; supporters, Two lions guardant gules. This bookplate was commissioned by his son and heir, the Marquess of Lorne, perhaps as a seventieth birthday present, but was never used. Since, however, it is familiar in bookplate collections it seemed right to include it, with this explanation. It is illustrated in half-tone in *The Ex Libris Journal*, Vol. 5, 1895, and prints from the copper are illustrations in Egerton Castle's *English Book-plates*, 1893 edition, and in George H. Viner's *A Descriptive Catalogue of the Bookplates designed and etched by George W. Eve, R.E,* 1916. It occurs printed in black and in brown, and the original copper is now at Inverary Castle.

George Douglas Campbell, 8th Duke of Argyll, second son of the 7th Duke and his second wife, Joan, daughter and heir of John Glassel, of Long Niddry, was born on 30 April 1823. He married firstly in 1844 Lady Elizabeth Georgiana Sutherland-Leveson-Gower, eldest daughter of the 2nd Duke of Sutherland. There were five sons and seven daughters of the marriage. He married secondly in 1881 Amelia Maria, daughter of the Rt Revd Thomas L. Claughton, Bishop of St Albans, widow of the third son of the 1st Earl of Lichfield. He married thirdly in 1895 Ina Erskine, youngest daughter of Archibald McNeill of Colonsay. He succeeded his father in 1847, was Postmaster-General, Lord Privy Seal three times, and Secretary of State for India 1867–74. He was also Chancellor of the University of St Andrews. His eldest son, John Douglas Sutherland Campbell, Marquess of Lorne (later 9th Duke) was married to Princess Louise (117), fourth daughter of Queen Victoria. The family seat is Inverary Castle, Argyll. His Grace died on 24 April 1900.

For a note on George W. Eve see (53).

183

Anonymous (The Duke of Fife)

Unsigned process reproduction of a larger armorial designed by George W. Eve and engraved by Alfred D. Downey (see below). Armorial: two shields accolé: dexter, within the ribbon and collar of the Thistle, quarterly, 1st and 4th, Or, a lion rampant gules (Dukedom of Fife); 2nd and 3rd, Vert, a fess dancettée ermine between a hart's head cabossed in chief and two escallops in base or (Duff of Braco); sinister, within a wreath the Royal arms with the inescutcheon of Saxony and over all a label of five points argent, the centre and two outer points charged with a cross gules and the other two with a thistle slipped and leaved proper; with coronet, helm, crest, motto and supporters of the Dukedom of Fife. Beneath are the badges of the Orders of the Thistle, the Royal Victorian Order and the Royal Order of Victoria and Albert – the first two appertaining to the Duke and the last to Princess Louise. The original, larger version was engraved by Downey as illustration in A. C. Fox-Davies' *Armorial Families*, in which it occurs in the 4th and perhaps other editions; and separate prints of this occur with 'Geo W. Eve del' at lower left, but it is not evident that the larger size was ever used as a bookplate.

Alexander William George Duff, 1st Duke of Fife, only son of the 5th Earl Fife and Lady Agnes Georgiana Elizabeth Hay, daughter of the 18th Earl of Erroll, was born on 10 November 1849. He succeeded his father as Earl Fife in 1879, was created Earl of Fife in the peerage of the United Kingdom in 1885 and Duke of Fife in 1889. He married at Buckingham Palace in 1889 Princess Louise, later Princess Royal (119 and R), the eldest daughter of the future King Edward VII and Queen Alexandra. There were two daughters of the marriage: Alexandra, later Duchess of Fife, and Lady Maud Carnegie, later Countess of Southesk (both were given the title of Princess and the qualification of Highness in 1905). The Duke was a great-grandson of King William IV on the distaff side, for his grandmother was Elizabeth FitzClarence. In December 1911, as the family was travelling to Egypt, their ship was wrecked in a gale near Cape Spartel, and the Duke's death at Aswan on 29 January following was hastened by that misadventure. He was buried in St George's Chapel, Windsor, but his remains were later transferred to Scotland.

For a note on George W. Eve see (53).

Alfred Dyer Downey joined the family engraving business of Thomas and Edward Downey in 1889 at 47 Berwick Street, Soho. They moved in 1901 to 63 Berners Street, by which time he had specialized in heraldic engraving. For further details of the family see (28).

184

JOHN EVELYN GIBBS

Signed 'WPB 1920', and thus from Messrs J. & E. Bumpus, but engraved by Robert Osmond. Armorial: Gibbs (Argent, three battleaxes sable, a bordure nebuly of the last) impaling the Royal arms quartering Württemburg and Swabia with an inescutcheon of Teck (1st and 4th, the Royal arms as borne by George III after 1801 with over all a label of three points argent, the centre point charged with a cross and each of the others with two hearts in pale gules (Cambridge); 2nd and 3rd, Per pale, dexter, Or, three stag's attires fesswise in pale points to the sinister sable (Württemburg); sinister, Or, three lions passant in pale sable the dexter forepaws gules (Swabia); over all an inescutcheon Paly bendy sinister sable and or (Teck)). Helm, crest and motto, with rich mantling. Proofs from Osmond's workshop, lacking 'WPB 1920', are known. Author's coll.

Colonel John Evelyn Gibbs (1879-1932), fourth son of Antony Gibbs of Tyntesfield and Charlton, Somerset, and Pytte, Clyst St George, Devon, married at Windsor Castle on 2 September 1919 Lady Helena Frances Augusta Cambridge (formerly Her Serene Highness Princess Helena of Teck), the second daughter of Adolphus, 2nd Duke of Teck, and Lady Margaret Grosvenor. He died without issue at Tetbury, Gloucestershire, on 11 October 1932. Lady Helena Gibbs died at Badminton House, Gloucestershire, on 22 December 1969.

The Gibbe family (claiming descent from John Gibbe, of Venton or Fenton, Darlington, Devon in the time of Richard II) settled at Exeter in the fifteenth century; and early in the reign of Henry VIII members of the family were in the nearby parishes of Woodbury and Clyst St George. (For a note on Robert Osmond see (64).)

185

LIBER E BIBLIOTHECA HENRY VISCOUNT LASCELLES (later Earl of Harewood)

Unsigned. Pictorial–armorial: a mediaeval knight with tilting spear and caparisoned horse; motto and armorial shield (Sable, a cross patonce, within a bordure or, a label for cadency) at lower left, the inscription within the rectangular border, which also encloses the crest and 'Ao Dmi: 1899'. His later and more familiar bookplate follows. Uncommon. Viner Coll.

Henry George Charles Lascelles, 6th Earl of Harewood, the elder son of Henry Ulick Lascelles, the 5th Earl, and his wife Lady Florence Katharine Bridgeman, the second daughter of the 3rd Earl of Bradford, was born on 9 September 1882. He became Viscount Lascelles in 1892, on his father's elevation to the Earldom, was educated at Eton and the Royal Military College, and could not have been above 17 years of age when this bookplate was made for him. He served with distinction in the First World War, in which he was twice wounded, and he was awarded the Croix de Guerre and D.S.O. with Bar. His great-uncle, the last Marquess of Clanricarde, left him a great fortune in 1916, they having become close friends through their love of the arts. In 1922 he married at Westminster Abbey Princess Mary, later the Princess Royal (130), the only daughter of King George V and Queen Mary. There were two sons of the marriage: Lord Harewood and the Hon. Gerald Lascelles. The Earl — who succeeded his father in 1929 — was a thorough connoisseur, as was his wife; but he also loved the countryside, racing and Freemasonry, and much supported Princess Mary in her Royal engagements. Their homes included Harewood House, near Leeds, and Goldsborough Hall, Knaresborough. Lord Harewood died at the former residence on 24 May 1947, and was buried in the family vault in Harewood Church.

186

Henry George Charles Viscount Lascelles, K.G. D.S.O. (later Earl of Harewood)

Signed 'C. HELARD 1922', but engraved by A. Dyer Downey. Armorial, two shields accolé: dexter, within the ribbon of the Garter, Sable, a cross patonce, within a bordure or (though no tinctures are indicated), a label for difference; from the ribbon depend the Croix de Guerre and D.S.O.; sinister, in a beribboned wreath with Royal coronet above, the Royal arms with over all a label of three points argent each charged with a cross gules. Helm, crest, motto and supporters: dexter, A bear ermine, muzzled and collared gules, buckled and chained, the chain reflexed over the back or, the collar studded and rimmed or and pendent therefrom an escutcheon sable, charged with a cross patonce or, charged on the shoulder with a label; sinister, The unicorn of the Royal arms, gorged with a coronet of rank and charged on the shoulder with a label as on the arms.

The above motto, which translates 'One king, one faith, one law', was probably adopted out of respect for his great-uncle, the last Marquess of Clanricarde (see the foregoing for the Lascelles motto and a biographical note). The said progenitor of the Clanricardes, Baron de Tousburgh, was governor for William the Conqueror's father of many of Normandy's chief towns, assuming the name de Burgo. He may have adopted his motto from that of the town of Caen: 'Un Dieu, ung foy, ung loy'. His grandson brought it to England with the Conqueror.

C. Helard was the name used as an artist by Mary Ellen Blanche (b.1870), eldest daughter of Capt Septimus Wilkinson Crookes of Shifnal in Shropshire. She designed bookplates from 1895, and six years later married Arthur Charles Fox-Davies, the author of *Armorial Families*, 1895, to which she had provided illustrations. Shunning publicity, she continued her work until 1932, four years after her husband's death. Her bookplates – some of them engraved by Alfred Dyer Downey (see (183)) and his son Alfred J. Downey – are listed by Colin Lattimore in *The Bookplate Society Newsletter* for March and September 1979.

Bookplates of related families

II
Illegitimate descendants
of Charles II and James II
and of marriages contravening
the Royal Marriages Act 1772

187

(Anonymous (Charles Beauclerk, 2nd Duke of St Albans)

Unsigned. Armorial: the Royal arms as borne by King Charles II debruised by a baton sinister gules charged with three roses argent, barbed and seeded proper; crest: On a chapeau gules turned up ermine, a lion statant guardant or, ducally crowned per pale argent and gules, gorged with a collar gules charged with three roses argent, barbed and seeded proper; supporters: dexter, An antelope argent attired and unguled or, sinister, A greyhound argent, both gorged with a collar as on the crest; motto on a ribbon below. It is impossible to be certain whether this bookplate belonged to the 2nd or 3rd Duke. Lack of the ribbon of the Garter would suggest the 3rd, for only the 2nd Duke was a Knight of the Garter (1741). On the other hand, the style of the ex-libris is transitional Jacobean–Chippendale, and *c.*1740 would not be an unreasonable supposition of date. It may well have been used by both in course of time. Franks Coll. 1946.

Charles Beauclerk, 2nd Duke of St Albans, was born on 6 April 1696, the eldest son of the 1st Duke and Lady Diana de Vere, eldest surviving daughter and sole heiress of Aubrey, 20th and last Earl of Oxford. Charles, the 1st Duke was the elder natural son of King Charles II (F–G) by his mistress Eleanor – 'Nell' – Gwyn; and it is said that when the King visited Nell and her little son she called the boy, saying,'Come hither, you little bastard, and speak to your father'. The King remonstrated at the nomenclature, Nell replied that he had given him no other name, and thereupon the King named him Beauclerk and created him Earl of Burford. The 2nd Duke was educated at Eton and matriculated from New College, Oxford, in 1714, but did not graduate. In 1722 he married Lucy, eldest daughter of Sir John Werden, 2nd and last Bart., and she bore him one son, who succeeded him, and a daughter. Sometime MP for Bodmin and for Windsor, the Duke carried the Queen's crown at the coronation of King George II, became a Lord of the Bedchamber in 1738, and was Governor of Windsor Castle and Warden of the Forest of Windsor. He died on 27 July 1751 at his house in St James's Place.

188

The Rt. Honourable Lord JAMES BEAUCLERCK. (sometime Lord Bishop of Hereford)

Unsigned. Jacobean armorial: the Royal arms as borne by King Charles II debruised by a baton sinister gules charged with three roses argent, barbed and seeded proper. Crest: On a chapeau gules turned up ermine, a lion statant guardant or, ducally crowned per pale argent and gules, gorged with a collar gules charged with three roses argent barbed and seeded proper, as on the arms. The mantling is rich, and the motto is on a ribbon below. *c.*1730. Franks Coll. 1944.

Lord James Beauclerk was born in 1709, the eighth of nine sons of Charles Beauclerk, 1st Duke of St Albans, and Lady Diana de Vere, eldest surviving daughter and sole heiress of Aubrey, 20th and last Earl of Oxford. The 1st Duke was the elder illegitimate son of King Charles II (F–G) by Eleanor – 'Nell' – Gwyn, sometime Lady of Queen Catherine's Privy Chamber. Lord James was educated at Queen's College, Oxford (BA 1730, MA 1733, DD 1744), and then entered the Church. He became Prebendary of Windsor in 1733, Canon of Windsor in 1738, Chaplain in Ordinary to King George II in 1739 and Deputy Clerk of the Closet in 1744. In 1746 he was appointed Bishop of Hereford. He resigned in 1785 and died, unmarried, on 20 October 1787.

189

Anonymous (Lord James Beauclerk as Bishop of Hereford)

Unsigned. Chippendale armorial: the arms of the See of Hereford (Gules, three leopards' faces reversed jessant-de-lis or) impaling the quarterly arms of Beauclerk, Duke of St Albans: 1st and 4th, Quarterly, the Royal arms as detailed above; 2nd and 3rd, Quarterly, gules and or, in the first quarter a mullet argent (de Vere); a mitre replaces the crest. This was most probably engraved quite late in his life, for the Chippendale frame has festoons of flowers. Franks Coll. 1945. Lord James was the last surviving grandson of King Charles II (F–G).

209

190

The Right Honble Bridgit Countess of Dowager of Plymouth

Unsigned. Armorial: within a lozenge the Royal arms as borne by King Charles II differenced by a baton sinister vairé (FitzCharles), impaling Ermine and azure a cross or (Osborne); with motto, an earl's coronet, and supporters: dexter, A dragon gules, armed and langued azure, gorged with a collar vairé affixed thereto a chain (FitzCharles); sinister, A griffin or, gorged with a ducal coronet azure (Osborne). This bookplate, despite its compositional lack of ambition, has characteristics — especially its name cartouche and motto ribbon — which suggest it may have come from the workshop of William Jackson (see (139)); and this tentative ascription is encouraged by the fact that her father used ex-libris in two sizes from that source (Franks Coll. 22435, *14 and *21). Franks Coll. 10606 and author's coll.

Bridget, the second daughter of Sir Thomas Osborne, later the 1st Duke of Leeds, and Bridget, daughter of Montagu Bertie, Earl of Lindsey, married at Wimbledon in 1678 Charles FitzCharles, Earl of Plymouth, the natural son of King Charles II (F–G) by Catherine Pegg. He had been brought up abroad, and trained as a soldier, but his marriage was short-lived and without issue: he became ill at Tangier, when it was besieged by the Moors, and died aged only 23. He was buried in Westminster Abbey. The Countess remained a widow for twenty-six years. Her bookplate cannot, however, be later than 1706, for in that year she made a second marriage to Philip Bisse, when her chaplain, who in 1710 became Bishop of St David's, and was later translated to Hereford. He used a bookplate in the Jacobean style as Bishop of St David's (Franks Coll. 2644). She died on 9 May 1718, and was buried in Hereford Cathedral.

191

Adolphus FitzClarence (natural son of King William IV)

Unsigned. Armorial: the Royal arms as borne by William IV, without the Electoral inescutcheon and crown of Hanover, debrusied by a baton sinister azure charged with an anchor and two roses. Crest: On a chapeau gules turned up ermine, a lion statant guardant, ducally crowned or and gorged with a collar as on the arms. The arms are encircled by the collar of the Royal Guelphic Order, from which its badge depends; and there is a second badge of an unidentified order. Supporters: dexter, A lion guardant, ducally crowned or; sinister, A horse argent; each gorged with a collar as detailed above. The name below is in the form of a facsimile signature. The bookplate cannot be earlier than 1832, when he was made a Knight Grand Cross of the Royal Guelphic Order. Franks Coll. 10610. Winterburn Coll. 80.

Lord Adolphus FitzClarence was born on 18 February 1802, the seventh child and fourth son of the future King William IV (169–170) and his mistress Mrs Jordan.

Dorothy Jordan was, in fact, the name she used as an actress. Her real name was Dorothy Bland, and she was the third daughter of Francis Bland, actor or stage underling, and Grace Phillips. The young FitzClarences lived with their parents at Bushey Park. Lord Adolphus entered the navy in 1814, serving on the *Impregnable,* and later saw service in the Mediterranean, on the North American Station and the coast of Portugal. He was made Commander in 1823 and Captain the following year. In 1830 he took command of the *Royal George* yacht, later becoming Captain and Commodore of the Royal yacht *Victoria and Albert* (see (138)), in which he continued until 1853 when he attained flag rank. After his father's accession in 1830 he was in 1831 granted the title and precedence of a younger son of a marquess, and the same year became groom of the robes; he was naval A.D.C. to Queen Victoria 1846–53. Lord Adolphus died, unmarried, at Newburgh Park near Easingwold, Yorkshire on 17 May 1856. The bookplates of three of his brothers follow.

192

Sigillum domini augusti de fitz clarence (Lord Augustus FitzClarence)

Unsigned, but engraved in London. Seal armorial: the arms identical to those of his brother on the foregoing bookplate, but the baton is charged, like the bookplate for his brother, Lord Frederick, which follows, with a cross between two anchors (like the label assigned to his father); the shield and motto scrolls are set at an angle, and the motto reads 'Nec timere nec timide' instead of the usual 'nec temere nec timide'; the inscription runs around the inner border of the seal. Franks Coll. 10611. Winterburn Coll. 81.

Lord Augustus FitzClarence was born on 1 March 1805, the fifth son of the future King William IV (169–170) by his mistress Mrs Jordan. His early life was spent at their home at Bushey Park in Surrey, and on 28 June 1824 he matriculated from Brasenose College, Oxford. Later of Trinity Hall, Cambridge, he obtained his LL.B. in 1828 (LL.D 1835). Lord Augustus was ordained, became rector of Mapledurham, Oxfordshire in 1829, and was a Chaplain to the Queen from 1837 until his death. He married in 1845 Sarah Elizabeth Catherine, the eldest daughter of Lord Henry Gordon, and she bore him two sons and four daughters. Like other younger sons and daughters of the family he was given in 1831 the rank and title of the younger child of a marquess. He died at Mapledurham on 14 June 1854.

*This belonged to my Father
when Duke of Clarence, and
was left to me by the Will of Queen Adelaide.*

Lord Frederick Fitzclarence.

193

**Lord Frederick Fitzclarence. This belonged to my father when Duke of Clarence
and was left to me by the Will of Queen Adelaide**

Unsigned. Armorial: within the ribbon and collar of the Royal Guelphic Order, from which the badge depends, the Royal arms as borne by William IV debruised by a baton sinister azure charged with a cross between two anchors. Crest: On a chapeau gules turned up ermine, a lion statant guardant, ducally crowned or and gorged with a collar azure charged as on the arms. Supporters: dexter, A lion guardant, ducally crowned or; sinister, A horse argent; each gorged with a similar collar. The motto differs from the usual, like the foregoing plate. Queen Adelaide died on 2 December 1849, so this bookplate cannot be earlier than 1850. Rare. Winterburn Coll. 78.

Lord Frederick FitzClarence was born on 9 December 1799, the fifth child and third son of the future King William IV (169–170) and his mistress Mrs Jordan. He entered the Army in 1814, becoming an ensign in the Coldstream Guards, assisted at the arrest of the Cato Street conspirators in 1820, and rose to the rank of Lieutenant-Colonel – in the 7th Foot Guards – in 1825. In 1821 he married Lady Augusta Boyle, daughter of the 4th Earl of Glasgow. She bore him one daughter, who died unmarried. Granted the rank and precedence of a younger son of a marquess in 1831, he was made a Knight Grand Cross of the Royal Guelphic Order in the same year. FitzClarence was appointed Military Governor of Portsmouth in 1840, became Colonel of the 36th Foot in 1841, and was Commander-in-Chief at Bombay from 1852 until his death. He was the author of several works, including *A Manual of Out-Post Duties*. Lord Frederick died at Poorundhur near Poona on 30 October 1854, and his body was shipped back to England and buried at Ford, Northumberland, the following February.

Earl of Munster.

Col. Fitz Clarence.   *Lt. Col. Fitz Clarence.*

194

Earl of Munster. (FitzClarence)

Unsigned. Armorial: the Royal arms as borne by King William IV, without the electoral inescutcheon and crown of Hanover, debruised by a baton sinister azure charged with three anchors or; with earl's coronet, motto and supporters: dexter, A lion guardant, ducally crowned or; sinister, A horse argent; each gorged with a collar azure charged with three anchors or. Franks Coll. 10607. A variant, perhaps from a different copper, is Franks Coll. 10609.

195

Col. Fitz Clarence

Engraved label without border. This sometimes occurs printed together with the above. Franks Coll. 10608; Winterburn Coll. 79 (with (194), above).

196

Lt. Col. Fitz Clarence

Engraved label without border. Franks Coll. 10612.

George Augustus Frederick FitzClarence was born in 1794, the eldest child of the future King William IV (169–170) by his mistress Mrs Jordan. His early life was spent at Bushey Park, and he went to a private school at Sunbury and afterwards to the Royal Military College at Marlow. He entered the army aged thirteen in 1807, was at Corunna, and served later in India, where he was A.D.C. to Lord Hastings when Governor-General at the time of the Mahratta war of 1816–17. In 1819 he married Mary Wyndham, the natural daughter of George, Earl of Egremont. There were four sons and three daughters of the marriage. Created Earl of Munster in 1831, he was sometime Lieutenant of the Tower of London, A.D.C. to Queen Victoria, and Governor of Windsor Castle. A fellow of the Royal Society and other learned institutions, he furthered Asiatic studies and became President of the Royal Asiatic Society the year before his death. A companionable man, and the author of several works, he lived at Upper Belgrave Square. It was there that he committed suicide by shooting himself on 20 March 1842. He was buried in the parish church at Hampton.

197

Thos. Dunckerley Fitz George

Signed 'LEVI SCU. PORTS'. Chippendale armorial: the Royal arms as borne by King George II debruised by a baton sinister argent. Crest: On a chapeau gules turned up ermine a lion statant guardant or crowned. The name and engraver's signature are in a cartouche below. Franks Coll. 10613. Winterburn Coll. 102.

Thomas Dunckerley FitzGeorge was born in 1724, the son of a domestic in Sir Robert Walpole's household at Houghton. King George II (J) was claimed as father, but the girl made a marriage and her husband got a position as a porter at Somerset House. Losing his mother young, his grandmother brought him up, and he was apprenticed to a barber. He ran away, however, and got aboard Sir John Morris's ship. Sir Robert Walpole was told, and requested Morris to give him training as a sailor. The brief account of his life from which the foregoing was gleaned, in the *Gentleman's Magazine* for 1793 (Pt. 2, pp. 1052–3) continues:

> He seems to have continued in the sea-service, as the next thing we have heard of him was his being at the siege of Quebec by Wolfe, where he behaved so well as to have had a recommendation to fill some employment in the naval academy at Portsmouth, which he did with credit. About 20 years ago he availed himself of the remarkable likeness he

bore to the Royal Family, to get it represented to his Majesty that the late King was in truth his father, and that he owed his existence to a visit which the King when Prince had paid to Houghton; and he ventured to refer to Sir Edward Walpole.

Though Sir Edward was unhelpful, after the King's kind enquiry into the matter FitzGeorge was given a pension and an apartment at Hampton Court. He was later called to the bar, but did not proceed long. In the same magazine for 19 November 1795 there is record of his death: 'At Portsmouth, in his 71st year, Thomas Dunckerley Esq., provincial grand master of masonry; and pretty generally supposed to have been a natural son of King George II.' Notice of his widow's death, in the same magazine for 24 February 1801 refers, incidentally, to his use of the Royal arms.

Levi of Portsea was probably Isaac Levi (d.1785), by whom five ex-libris signed with his name alone are recorded by Fincham. If the attribution is correct he was the brother of Elias Levi and son of Benjamin Levi (d.1784), both of Portsmouth. He was also almost certainly associated sometime with Mordecai Moses of Portsmouth, who shares the signature of four ex-libris with I. Levy (sic).

Louisa.

198

Louisa. (Mrs Louisa FitzGeorge, wife of the 2nd Duke of Cambridge)

Unsigned. Armorial. This is simply another rendering of the bookplate of Prince George, 2nd Duke of Cambridge (for details of which see (87)) with the name substituted; and it is an example of crass impertinence. The marriage (see below) was illegal, and yet Mrs FitzGeorge adopts not only the Royal arms but the ribbon and collar of the Garter! One hopes that this travesty never came to the attention of Queen Victoria. It should, moreover, be noted that it is from a different copper, for the engraving of the lion's head and the length of the unicorn's horn, etc., very evidently differ. Extremely rare, the only print noted being in the library at Wolfenbüttel. The ex-libris is No. 157 and is illustrated in *Ex Libris Wolfenbüttel*, Heinemann, 1895. It probably dates from 1847–50, for on her husband's succeeding his father as Duke he would drop the second label.

Sarah (called Louisa) Fairbrother, the daughter of Robert Fairbrother, a theatrical printer, by his wife, née Freeman, was born at Bow Street, Covent Garden in 1816. Having been an actress, she married morganatically (in contravention of the Royal Marriages Act) in 1847 at St John's Church, Clerkenwell, Prince George William Frederick Charles, 2nd Duke of Cambridge, son of Prince Adolphus, Duke of Cambridge (seventh son of King George III) and Princess Augusta of Hesse-Cassel. There were three sons of the marriage, who bore the name FitzGeorge, the second of them Sir Adolphus (199). Mrs FitzGeorge lived at 6 Queen Street, Mayfair, until her death on 12 January 1890, and she was buried at Kensal Green Cemetery.

Sir Adolphus Fitz-George.

199

Sir Adolphus Fitz-George

Unsigned. Armorial: within the ribbon of the Garter, the Royal arms as borne by his father, George, Duke of Cambridge (87), but debruised by a baton sinister argent and undifferenced by a label, with a cap of maintenance and Royal lion as crest and the Royal supporters with coronets but not charged on the shoulder with a label. This is a curious bookplate in not only, it seems, adopting arms, supporters and a crest to which he was unentitled, but also placing them in the ribbon of the Garter, of which he was of course never a Knight. The inscription indicates that it was engraved not earlier than 1904, when he was made a Knight Commander of the Royal Victorian Order, so he could legitimately have placed his arms in that Order's ribbon. Winterburn Coll. 82.

Sir Adolphus Augustus Frederick FitzGeorge was born in London on 30 January 1846, the second of three sons of Prince George, 2nd Duke of Cambridge, and Sarah (called Louisa) Fairbrother (198), the daughter of Robert Fairbrother, a theatrical printer. Their marriage was, needless to say, in contravention of the Royal Marriages Act 1772. Adolphus entered the Royal Navy in 1859, rising by 1896 to the rank of Rear-Admiral; and he was Equerry to his father and Deputy Ranger of Richmond Park. He married firstly at Hessle in Yorkshire in 1875 Sophia Jane, the daughter of Thomas Holden, of Winestead Hall, Hull, Yorkshire, and by her he had one daughter. After his wife's death in 1920 he married, at Pimlico in London, Margarita Beatrice, the daughter of John Watson. Sir Adolphus died in London on 17 December 1922.

200

EX-LIBRIS DUC DE BERWICK. (James Fitzjames)

Printed label within a rectangular border of ornaments. 'No.' is below, and a print in the author's collection is numbered '8'. Extremely rare. Though this label is – not surprisingly – unreferred to in writings on British book-plates, it is illustrated in Francisco Vindel's *Ensayo de un Catalogo de Ex-Libris Ibero-Americanos*, Madrid, 1952, under Casa de Alba, other bookplates relating to his descendants also being detailed. It is there ascribed to the second half of the eighteenth century. If made for a descendant, however, surely the title would have been other than merely 'Duc de Berwick'. Moreover, this label is not dissimilar to labels produced in England during James Fitzjames' lifetime, and French examples of the period were probably comparable in their simple orna-ment and modesty. It is unlikely, though, that the Duke would have actually commissioned this ex-libris to serve in general in his library. More probably it was printed – as they were so often in this country – when books were sent for binding, and added as a small refinement to please and perhaps surprise a client.

James Fitzjames, Duke of Berwick and Marshal of France, the natural son of James, Duke of York, later King James II (P-Q), by his mistress Arabella Churchill, daughter of Sir Winston Churchill, was born on 21 August 1670 at Mou-lins in the Bourbonnais. He was educated in France at two Jesuit colleges and the Collège du Plessis, began a military career, visited England, and in 1687 was created Duke of Berwick. He served in Hungary before another visit to England the following year, when he was made a Knight of the Garter. Soon, however, he had to flee after the King to France. There followed service in Ireland, where he was present at the Battle of the Boyne, and then in the Nether-lands. In 1695 he married Lady Honora Sarsfield, daughter of the Earl of Clanricarde, but she died three years later; and in 1700 he married secondly Anne, the daughter of the Hon. Henry Bulkeley. He became a naturalized Frenchman in 1703. He spent much time in Spain, and gained a great victory at Almanza, after which King Philip V of Spain created his son Duke of Liria. In 1733 he was in the war of the Polish succession, commanding his army; but on 12 June 1734 at Philippsburg he was decapitated by a cannon-ball. He was buried in the church of the Hôpital des Invalides in Paris. His descendants in Spain were Dukes of Liria, and in France Ducs de Fitzjames.

201

**The Most Noble Charles Fitz Roy Duke of Southampton Knight of the most Noble
Order of ye Garter 1704**

Unsigned, but from the workshop of William Jackson. Armorial: the Royal arms as borne by King Charles II debruised by a baton sinister ermine, impaling Argent, a fess indented (should be) gules (not sable), in chief three leopards' faces sable; ducal coronet, helm, blank motto ribbon, and crest, On a chapeau gules turned up ermine, a lion statant guardant ducally crowned azure, gorged with a collar componée ermine and azure; supporters, dexter, A lion guardant or ducally crowned azure, gorged with a collar componée ermine and azure; sinister, A greyhound argent, collared as the dexter. Only one print recorded. Franks Coll. *22.

There is a variety, which reads: *The Most Noble Ann Duchess of Southampton 1704*. It is from the same copper as the above, but with the inscription re-engraved. Very rare. Franks 10718 & *24 (a duplicate) and author's coll.

Charles, Duke of Cleveland and of Southampton, the eldest natural son of King Charles II (F–G) by his mistress Barbara Villiers, Countess of Castlemaine, was born in 1662 and surnamed Palmer, in right of his legal father, the Earl of Castlemaine. King Charles II acknowledged paternity, and on Barbara Villiers' elevation as Baroness Nonsuch, Countess of Southampton and Duchess of Cleveland in 1670, he forsook the title Lord Limerick and became Earl of Southampton, with the surname FitzRoy. He became a Knight of the Garter in 1673, Duke of Southampton in 1675, and also Duke of Cleveland on his mother's death in 1709. Despite these great dignities, however, his life was not markedly eventful. He married firstly in 1671 Mary, the only daughter of Sir Henry Wood, Bart. A great heiress, she was but about seven at the time, and he about nine; so the ceremony was repeated at the age of legal consent, but she died of smallpox when scarcely seventeen. He married, secondly, in 1694, Ann, daughter of Sir William Pulteney, of Misterton, Leicestershire. Ann Pulteney was born on 25 November 1663 and died on 20 February 1746. She bore him three sons and three daughters. The Duke died in 1730, and was succeeded by his only surviving son, William (202), the second and last Duke of Cleveland of that creation.

For a note on William Jackson see (139).

His Grace
The Duke of Cleveland.

202

His Grace The Duke of Cleveland. (FitzRoy)

Unsigned. Armorial: on a mantle, the Royal arms as borne by King Charles II debruised by a baton sinister ermine; with ducal coronet, motto, and supporters: dexter, A lion guardant or ducally crowned azure, gorged with a collar componée ermine and azure; sinister, A greyhound argent, collared as the dexter. The motto of the Dukes of Cleveland of this creation was 'Secundis dubiisque rectus' (Upright both in prosperity and in perils); the Dukes of the second creation used 'Nec temere nec timide' (Neither rashly nor timidly), the motto also used by the FitzClarences. Rare. Author's coll.

William FitzRoy, 2nd Duke of Cleveland and of Southampton, was born on 19 February 1698, the eldest son of Charles, Duke of Cleveland and of Southampton (201) — eldest natural son of King Charles II (F–G) by Barbara Villiers — and Ann, daughter of Sir William Pulteney of Misterton, Leicestershire. Known as the Earl of Chichester before he succeeded his father in 1730, he married in 1732 Henrietta, the fifth daughter of Daniel Finch, 7th Earl of Winchilsea. There was no issue of the marriage, and the Duchess died of miliary fever in 1742. Sometime Receiver General of the Profits of the Seals in the King's Bench and Common Pleas, and Comptroller of the Seal and Green Wax Office, the Duke died in 1774 at Raby Castle, Co. Durham, the residence of his nephew, the Earl of Darlington. The Dukedom of Cleveland of the second creation (1833) is in descent from William Fitz-Roy's sister, Lady Grace, who married the 1st Earl of Darlington.

203

Charles Lennox Duke of Richmond, Lennox and Aubigny Knight of ye most noble order of the Garter

Unsigned. Armorial: within the ribbon of the Garter the Royal arms as borne by King Charles II differenced by a bordure componée argent and gules, the first charged with roses of the second barbed and seeded proper, and over all an inescutcheon gules charged with three buckles or, for the Dukedom of Aubigny; on a shaded rectangular ground, with ducal coronet above, the inscription on a mantle below. Engraved 1734–50. This rare bookplate is No. 79 in *83 Examples of Armorial Book Plates*, privately printed in an edition of sixty copies by W. Griggs, Peckham, 1884. Franks Coll. 18141.

Charles Lennox, 2nd Duke of Richmond, Lennox and Aubigny, was born at Goodwood on 18 May 1701, the only son of Charles Lennox, 1st Duke of Richmond, a natural son of King Charles II (F–G) by Louise de Ker-ouaille, Duchess of Portsmouth. His mother was Anne, the daughter of Francis, Lord Brudenell, and widow of Henry, son of John, Lord Bellasis. He entered the Army, became an MP, succeeded his father in 1723, and three years later was made a Knight of the Garter. Appointed Lord High Constable of England for the coronation of King George II, he became a Lord of the Bedchamber and later Master of the Horse. Lennox became Duke of Aubigny in France on the death of his grandmother in

1734. He married in 1719 Sarah, eldest daughter and coheir of William, 1st Earl of Cadogan. The marriage began curiously, as payment of a gambling debt between their parents, and Lennox repaired at once to the Continent with his tutor. Returning three years later he betook himself to the theatre, having unpleasant recollections of his wife, and was astounded by the beauty of a lady who turned out to be none other than she. They were thereafter entirely devoted, and she bore him twelve children. An entertaining but not highly intelligent man, he was present at the Battle of Dettingen, and was several times one of the lord justices of the Kingdom during the King's absences. He died on 8 August 1750, and was buried in Chichester Cathedral, where his father's remains then were.

NB A Jacobean trophy plate, occurring in two states, reading 'Du très-haut, très-puissant et très noble Prince Charles Lenos, Duc de Richmond et Lenox', etc., which probably appertained to his father (d.1723) was Lot 557 in the Marshall Collection, auctioned by Sotheby, Wilkinson & Hodge in 1906. No print of it has, however, been seen, and it was probably not a bookplate. Its inscription is reminiscent of the armorial for Prince William, Duke of Gloucester (JJ).

204

L M (Princess Louise Maximilienne Caroline Emmanuèle of Stolberg-Gedern, wife of Prince Charles Edward, 'The Young Pretender')

Signed: 'Inv et gr. P.S.A.R'. Initials in a shaded lozenge within an oval, with festoons, doves and 'EX LIBRIS' above, and a cherub, globe and books, etc., on a cloud below. Most copies of this ex-libris encountered are nineteenth-century reprints. Author's coll.

Princess Louise Maximilienne Caroline Emmanuèle of Stolberg-Gedern (d.1824), daughter of Gustav-Adolf, Prince of the same, married in 1772 Prince Charles Edward Louis Philip Casimir (1720–88), known as 'Bonnie Prince Charlie' or 'The Young Pretender', the elder son of 'The Old Pretender', James Francis Edward Stuart, Prince of Wales, and Maria Clementina Sobieska (who later became a nun), the daughter of James Sobieski, son of the King of Poland. For a short time the marriage was happy, but the

Countess of Albany (as she became) found the Prince's alcoholism and ill-usage too much to bear, and in 1777 she met the Italian poet Vittorio Alfieri, with whom she fell in love. An incident with the Prince in 1780 caused her for a time to go into a convent, but a separation was arranged and she subsequently lived twenty years with Alfieri until his death in 1803.

The Stolberg family originated in the Harz and its lineage is traceable from 1200. The Stolberg-Gedern line is now extinct, but two branches survive: Stolberg-Wernigerode and Stolberg-Stolberg. The rank of Prince of the Empire was conferred on Friedrich-Karl, Count of Stolberg-Gedern in 1742.

205

The Right Honble. Edward Radcliffe Earl of Darwentwater Viscount Radcliffe and Langley Baron of Tyndale, 1702

Unsigned, but from the workshop of William Jackson. Armorial: Argent a bend engrailed sable, with earl's coronet, helm and crest: out of a ducal coronet a bull's head sable armed or; supporters, Two bulls pean gorged with ducal coronets, armed and chained argent. This must be the bookplate of the 2nd Earl, though both Burke and the Official Baronage give his Christian name as Francis. Uncommon. Franks Coll. 24441 and *45 (both the same).

Edward Radcliffe, 2nd Earl of Derwentwater, was the eldest son of Sir Francis Radclyffe (d.1696), whose peerage was one of the few created by King James II. He married in 1687 Lady Mary Tudor, a natural daughter of King Charles II (F–G) by Mary Davies or Davis, 'Moll Davis' the actress, whom Mrs Pepys described as 'the most impertinent slut in the world'. Lady Mary was granted by her father the precedence of a duke's daughter. Though not famed for her faithfulness to her husband, she bore him three sons, the eldest of whom, James, the 3rd Earl, was born in Arlington Street, London. He was brought up at the exiled court of St Germain, as a companion to James Edward, The 'Old Pretender', but he joined in the conspiracy of 1715, and was beheaded on Tower Hill in 1716. The family had estates in Cumberland, and Dilston Hall was built by the 1st Earl. The 2nd Earl died in 1705.

For a note on William Jackson see (139).

John Sheffield,
Duke of
Buckingham & Normanby.

206

John Sheffield, Duke of Buckingham & Normanby

Unsigned. Armorial: within the ribbon of the Garter, Quarterly of fifteen: 1st, Argent, a chevron between three garbs gules (Sheffield); 2nd, ? ; 3rd, Gower; 4th, Moyne; 5th ? ; 6th, Beltoft; 7th, Lownde(s); 8th, ? ; 9th, ? ; 10th, Beltoft; 11th, Rocheford?; 12th, Delves; 13th, Babbington, Giffard or Gifford; 14th, Pigot; 15th, Gibthorp?; with ducal coronet, helm, crest, motto and supporters: Two boars or. A pedigree of the ancestry of John Sheffield is given on p. 267 of *The Banner Displayed, or Gwillim Abridged,* 1726. The Gower, Moyne, Beltoft, Lownde and Delves coats can there be seen to relate to marriages, but on the bookplate above not all are placed precisely in order. Most copies of this bookplate encountered are clearly reprinted from the original copper. Franks Coll. 26643.

John Sheffield, 3rd Earl of Mulgrave, later 1st Duke of Buckingham and Normanby, only son of Edmund Sheffield, 2nd Earl, and Elizabeth, daughter of Lionel Cranfield, 1st Earl of Middlesex, was born on 8 September 1647. He succeeded his father in 1658, became captain of a troop of horse in 1667 and in 1673 became a Gentleman of the Bedchamber to the King. In 1680 he commanded an expedition to relieve Tangier from the Moors, and later did well as a result of Monmouth's disgrace, but was sent from Court for courting Princess Anne. Later allowed back, he was Lord Chamberlain under King James II. Created Marquess of Normanby in the next reign, Queen Anne also favoured him and created him Duke. In 1710 he became Lord Steward of the Household and Lord President of the Council, but was removed from all posts on King George I's arrival. Thrice married, his third wife was Catharine Darnley, natural daughter of King James II (P–Q) by Catharine Sedley. By her, whom he married in 1706, he had three sons, of whom Edmund survived him and succeeded as 2nd Duke of Buckingham on 24 February 1721.

NB   An early armorial, the shield in the Garter, reading 'The Most Honble. John Marquiss of Normanby Earle of Mulgrave Lord Privy Seale and Knight of the Most Noble Order of the Garter. 1702', was engraved in William Jackson's workshop, but was perhaps never used. Only one print is recorded. Franks Coll. *19

207

Walter Smythe Esqr.

Unsigned. Chippendale armorial (Sable, three roses argent, with a crescent for difference, as second son), with floral decoration and cherubs pursuing learning, the name in a cartouche below. Uncommon. Author's coll.

Walter Smythe was the second son of Sir John Smythe, 3rd Bart., of Eshe Hall, Co. Durham, and Constantia, daughter of George Blount. He married Mary, the daughter of John Errington. There were four sons and two daughters of the marriage, and he died on 14 January 1788. His inclusion here may, therefore, seem rather mysterious; but he happened to be the father of the famous Mrs Fitzherbert. His elder daughter, born in 1756, she first married Edward Weld, of Lulworth Castle, and after his death Thomas Fitzherbert, of Norbury, Derbyshire. When George, Prince of Wales, later Prince Regent and King George IV (42, 78–86), met her in 1783–4 she had been widowed twice. She had such an electric effect on him that she retired for a while to the Continent to resist his advances; but he was inconsolable, sent her a forty-two page letter, and a miniature, and in due course she returned. They went through a form of marriage at her house in London in December 1785. The marriage was, of course, in contravention of the Royal Marriages Act, and it was gross folly for the heir to the throne to marry a Catholic; but she realized the marriage was invalid and settled for being his mistress. He bought her a mansion in Pall Mall, treated her as his wife, and expected others to do so; and she behaved with dignity and was well liked, even by those in the Royal family. They parted in 1794, before his marriage to Princess Caroline of Brunswick, but in 1800 were reconciled as friends. In his will he wrote: 'How I have ever loved and adored you God only knows, and how I do now he also knows.' She was perhaps the only woman he was sincerely attached to, and he died in 1830 with her portrait round his neck. Mrs Fitzherbert died on 29 March 1837, and was buried in St John the Baptist's Roman Catholic Church at Brighton.

208

The Right Honble. James Lord Waldegrave Baron of Chewton 1728

Unsigned, but from the workshop of William Jackson. Early armorial: Per pale argent and gules; with baron's coronet, helm and crest, (should be) out of a ducal coronet or, five ostrich feathers, the two first argent the centre one per pale argent and gules and the last two gules; supporters, Two talbots sable eared or, each gorged with a mural crown argent; motto ribbon blank. The date was first engraved '1727' but has been amended to '8', the '7' still being evident. Uncommon. Franks Coll. 30536 – a reworking of Franks Coll. 30535 and *67 (two identical prints), dated 1707.

James, Baron Waldegrave, later 1st Earl, was born in 1685, the elder son of Henry, 1st Baron Waldegrave, sometime Comptroller of King James II's Household, and Lady Henrietta Fitzjames, natural daughter of King James II (P–Q) by Arabella Churchill, sister of John, Duke of Marlborough. He was thus a grandson of the King.

Educated in France, he married in 1714 Mary, second daughter of Sir John Webbe, Bart., of Hatherop in Gloucestershire. There were three sons and a daughter of the marriage; and Maria, the wife of his eldest son, James, the 2nd Earl, later became the Duchess of Gloucester (120–121). Lord Waldegrave in 1718–19 declared himself a Protestant, took the oaths and entered the House of Lords, infuriating the Jacobites and not least his uncle, the Duke of Berwick (200). He became a Lord of the Bedchamber to King George I, and later became ambassador and minister-plenipotentiary at Vienna, where he spent three years. Created Earl in 1729, he then went as ambassador to Paris, where he served until 1740. He died at Navestock on 11 April 1741 and was buried in the chancel of the church there. His monument there was erected by Maria, later Duchess of Gloucester.

For a note on William Jackson see (139).

Lord Truro.

209

Lord Truro. (Thomas Wilde)

Unsigned. Armorial: Ermine on a cross sable a plate, a chief of the second charged with three martlets argent (Baron Truro) impaling, Azure an eagle displayed argent armed and crowned or (sometimes holding a sceptre and orb (d'Este)); baron's coronet, motto and supporters: Two ermines proper. There is a hatchment for Lord Truro at Ramsgate, showing the arms impaled. 1850–55. Franks Coll. 31747.

Thomas Wilde, 1st Baron Truro, second son of Thomas Wilde, an attorney, of London and Saffron Walden, by his wife Mary Ann Knight, was born in Warwick Square, Newgate Street, London on 7 July 1782. He was educated at St Paul's School 1785–96, was articled to his father, and became an attorney; and he was called to the bar from Inner Temple in 1817. Though unprepossessing, and with a speech impediment, he had great natural skill. He defended Queen Caroline in 1820. In 1831 he entered Parliament, representing Newark-on-Trent twice, and

Worcester once. Later Solicitor-General, he was knighted in 1840, and was instrumental in the movement of the Courts of Justice to the Strand. He was briefly Attorney-General in 1841, supported Rowland Hill's postal reforms and the suppression of the slave trade, and subsequently became Chief Justice of the Common Pleas and a Privy Councillor. Wilde rose to the rank of Lord Chancellor in 1850, in which year he was created Baron Truro, of Bowes, Middlesex. His first wife, whom he married in 1813, was Mary, the daughter of William Wileman, widow of William Devaynes; his second wife, whom he married in 1845, was Augusta Emma D'Este, the daughter of Augustus Frederick, Duke of Sussex (23–26) by his marriage – invalid under the Royal Marriages Act 1772 – with Lady Augusta Murray, second daughter of the 4th Earl of Dunmore. There was issue of the first marriage, but not of the second. He died at his residence in Eaton Square on 11 November 1855, and was buried in the Dunmore vault in the churchyard of St Laurence, near Ramsgate.

APPENDIX

Armorials and other designs of questionable authenticity or in the past wrongly recorded as bookplates

In order to avoid confusion between genuine bookplates and items wrongly ascribed in earlier writings and in the Franks and other well-known collections, the questionable or fraudulent armorials or pictorials which follow are listed alphabetically rather than numerically. By way of preamble, however, it may be useful to make a few general comments on the contents of the three works on bookplates published within the last fifty years which deal at some length with Royal ex-libris.

Percy Neville Barnett's *Australian Book-plates and book-plates of interest to Australia*, Sydney, 1950, illustrates thirty-two Royal plates, all of which are genuine; though as the catalogue indicates the gift ex-libris from the Australian Ex Libris Society, although accepted by the members of the Royal family for whom they were made, were probably never used. Useful documentation in this work is, however, scant. Moreover, the bookplate illustrated on p. 102 is erroneously ascribed to King George III, though it is the ex-libris of his wife, Queen Charlotte Sophia (35). The bookplate of William IV as King, shown on p. 106, is, without it being mentioned, shown in reduced size, and its real dimensions are as illustrated here (170); other than this, only the plates used by Queen Elizabeth II as Princess and Princess Margaret, both by Gooden, and the ex-libris of Prince Philip, Duke of Edinburgh, by Colonel C. J. Barton-Innes, lie beyond the scope of this study.

Arvid Berghman's *Kungliga och Furstliga Exlibris*, Svenska Exlibrisföreningens Utställning, 1955, lists fifty-two British Royal plates, of which it illustrates fourteen, several in slightly reduced size. Of the illustrations, all but the Gooden ex-libris for Queen Elizabeth II as Princess and Queen (the latter the largest of the Windsor series without cypher) and Princess Margaret's plate are included in the catalogue. Amongst those simply described, No. 73, for Prince Edward Augustus, Duke of York (1739–67), has not been seen, and was probably not a bookplate or incorrectly ascribed, though all other ex-libris before 1952 which Berghman listed are included here.

Christine Price's *Catalogue of Royal Bookplates from the Louise E. Winterburn Collection*, printed for the California Bookplate Society by the Saunders Press, Claremont, California, 1944, has 103 examples in its Great Britain section. Items 31 and 32, ex-libris for the Maharajah of Kapurthala, are of course not eligible for inclusion here. Of the others, the following are excluded since they are either not Royal bookplates or their use as ex-libris is at least uncertain: 2 (see (O)), 8 (see (K)), 13 (see (A)), 19, for Alexandra House, Kensington Gore (see (15)), 30 (see (E)), 40 (see (R)), 58 (see (L)), 59 (see (GG)), 72 (see (FF)), 83, which is a stamp for the boards of a book, 86 (see (H)), 88 (see (BB)), 90 (see (CC)), 93 (see (S)), 94 (see (Z)), 97 (see (T)) and 101 (see (I)). All other bookplates recorded in the catalogue of the Winterburn Collection will be found in the catalogue.

The holdings in the Franks Collection at the British Museum, listed in E. R. J. Gambier Howe's *Franks Bequest. Catalogue of British and American Book Plates bequeathed to the Trustees of the British Museum by Sir Augustus Wollaston Franks*, 1903–4, also deserve special mention, as that work remains the major source for the recording of ex-libris. As stated in the Introduction, of the seventy-eight examples included within the 'Royal Plates' classification, three are admittedly not ex-libris, eight are described as 'probably not', five more are questioned, and nine are prints from book-stamps. The impressions from book-stamps rightly have no place in this work. In order to help collectors the other sixteen fradulent or doubtful ex-libris are all illustrated here, for the detailing in the Franks Collection Catalogue is of totally unhelpful brevity. They are as follows: Franks Coll.33166A (see (D)), 33167 (see (Q)), 33168 (See (LL)), 33169 (see (T)), 33173 (see (HH)), 33174 (see (JJ)), 33175 (see (J)), 33176 (see (U)), 33182 (see (K)), 33187 (see (KK)), 33209 (see (C)), 33213 (see (X)), 33214 (see (AA)), 33215 (see (W)), 33216 (see (V)), 33217 (see (70)), 33224 (see (Y)), 33237 (see (N)), 33238 (see (DD)) and 33239 (see (EE)). This, as will immediately be noticed, exceeds the sixteen by four, due to the fact that four of the examples which are unquestioned as bookplates in the Catalogue are also relegated to the 'doubtful' class in the absence of any evidence of their service for this purpose.

Several other questionable ex-libris are added to those listed above, and it may well be that several items relegated to this category will subsequently be proven as authentic. This eventuality is, however, both one of the inevitabilities and joys of any pioneer work – for it is not until attention is focussed upon a subject that evidence of usage comes to hand. Whilst illustrations within this section are reduced in size – chiefly to avoid confusion as to authenticity – the actual dimensions of a composition are given to enable precise identification.

A
H.R.H. ALBERT. PRINCE CONSORT. Always Labouring for the GOOD of others. V.R.

Unsigned, but engraved perhaps *c*.1865. Portrait of the Prince within a decorative rectangular border. This composition is No. 13 in the Winterburn Collection, and its inscription and design suggest that it was used in memoriam for a donatory purpose, perhaps in books; no other print has, however, been seen, nor is it referred to in any work on bookplates, so its usage is as yet unproven. It is the same size as the illustration, and is printed in black.

See (2) for a note on Prince Albert's life. The bookplates he is known to have used are (2–6 and 8). (7) was for additions to his military library after his death, and (9) marks books given to Wellington College in memory of him.

B
A R (Queen Anne)

Unsigned. Armorial: within the ribbon of the Garter, the Royal arms as used by Queen Anne 1702–1707, before the arms of France were relegated to the second quarter; with helm, four-arched crown, the Royal crest, supporters, and the motto 'SEMPER EADEM' which Queen Elizabeth I had used. 114 × 59mm. There are examples of this in the Wolseley Collection at Hove Public Library and in the

author's collection, but it was probably engraved as a frontispiece or dedicatory plate. No print is recorded serving as an ex-libris. An 1821 copy of this engraving by Thomas Willement is illustrated on p. 215 of C. Hasler's *The Royal Arms*, 1980.

Her Royal Highness Princess Anne was born at St James's Palace on 6 February 1665, the second daughter of the future King James II (P–Q) and Anne Hyde, eldest daughter of Edward Hyde, 1st Earl of Clarendon. Brought up like her sister Queen Mary in the Anglican faith, she married at the Chapel Royal, St James's, in 1683 Prince George of Denmark, second son of Frederick III, King of Denmark. There were seventeen children of the marriage, but twelve were stillborn, and the longest-lived was Prince William of Gloucester (JJ), who died of smallpox at the age of eleven. Rather dominated by her friend Sarah Churchill, later Duchess of Marlborough, Queen Anne succeeded her brother-in-law King William III (HH–II) to the throne in 1702. Marlborough was supreme in the early years of her reign, for her own personality was unassertive and domestic, though kindly. She cared little for art and letters. Smollett described her as 'of the middle size, well proportioned. Her hair was of dark brown colour, her complexion ruddy; her features were regular, her countenance was rather round than oval, and her aspect more comely than majestic'. Ill-health much troubled her latter years, and she died on 1 August 1714. She was buried in the vault on the south side of King Henry VII's Chapel at Westminster Abbey.

232

C
Princess Augusta Sophia (daughter of King George III)

Unsigned. Armorial: within a lozenge the Royal arms as borne 1801–37, without an inescutcheon in the Hanoverian quarter, and over all a label of three points argent, the centre point charged by a rose gules and the others with an ermine spot sable; coronet above; the Royal supporters charged on the shoulders with a label as on the arms. Franks Coll. 33209, where it is described as 'probably not a bookplate'. It is almost certainly the work of the engraver of her sister Princess Elizabeth's second bookplate (63), with which it compares very closely in design. No print has, however, been seen in a book or in any bookplate collection other than the Franks Coll.

Princess Augusta Sophia was born at The Queen's House, St James's Park, on 8 November 1768, the second daughter and sixth child of King George III (75–77) and Queen Charlotte (35–36). She never married. Her brother, later King William IV (169–170), commented of her in 1789: 'She looks as if she knows more than she would say. I like that character.' She was an extreme Tory, but private in her life, assisting her father during his illness, and pleasant and patient withal. She resided latterly at Frogmore and at Clarence House, and died at the latter on 22 September 1840. She was buried at St George's Chapel, Windsor.

D
C R (Queen Catherine of Braganza)

Unsigned. Lozenge armorial: the Royal arms as borne by King Charles II impaling Argent, five escutcheons in cross azure, each charged with as many plates in saltire, all within a bordure gules charged with seven castles or (Portugal); with lac-d'amour and Royal crown above, the arms supported by cherubs, and two curious lion supporters couchant regardant holding in their paws ovals bearing a 'C' and 'R'. It is of Portuguese engraving, and

was at one time – especially in Portugal – thought to be an ex-libris, thought it is not. It occurs as a dedication plate for Padre Antonio Veira's *Sermoens a undecima parte oferecida Serenissima Rainha de Gran Bretanha*, Lisbon, 1696. For full details see *A Arte do Ex-Libris*, Vol. X, No. 2, Ano XXI, 1976, 2° Trimestre, No. 74, pp. 41–3. 180 × 127mm. Franks Coll. 33166A.

Princess Catherine was born at the Palace of Villa Vicosa on 15 November (25 Gregorian Calendar) 1638, the third child of the future John IV, King of Portugal, and Louisa de Gusman, daughter of the Duke of Medina Sidonia. The family's long desire for her marriage to Charles, Prince of Wales, was not realized until he had succeeded as King Charles II (F–G), the wedding – a Catholic ceremony – taking place in her bedchamber in 1662, followed by the semblance of an Anglican wedding. There were no children of the marriage. Ill-educated for the position she was to occupy, she seemed out of place at court, but had a simple piety which did not eschew sociability and enjoyment. Demanding of her courtiers, and wondrously long-suffering over the question of her husband's mistresses, the extension of anti-Catholic feeling understandably troubled her. She stayed in England after her husband's death in 1685, but in 1692 embarked for the Continent, settling finally at the new palace of Bemposta near Lisbon. Queen Catherine died on 31 December 1705.

E
Charles R (King Charles I)

Signed 'Will Marshall. Sculpsit'. Armorial: within the ribbon of the Garter, the Royal arms as borne by King Charles I, with helm, Royal crown and crest, supporters, and motto beneath on a ribbon. This is No. 30 in the Winterburn Collection, but is there admitted not to be a bookplate, so one wonders why it was included; and it need not be illustrated here. The engraved lettering of it is quite explicit:

> Charles R Haveing caused this Translation of the Psalmes (whereof oure late deare Father was Author) to be perused, and it being found to be exactly and truely done, wee doe hereby authorize the same to be Imprinted according to the Patent graunted thereupon, and doe allow them to be song in all the Churches of oure Dominiones, recommending them to all oure goode Subjects for that effect.

It occurred printed in this form at the front of the 1630 edition of the King James I translation of the Psalms. 134 × 71mm.

For a bookplate of King Charles I as Prince, and a note on his life, see (33).

F
C R (King Charles II)

Unsigned woodcut or soft metal engraving. Armorial: within the ribbon of the Garter the Royal arms as borne 1603–89 with over all an inescutcheon of Portugal; two-arched Royal crown and 'C R' above, supporters, rose and thistle and motto below, the last in a cartouche extended below to add a number. The only illustration seen is in *A Arte do Ex-Libris*, Vol. X, No. 2, Ano XXI, 1976, 2° Trimestre, No. 74, pp. 41–4. It is there described as 'an evident fraud. . . a simple adaptation, in ex libris form, of the . . . arms . . . used by King Charles II. The authors of this forgery implemented in the centre of the escutcheon a minute escutcheon with the arms of Portugal'. The question is, however, not quite so simply resolved. The composition was first used on the first leaf of the full-sized 1649 octavo edition of *Eikon Basilike*. That variety

(though not a bookplate) is illustrated on p. 49 of Almack's *Bookplates*, 1904. It differs most in having a small crown above the 'C' and 'R'. It occurs subsequently, as shown here, and in a version without the extension of the cartouche to include a number. A later variety is as the last but with the inescutcheon of Portugal removed. All three of the last described versions are shown in the above-mentioned periodical; but the inescutcheon's removal is not commented upon, and was probably not noticed. All show notable wear to the block or plate, which evidences clumsy recutting here and there, but all are from the same block or plate. This armorial is not a 'fraud' in the sense implied, but there seems no reason to doubt that all the alterations date from the reign of King Charles II. (Incorporation of the Portuguese arms cannot, of course, be earlier than 1662.) Moreover, there could have been little incentive for someone to perpetrate a fraud by adding the inescutcheon and then bothering to remove it before undertaking a further printing. The final discouragement to accepting the idea of falsification is the incorporation of 'No.' below, the character of which seems contemporary with the rest. We may never know the purpose for which the numbered variety was used. If it was for books, it is odd that no print has been seen elsewhere. It was, of course, quite usual for old woodcuts and engravings to be kept in printing shops in case they could be re-used later, perhaps with slight modifications. Royal arms were used then as now for such multifarious purposes by printers that retention would seem worthwhile – nor did many of the publications in which they appeared require engravings of finesse. 73 × 62mm.

His Royal Highness Prince Charles was born at St James's Palace on 29 May 1630, the second but eldest surviving son of King Charles I (33 & E) and Queen Henrietta Maria, the youngest daughter of Henry IV, King of France and Navarre. Created Prince of Wales in 1640, he withdrew to the Continent in the Civil War. He was crowned at Scone in 1651, had narrow escapes in England after the Battle of Worcester, but got to Normandy and remained abroad until he became King Charles II at the Restoration in 1660. He married in 1662 Catherine of Braganza (D), third child of John IV, King of Portugal. There were no children of the marriage, but he had a succession of mistresses and fourteen natural children over a period of thirty years. See (187–190, 201–203 and 205) for bookplates relating to his illegitimate descendants. His reign saw a modification in the power of the Crown, he worked towards religious tolerance, having Catholic tendencies himself, but was too dependent upon France. Evelyn described him as 'debonnaire and easy of access', and he was undeniably popular, intellectual and artistic in his tastes, but he had a selfish streak and a sense of humour of no marked refinement. He died, at last a professed Catholic, on 6 February 1685, and was buried in the Henry VII Chapel at Westminster Abbey.

G
C R (King Charles II)

Unsigned. Armorial: within the ribbon of the Garter the Royal arms as borne 1603–89, with a four–arched Royal crown, Royal crest, and 'C' and 'R' surmounted by crowns above; supporters, roses and thistles, and motto in a cartouche below, all within a double line rectangular border. There are two varieties, the small differences so many that it seems likely they are from different coppers. The one shown lacks detailing of the bars of the helm etc. Both occur in bookplate collections, but it is most unlikely they were ex-libris. More probably, like comparable armorials for King James II (P), King William III (II) and Queen Anne (B), they were frontispieces or dedicatory plates in books. 133 × 76mm (both).

For a note on the life of King Charles II see immediately above.

H
A E (King Edward VII as Prince of Wales)

Unsigned. Within the ribbon of the Garter the Prince of Wales's feathers, both enclosed within the collar of the Order of the Star of India, from which the Order's badge depends; Prince of Wales's coronet above, and 'A E' (for Albert Edward) at the sides. This composition is No. 86 in the Winterburn Collection, but it is most unlikely that it was ever used as a bookplate, and it is a curiously inele-

gant piece of etching, the purpose of which cannot be surmised. The Most Exalted Order of the Star of India was instituted by Queen Victoria in 1861, and the Prince of Wales was early created Knight Grand Commander (G.C.S.I.), a class limited, apart from members of the Royal family and ex-Viceroys, to forty-four members, about half of whom were native Princes in India. It was the premier Indian Order, taking precedence between the Orders of the Bath and St Michael and St George. The other Indian Orders were the Most Eminent Order of the Indian Empire (instituted 1877) and the very exclusive Imperial Order of the Crown of India (instituted 1878) for ladies. The Prince of Wales undertook visits to that country, and did much to cement its links with the Crown. It may well have been that this etching was used to ornament a publication or document in connection with one of his tours. c.160 × 116mm.

For a note on the life of King Edward VII see (48).

I
Frederick Lewis Prince of Wales, Duke of Cornwall & Edinburgh, Marquess of ye Isle of Ely, Earl of Chester & Eltham, Viscount Launceston and Baron of Snaudon

Unsigned. Jacobean armorial: within the ribbon of the Garter, the Royal arms as borne by King George II, the inescutcheon Gules added to the Hanover quarter showing he was heir to the Elector, and over all a label of three points argent; with coronet, helm and Royal crest above;

supporters, charged on the shoulders with labels as on the arms, resting on a bracket from which the motto ribbon depends; in a double line rectangular border. This armorial is No. 101 in the Winterburn Collection, but is clearly not a bookplate. Its inscription leaves little doubt that it is cut from an armory of some sort of the 1730–45 period. A virtually identical armorial, with a less shaped motto ribbon, is shown, as the arms of his father as Prince of Wales in C. Hasler's, *The Royal Arms*, 1980. 96 × 89mm.

Prince Frederick Louis was born at Hanover on 20 January 1707, the eldest son of the future King George II (J) and Queen Caroline of Brandenburg-Ansbach. He became Duke of Gloucester in 1717, Duke of Edinburgh in 1726, and Prince of Wales in 1729. A marriage long planned for him by King George I to the Princess Royal of Prussia was cancelled after the King's death; and in 1736 he married at the Chapel Royal, St James's Palace, Princess Augusta, the youngest daughter of Frederick II, Duke of Saxe-Gotha-Altenburg. There were five sons and four daughters of the marriage, the eldest son becoming King George III. More than unpopular with his parents and sisters, the family's wrangles make embarrassing reading; and though Prince Frederick was popular with the people, it was largely a result of the King's financial meanness towards him and comparison of Frederick with his brother, 'Butcher' Cumberland. They lived sometime at St James's Palace, Kew, and Norfolk House, St James's Square, and the Prince died at Leicester House – predeceasing his father by nine years – on 20 March 1751. He was buried in the Henry VII Chapel at Westminster Abbey.

J
Anonymous (King George II)

Signed 'P Fourdrinier fecit'. Pictorial–armorial: Father

Time, within a classical landscape with zodiacal signs at top right, supports a cartouche bearing two shields accolé beneath the crown: 1) within the ribbon of the Garter the Royal arms as borne by King George II; 2) Quarterly of fifteen, for Brandenburg-Ansbach. The poorly engraved arms appear to be: 1st, Magdeburg; 2nd & 3rd, Brandenburg; 4th, Cassuben?; 5th, Principality of Wenden; 6th, ?; 7th, Prussia; 8th, ?; 9th, Brandenburg; 10th, Halberstadt; 11th, Nuremburg; 12th, Minden; 13th, Hohenzollern; 14th, ?; 15th, Sovereign rights. This armorial occurs pasted on the cover of a book with, as manuscript mark of ownership at top left, 'Ar: Onslow. No. 413', but whether it was ever used as a bookplate by King George II seems very doubtful. Arthur Onslow (1691–1768) was Speaker of the House of Commons for thirty-three years, and his own fine bookplate, designed by William Kent and engraved by Benjamin Cole, is familiar to collectors. One wonders whether perhaps he himself placed this engraving into a volume perhaps given to him by the King, who held him in high regard. No other print has been seen. Franks Coll. 33175.

Prince George Augustus was born at Hanover on 30 October 1683, the only son of King George I (71–74) and Sophia Dorothea, the only surviving daughter of Georg Wilhelm, Duke of Brunswick-Lüneburg and Celle. He became Electoral Prince (Kurprinz) of Hanover in 1698 and a British subject in 1705, being created Duke and Marquess of Cambridge. On his father's accession in 1714 he was made Duke of Cornwall and of Rothesay and shortly afterwards Prince of Wales. He spent much of his youth with his grandparents and – like his own eldest son – did not accord with his father. He married at Hanover in 1705 Princess Wilhelmina Charlotte Caroline, the third daughter of Johann Friedrich, Margrave of Brandenburg-Ansbach, and she bore him four sons (one stillborn) and five daughters. His eldest son was Prince Frederick Louis (see immediately above). King George II succeeded to the throne in 1727. Small and stiff, he enjoyed pageantry and military affairs, and was the last English king to lead his troops into battle, at Dettingen in 1743. He had little grace of person or manner except when confronted with attractive women, and was not in the least addicted to books; but he was regular in his habits and hard-working as King. He died at Kensington Palace on 25 October 1760, and was buried in the Royal vault in Henry VII's Chapel at Westminster Abbey.

Paul Fourdrinier (1698–1758) was born in France but settled in England in 1719. He illustrated Fiddes' *Life of Wolsey*, 1724, and engraved frontispieces for the three volumes of Trapp's *The Works of Virgil*. His beautiful trade card, drawn by William Kent in 1731, takes as subject the Goddess of Engraving with cherubs etc., and gives his address as the corner of Craggs Court, Charing Cross. Described there as engraver and stationer, all sorts of prints and maps were to be had from him. The card is illustrated in Ambrose Heal's *The Trade Cards of Engravers*, reprinted from *The Print Collector's Quarterly*, July 1927. Fincham lists no ex-libris by any of the Fourdrinier family, which included his son and grandson, both named Charles, who worked as engravers.

K
Anonymous (King George III)

Signed 'F Bartolozzi inv sculp'. Armorial: the Royal arms as borne to 1800, framed by a mantle and supported, like the crown, by cherubs, with Fame trumpeting at top right. An elegant composition. 156 × 169mm. Winterburn Coll. 8. Lord de Tabley, in his *A Guide to the Study of Book-Plates*, 1880, the first book on the subject published in England, refers to this armorial and describes it, assuming it to be an ex-libris. In W. J. Hardy's *Book-plates*, 1893, it is again commented upon, but Hardy suggests it may have been a complimentary gift to the King and was too large to have been of much use. The composition was illustrated in *The Ex Libris Journal*, Vol. IV, 1894, from a print in the Thairlwall Collection. It is not, however, a book-plate. As James Roberts Brown pointed out later in the same volume of the journal, the armorial comes from the

title page of *Court of Henry VIII, a collection of 36 portraits of Nobility and Statesmen of that Reign from original drawings by Hans Holbein in the collection of his Majesty*, large folio, 1792. A second anonymous armorial for King George III by Bartolozzi (Franks Coll. 33182) is likewise not an ex-libris; nor is the same engraver's armorial of 1784 for the Duke of York as Bishop of Osnaburgh, which is listed by Fincham.

For a note on the life of King George III see (75).

Francesco Bartolozzi (1727–1815) was born in Florence, but came to England in 1764 at the invitation of Mr Dalton, King George III's librarian, who offered him appointment as 'Engraver to the King' and, independently, a salary of £300 a year. He spent forty years in London, became famed for his 'red-chalk manner of engraving' (a soft-ground etching process), and did some of his finest work for Alderman Boydell. Elected to the Royal Academy, he was patronized much by Reynolds, but though he amassed wealth he was spendthrift. Bartolozzi left England in 1802, and died at Lisbon. Fincham lists ten bookplates by him, but the Royal examples may be deleted from the list, and several more created for other purposes.

L
H K (King Henry VIII and Katherine of Aragon)

Unsigned. Badge: a leafy stem bearing on the left side the Tudor rose and on the right a cleft pomegranate (the arms of Granada are Argent, a pomegranate or); Royal crown above. 64 × 50mm. This composition is No. 58 in the Winterburn Collection, and is illustrated in Christine Price's book on it, but it is patently not a bookplate, and one wonders why it was considered for inclusion at all. Its engraving is most likely early nineteenth century, and this and other badges are not unfamiliar as illustrations and on carvings etc. Catherine of Aragon also used as a badge a sheaf of arrows argent, again found combined with the Tudor rose.

Prince Henry was born at Greenwich on 28 June 1491, the

second son of King Henry VII and Queen Elizabeth of York. His elder brother Prince Arthur died in 1502, and in 1509 he married his brother's widow Princess Catherine, daughter of King Ferdinand and Queen Isabella of Spain. She bore him six children, but only the future Queen Mary I survived. They married within two months of his accession as King Henry VIII. By 1527 he was seriously considering divorce, but he did not marry Anne Boleyn – of whom he had been enamoured for some years – until 1533. His marriage to Catherine had not been annulled by Rome, but he simply assumed he had not been legally married to her at all, and left others to settle the matter to his satisfaction. Catherine died in 1536, and Henry's later acquisition and disposal of wives require no recounting here; like his proclaiming himself Head of the Church and his dissolution of the monasteries they are the stuff of traditional history lessons. He died at Westminster at midnight on 28 January 1547, and was buried at Windsor in St George's Chapel.

M
Anonymous (Henry Benedict, Cardinal York)

Unsigned. Armorial: the Stuart Royal arms within a cartouche, with continental crown and cardinal's hat above, the arms supported by Fame and a cherub. There are two varieties. The earlier is illustrated in *The Ex Libris Journal*, Vol. 7, p. 17, 1897, and differs from the print shown here in several respects; there is a crescent argent on the fess point, the dots indicating or on the second quarter's ground are lighter, and the coronet lacks arches, etc. It was illustrated in the journal in the belief that its genuineness was almost certain. However, in the same journal the following year, Vol. 8, pp. 47–8, there is a letter from Hartwell D. Grissell stating that the armorial had evidently been cut from the title-page of a book dedicated to the Cardinal by Pierniccolo Capocci entitled *Del Cantico di Mosè*, published in Rome by Salamoni in 1782. The writer possessed the original presentation copy, handsomely

bound in red morocco with the Cardinal's arms on it embossed in gold, and the supposed ex-libris ornamenting the title-page. He added that he possessed several relics of the Cardinal, including a wood-block he used for stamping notifications and pastoral letters as Bishop of Frascati. The arms of these were illustrated, but the cardinal's hat and its tassels were on a separate block. The variant shown here, in the Viner Collection, probably served a similar purpose, and if from the same copper is much reworked. 75 × 92mm. The Cardinal had a valuable library, but no genuine ex-libris is known. See also the following illustration.

Henry Benedict Maria Clement was born at Rome on 6 March 1725, the second son of the Chevalier de St George ('The Old Pretender', called by his adherents James III) and Princess Clementina, daughter of Prince James Sobieski. He took orders in the Roman Church in early life, soon became a bishop, and was made cardinal by Pope Benedict XIV in 1747. On his brother's death he had medals struck which declared him King of England. After the French Revolution he became penurious, but was generously supported financially by King George III. With his death at Frascati on 13 July 1807 the male line of James II ended. He was buried at St Peter's, Rome.

N
EX LIBRIS H. CARD. DE YORK (Henry Benedict)

Etching signed 'C Carelli ft'. Pictorial: landscape with a ruined tower etc., with two figures dimly discerned, one on a horse, the other walking. The inscription is letterpress. 50 × 104mm. Franks Coll. 33237 and author's coll.

This fraudulent bookplate for Henry Benedict, Cardinal York, is illustrated and commented on in *The Ex Libris Journal*, Vol. 6, pp. 150–1, 1896. Sir Ross O'Connell, Bart. purchased the print for the equivalent of 2½d. in a Rome shop, and believed it to be genuine; but the editor was less convinced. The pictorial is also illustrated on p. 59 of A. Bertarelli's *Gli Ex Libris Italiani*, Milan, 1902, where it is with other entirely fraudulent ex-libris singled out to warn collectors. J. Gelli, in his book of the same title, published in Milan, 1930, suggests the fraud dates from about 1890. A print in the author's collection is on paper which appears to have been deliberately 'antiqued'; but beyond this the lettering is entirely unconvincing and inappropriate to the period of the Cardinal's life, and it seems inconceivable that the last of the Stuarts – Cardinal and producer of medals stating his kingship – would have commissioned such a design. He would surely have used an armorial.

For a note on Henry Benedict's life see immediately above.

O
Anonymous (King James I of England and VI of Scotland)

Unsigned. Armorial: within the collar of the Order of the Thistle, from which the badge depends, the Royal arms of Scotland (Or, a lion rampant within a double tressure flory counterflory gules) with Royal crown and crest: a lion sejeant affrontée gules, Imperially crowned or, holding in the dexter paw a sword and in the sinister paw a sceptre both erect and proper; motto 'In defence'; the Royal supporters of Scotland, Unicorns argent, armed, unguled and crined or, gorged with open crowns of crosses patée and fleurs de lys alternately and attached thereto a chain reflexed over the back also or, supporting tilting lances proper flying banners, (here), dexter, the arms of Scotland, sinister, the Cross of St Andrew crowned centrally, incorporating 'I R 6' and a thistle. 233 × 155mm. Winterburn Coll.2. The authenticity of this armorial as a bookplate is not questioned in the Winterburn Collection catalogue, but it is patently not an ex-libris, and was probably engraved as a dedicatory plate or frontispiece to a book. Its considerable size would, in any case, have rendered it useless as a mark of ownership in anything other than elephant folios.

His Royal Highness Prince James was born at Edinburgh Castle on 19 June 1566, the only son of Mary, Queen of Scots, and Henry Stewart, Lord Darnley, who was murdered in very mysterious circumstances the following year. He became King of Scotland at the age of one, on his mother's abdication. Though a markedly intelligent boy, the machinations of the nobles' striving for ascendancy made his minority difficult, but he assumed power in 1583. In 1589 he married by proxy at Copenhagen Princess Anne, the second daughter of Frederick II, King of Denmark. She bore him three sons and four daughters. The eldest son was Henry, Prince of Wales (see p. 2), the second the future King Charles I (33 and E). Their eldest daughter became Queen Elizabeth of Bohemia. King James achieved the supremacy of the State over the Kirk, but in his character he was given to favouritism, and there were several attempts on his life. He succeeded to the throne of England on the death of Queen Elizabeth I in 1603. The problems of his reign as King of England and Scotland were largely the result of his assertions of Divine Right and his alienation of the Puritans by his high church views, aided in the wider context by criticisms of his effeminacy. He died of a tertian ague at Theobalds on 27 March 1625, and was buried in Westminster Abbey.

P
I R (King James II)

Unsigned. Armorial: within the ribbon of the Garter, the Royal arms as borne 1603–89, with Royal crown and crest, and 'I' and 'R' surmounted by crowns above; supporters, roses and thistles with motto below, all within a single line rectangular border. This is clearly based on the armorial for King Charles II (G) in composition, and like it is most unlikely ever to have served as a bookplate. More probably it was a frontispiece or dedicatory plate in a book, as yet unidentified. 138 × 73mm.

His Royal Highness Prince James was born at St James's Palace on 14 October 1633, the third but second survi-

Q
Anonymous (King James II and Queen Mary of Modena)

Unsigned. Armorial–pictorial: two shields accolé beneath a Royal crown: 1) the Royal arms as borne 1603–89; 2) Quarterly, 1st and 4th, Or, an eagle displayed sable crowned or, 2nd and 3rd, Azure, three fleurs de lys or with a bordure indented point in point or and gules (Modena). The full arms of Queen Mary's father were modified – since the quarterings were divided by a pale gules charged with the Papal keys ensigned with a tiara – in recognition of the strong religious feelings of the time. The arms are within a cartouche with a flaming heart as ornament, and rest on a Jacobean bracket with festoons, framed by a leafy background. Supporters: dexter, The Royal lion of England, sinister, The eagle azure crowned or of the House of Este. Franks Coll. 33167, where it is noted that this is probably not a bookplate. Certainly no print has been seen or recorded serving in a book. 55 × 82mm.

R
Anonymous (Princess Louise, Duchess of Fife)

ving son of King Charles I (33 and E) and Queen Henrietta Maria. He was proclaimed Duke of York at birth, narrowly escaped capture at Edgehill in 1642, and though later apprehended escaped to Holland in 1648. He returned with King Charles II (F–G) to London in 1660, and the same year married Anne Hyde, eldest daughter of Edward Hyde, Earl of Clarendon. Two of the children she bore him – Mary and Anne (B) – survived infancy and later became Queens of England; but his wife died of cancer aged thirty-four, years before he became King. In 1673 he married secondly Mary of Modena, the daughter of Alphonso IV, Duke of Modena, and by her had two sons and five daughters. Of the sons, however, only James Francis Edward Stuart, Prince of Wales, survived infancy and he was later known as 'The Old Pretender'. By his mistress Arabella Churchill King James II had two sons and a daughter. His elder son was James, Duke of Berwick (200), and his natural daughter Henrietta married Sir Henry Waldegrave, later Lord Waldegrave of Chewton. James II ascended the throne on the death of his brother King Charles II in 1685, but his being a Catholic and in favour of Catholics, with his arbitrary rule, led to reaction, and he fled to France in 1688. He led a rising in Ireland the following year, but was defeated in 1690 at the Battle of the Boyne, thereafter remaining in exile in France. He died at St Germains on 6 September 1701, and was buried there.

Unsigned, but probably designed by George W. Eve. Armorial lozenge: the Royal arms with an inescutcheon of Saxony and over all a label of five points argent, the centre and two outer points charged with a cross gules and the other two with a thistle slipped and leaved proper; with Royal coronet above, and the Royal supporters charged on the shoulder with a label as on the arms, upon a bracket. Winterburn Coll. 40. Not made as a bookplate, it is an illustration in A.C. Fox-Davies's *Armorial Families*, 4th edition (and probably other editions as well). The coronet's form indicates the armorial was engraved before her father came to the throne in 1901. 103 × 105mm.

For a note on Princess Louise see (119), and for her husband's bookplate (183).

THE ROYAL ARMS

Examination of the authentic Royal bookplates illustrated reveals that their users almost invariably required of them a degree of precision in indication of ownership. Where a name, initials or cypher are absent, the arms themselves are as a rule those proper to the user. In the case of princes and princesses it has long been customary for a label of three or five points to be placed over the Royal arms, the charges of which are individually assigned (though, of course, the heir to the throne traditionally bears a label of three points argent without charges). It is understandable, in view of the wide usage of Royal arms referred to in the introduction, that prints of them lacking any of the distinguishing marks referred to above should have found their way into bookplate collections. Undoubtedly, very few of them were ever ex-libris; and to avoid undue repetition here eleven examples in this category are illustrated and briefly recorded below.

S

Anonymous. Unsigned. The Royal arms as borne 1603–89 within a lined oval border; four-arched crown above. Winterburn Coll. 93, where it is noted that this is probably not a bookplate. Illustrated actual size.

T

Anonymous. Unsigned. The Royal arms as borne 1603–89; four-arched crown above. Winterburn Coll. 97, where this handsome armorial is illustrated. The Winterburn print is dated in manuscript 1677. Franks Coll. 33169, where it is noted that the armorial is probably not a bookplate. Probably a frontispiece, book illustration or dedicatory plate. 147 × 100mm.

U

Anonymous. Unsigned. The Royal arms as borne 1714–1800; four-arched crown above. Franks Coll. 33176, where it is noted that this is probably not a bookplate. 47 × 65mm.

W

Anonymous. Unsigned. The Royal arms as borne 1801–16, when the Electoral Cap was replaced by the arched crown of the Kingdom of Hanover, with leafy ornament around the supporters and below. 40 × 87mm. Franks Coll. 33215. This is described as a bookplate in the Franks Collection catalogue, but if it is it was almost certainly not used by the King. More likely it would have been used by an institution entitled to adopt the Royal arms.

V

Anonymous. Signed 'Suffield sc. London'. The Royal arms as borne 1801–37 with over all a label of three points argent, Royal crown and Prince of Wales's feathers above; the Royal supporters – here not charged on the shoulder with a label as on the arms – and the Prince of Wales's motto. 50 × 75mm. Franks Coll. 33216. The curious character of this armorial reflects perhaps the lack of armorial precedent for a Regency. It is irregular in that the arms of the future King George IV are accompanied by a crown rather than a coronet and have supporters uncharged on the shoulder by a label. This almost certainly implies that the engraving dates from the years of the Regency, 1811–20. In 1816 the Electoral Cap was replaced by the four-arched crown of the Kingdom of Hanover, but only on the arms of the King. As indicated in the Franks Collection catalogue, the armorial's usage as a bookplate is uncertain. It seems, indeed, to have rather the character of a mast-head for a publication or advertisement of some kind.

For a note on King George IV see (79).

Suffield was a heraldic stationer and engraver in the 1800–40 period, with premises sometime at 233 Strand.

X

Anonymous. Unsigned. The Royal arms as borne 1816–37, in the ribbon of the Garter, Royal crown above. 74 × 40mm. Franks Coll. 33213. The Franks Collection cataloguer, Gambier-Howe, apparently believed this to be a bookplate, but if so its use – like the foregoing – was probably not personal. Beyond the shape of the crown, it differs from (AA) in being a little larger, in lacking the Royal crest and in having the crown of Charlemagne within the Hanoverian inescutcheon. Since no second print of either has been seen, loose or serving in a book, doubt must remain at present over both of them.

Y

Anonymous. Unsigned. The Royal arms as borne from 1837 within the collar of the Garter, Royal crown above.

Shown actual size. Franks Coll. 33224. Usage of this is not questioned in the Franks Collection catalogue, but no second print has been seen, and a degree of doubt must remain. The Franks print is on paper of usual bookplate size, but there is no inscription of any kind.

Z

Anonymous. Unsigned. The Royal arms as borne from 1837 within a compartmented decorative border contrived from a variety of decorative blocks, and reproduced by process in red, blue, green and gold. 72 × 108mm. Winterburn Coll.94, where it is described as 'probably not a bookplate'. It has the nature of a commemorative card of some kind.

AA

Anonymous. Unsigned. The Royal arms as borne 1816–37, in the ribbon of the Garter, Royal crown and crest above. 68 × 37mm. Franks Coll. 33214. The Franks Collection catalogue states that this is a bookplate, but see (X).

BB

Anonymous. Unsigned. The Royal arms as borne since 1837. 66 × 59mm. Winterburn Coll. 88, where it is ascribed to King George V. The character of the engraving certainly suggests this period, and it is printed on paper of typical bookplate size; but the armorial is not represented in the collection at the Royal Library at Windsor. See below.

CC

Anonymous. Unsigned. The Royal arms as borne since 1837. 70 × 52mm. Winterburn Coll. 90. Like the foregoing, this is printed on bookplate-size paper, and its character indicates that it is twentieth century work; but, again, there is no print in the collection at the Royal Library at Windsor. There surely would have been if Sir

Owen Morshead, who was Librarian at Windsor Castle for many years from 1926, had known of it – for he was most interested in the Royal bookplates.

DD

Anonymous. Unsigned. The Royal arms of Scotland as (O), except that the banners are reversed – the St Andrew's cross here plain – and the motto ribbon at the top is blank. This is a much later engraving, of the Early Armorial period, and is as the Franks Collection catalogue indicates a very doubtful item. Probably cut from a book. 98 × 81mm. Franks Coll. 33238. An additional reason for assuming that this and the following armorial could never have served as bookplates is that these examples would have been appropriate only for the monarch, and none of the period of their engraving would have been likely to have used a purely Scottish plate. It is, of course, possible that they were used by a Scottish institution entitled to use of the Royal arms; but no second print of either this or the following has been encountered.

EE

Anonymous. Unsigned. Armorial: the Royal arms of Scotland within a shaded cartouche, but without supporters and banners, etc.; Royal crown above. In character this would be described as Jacobean, but it is almost certainly of later engraving, and most likely served as a book illustration. 68 × 45mm. Franks Coll. 33239.

FF
R H G or R A G

Unsigned. Within the ribbon of the Garter entwined initials, a Royal crown above. This is No. 72 in the Winterburn Collection. Originally it was there suggested as the bookplate of King George III's son the Duke of Gloucester. That is, of course, absurd, for not only was he brother of King George III but the crown would have been inappropriate, and the engraving is in any case too late. Christine Price, who compiled the Winterburn Collection catalogue, no less ludicrously tentatively ascribed the bookplate to King George II on the supposition that the initials stood for 'Rex George Augustus'. In view of the style and composition of the plate one is drawn to a belief that it is probably a military bookplate. Perhaps for the Royal Horse Guards? 71 × 39mm.

GG
Anonymous (the Tudor Rose)

Unsigned. The Tudor rose surmounted by a Royal crown. Winterburn Coll. 59, where, unreasonably following its original ascription in the collection to King James I, Christine Price adds:

> but quite possibly the mark of Queen Elizabeth, who used a similar motif on her bookbindings, while King James combined the rose and thistle. Obviously an old plate, but it is to be recalled that the badge of the Tudor rose for England has been employed since Henry VII.

It is, of course, not a bookplate at all, but a cut from a work, probably on Royal heraldry etc., and is another instance of Louise Winterburn's travelling too hopefully in her quest. 62 × 38mm.

Gonzales van Heylen fecit. Antverpiæ.

HH
Anonymous (King William III)

Signed 'Gonzales van Heylen fecit. Antverpiae'. Armorial: within the ribbon of the Garter the Royal arms as borne 1689–1702 with the lion of Nassau (Azure, billetty and a lion rampant or) in pretence; surmounted by a four-arched Royal crown, with the Royal supporters and the Nassau

motto. 83 × 92mm. Franks Coll. 33173, where it states that it is 'probably not a bookplate'. Almost certainly a cut from a book, there is no reason to suppose it an ex-libris. If it had been, King William III would surely as King of England have used an unsigned armorial or one declaredly by an English engraver. An engraving of his arms made in England follows.

His Royal Highness Prince William Henry was born at the Hague on 4 November 1650, the posthumous son and only child of William II, Prince of Orange, and Mary, the eldest daughter of King Charles I (33 and E) and Queen Henrietta Maria. His mother died when he was ten. In 1677 he married Princess Mary, the eldest daughter of James, Duke of York, later King James II (P–Q). After two miscarriages, she had no children. They became joint sovereigns of the United Kingdom in 1689, but Queen Mary eschewed any part in politics, and in any case died of smallpox in 1694. He thereafter ruled alone – as in effect he had done before – and was an assured statesman. His health was not, however, robust. The King cleverly played the political parties against each other, and he campaigned in Ireland and in France in his endeavours to halt the threat of King Louis XIV's ascendancy over Europe. Indeed, saving the United Provinces from being overwhelmed by France was his prime concern. A man thoroughly dedicated to work, he had little time for learning, art and pleasure. King William III died at Kensington Palace on 8 March 1702, and was buried in the vault beneath the Henry VII Chapel at Westminster Abbey.

Gonzales van Heylen was born in Antwerp in 1661, and worked there, a member of the Guild of St Luke. For an account of his work and divergence of opinion on when he died see Thieme and Becker, *Allgemeines Lexikon der bilbender Kunstler*, Leipzig, 1924.

II
W R (King William III)

Signed 'F. H. Van Hove. Sculp'. Armorial: within the ribbon of the Garter the Royal arms as borne 1689–1702 with – as the last – the lion of Nassau in pretence, but here in an oval inescutcheon; with helm, four-arched Royal crown and Royal crest, the Royal supporters and the British Royal motto; all within a single line rectangular border. The 'W' and 'R' at top, surmounted by crowns, indicates that this was engraved after the death of Queen Mary in 1694, as of course does the omission of the impalement of the arms. It was probably engraved as a frontispiece or dedicatory plate, and is of the same pattern as the armorials for King Charles II (G) and Queen Anne (B), which in view of their close similarity of composition must have served a similar purpose. 116 × 60mm. Author's coll.

F. H. Van Hove, Sculp:

I. Sturt Sculp:

Du tres-haut, tres-puissant, et tres-illustre Prince;
GUILLAUME Fils de la Princesse ANNE,
par le Prince GEORGE de DANEMARC;
Chevalier du tres-noble Ordre de la JARTIERE:
Installé au Château de WINDESORE le 24.me jour
de Juillet, l'an MDCXCVI.

For a note on the life of King William III see immediately above.

Frederick Henry Van Hove (*c.* 1625–98) was born at Haarlem in Holland, but came and settled in London. He made many engraved portrait frontispieces from 1648. The collection of engraved British portraits at the British Museum contains thirty-six examples limned by him, and they include King Charles I, King Charles II, Cromwell and the Duke of Monmouth. Van Hove was found murdered on 17 October 1698.

JJ
Du tres-haut, tres-puissant, et tres-illustre Prince, GUILLAUME Fils de la Princesse ANNE, par le Prince GEORGE de DANEMARC; Chevalier du tres-noble Ordre de la JARTIERE: Installé au Château de WINDESORE le 24me jour de Juillet, l'an MDCXCVI (Prince William, Duke of Gloucester)

Signed 'I. Sturt Sculp'. Armorial: within the ribbon of the Garter the Royal arms as borne 1603–89, an inescutcheon of Denmark (simple), with over all a label of three points argent the centre point charged with a cross gules; with helm and coronet, the Royal crest and supporters charged on the shoulder with a label as on the arms. By later rules the coronet here is incorrect, being the one for a sovereign's child; and Prince William died before his mother came to the throne. 157 × 105mm. Franks Coll. 33174. Franks Coll. *2 is the same with the engraver's signature erased. It is not a bookplate, was probably engraved as

illustration to a book, and – as the inscription indicates – commemorates his admission to the Order of the Garter. Winterburn Coll. 100. Author's coll.

His Royal Highness Prince William was born at Hampton Court on 24 July 1689, and declared Duke of Gloucester soon afterwards. His birth – as eldest son of Princess and later Queen Anne (B) and Prince George of Denmark, second son of Frederick III, King of Denmark – eased fears of a papist succession. A frail child, he escaped smallpox in May 1695, and in 1698 Marlborough was appointed as his governor, and the Bishop of Salisbury as his preceptor. Prince William was given command of the Dutch regiment of footguards. On 26 July 1700 he was taken sick at Windsor, and he died three days later. Books on Queen Anne vary or are non-committal about his cause of death. *The Complete Peerage* states that he died of scarlet fever, but elsewhere smallpox is suggested. His death occasioned the Act of Settlement, to ensure that Queen Anne should have a Protestant successor (of her seventeen children twelve were stillborn, and of the others only Prince William survived infancy).

John Sturt (1658–1730) was born in London and became apprentice to the engraver Robert White. He engaged in making portrait frontispieces, engraved John Ayres' calligraphic books, and was remarkably adept in miniature delineation. His *Book of Common Prayer*, 1717, was his most ambitious work, using 188 silver plates. A prolific

246

engraver, he illustrated a number of fine books, and invented a class of prints called 'Medleys', the first of which appeared in 1706. He had premises in Golden Lion Court in Aldersgate Street, then in St Paul's Churchyard, and in the latter, with Bernard Lens, had at one time a drawing school; but he died in poverty in London.

to the severity with which he pursued the rebels. Once vastly popular, the country turned against him in his latter years due to his want of mercy. Though fond of women he never married. He died at his house in Upper Grosvenor Square on 31 October 1765, very suddenly, and was buried in Westminster Abbey.

KK
Anonymous (Prince William Augustus, Duke of Cumberland?)

Armorial: The Royal arms as borne 1714–1800 with over all a label of three points argent each charged with a cross (gules?); four-arched Royal crown above; the supporters rest on a ledge, but only the lion is charged with a label as on the arms. The shield's rather Chippendale style suggests a mid-eighteenth century date, but the armorial defies certain ascription. Why, one wonders, is there a crown above, and whom was the label intended to identify? Inclusion of the inescutcheon in the Hanoverian quarter is also mystifying. The Franks Collection catalogue suggests it was possibly intended for Prince William Augustus, but his label of three points argent should have been charged only on the centre point with a cross gules. It is, in any case, extremely unlikely that this armorial ever served as an ex-libris. 63 × 80mm. Franks Coll. 33187.

His Royal Highness Prince William Augustus was born at Leicester House in London on 15 April 1721, the third son of the future King George II (J) and Queen Caroline. He was nominated as the first Knight when the Order of the Bath was revived in 1725, was created Duke of Cumberland the following year, and became a Knight of the Garter in 1730. Educated for the navy, he preferred a military life, and rose quickly in rank. He served most bravely at Dettingen, suffering injury, and in 1745 became Captain General of the British Land Force at home and in the field. At Fontenoy he was in the thick of the battle, but the allied forces suffered defeat; and in 1746 at Culloden, the last battle of the Jacobite rebellion, he earned himself the sobriquet 'Butcher Cumberland', owing

LL

Anonymous. Unsigned. The Royal arms as borne 1603–89, with four-arched crown etc., the arms on a shaded ground within the ribbon of the Garter. This composition seems clearly to be based on the woodcut Stuart arms in Guillim's *A Display of Heraldrie*, London, 1610; and John Speed's interpretation published in 1627 is very similar. Engraved on copper, this armorial occurs in several bookplate collections, including Franks Coll. 33168, and two prints – one of them cut close – are in the author's coll. The latter seem to have been pasted down, perhaps in books; but evidence is lacking that it ever served as an ex-libris. 176 × c124mm.

MM
WA (Prince William Augustus, Duke of Cumberland).

Monogram with coronet above in a circle with double line border; volume and piece numbers incorporated below. This is not a bookplate but a label of classification for the

VOL:XII
60.

Duke's collection of maps. Only a handful of them survives, but where examples have been soaked off ultraviolet light shows 'ghosting' of the numeration. See 'Prince William, Royal Map Collector', by Yolande Hodson in *The Map Collector*, Autumn 1988, Issue No.44. King George III used a similar label, likely to have been of about the same size, but that had 'G R III' above the Royal crown.

Genealogical tables

Genealogical tables

This and the following tables, without dates and omitting many members of the Royal family, provide a simple guide to the relationships of those whose bookplates or supposed bookplates are recorded in the text. Their names are in capitals; others are in upper and lower case. Biographical details and dates will be found with their ex-libris, the numbers of which are in brackets below the names.

Table I
King James I to King George III

JAMES I (O) ══ Anne of Denmark

- Henry Frederick Prince of Wales
- CHARLES I (33, E) ══ Henrietta Maria of France
- Elizabeth ══ Frederick V Elector Palatine King of Bohemia

CHARLES II (F, G) ══ CATHERINE of Braganza (D) — See TABLE II

Anne Hyde dau. of Earl of Clarendon ══ JAMES II (P, Q) — See TABLE II ══ Mary of Modena

Others

WILLIAM III (HH, II) ══ Mary II

George of Denmark ══ ANNE (B)

James Francis Edward (The Old Pretender) ══ Maria Clementina Sobieska

Louisa

WILLIAM Duke of Gloucester (JJ)

LOUISA MAXIMILIENNE of Stolberg (204) ══ Charles Edward (The Young Pretender)

HENRY BENEDICT Cardinal York (M, N)

Others

Sophia ══ Ernest Augustus Elector of Hanover

Sophia Dorothea of Brunswick and Celle ══ GEORGE I (71–74)

Others

GEORGE II (J) ══ Caroline of Ansbach

Sophia Dorothea Queen in Prussia

THOMAS DUNCKERLEY FITZGEORGE (197)

Augusta of Saxe-Gotha ══ FREDERICK LOUIS Prince of Wales (I)

WILLIAM AUGUSTUS Duke of Cumberland (KK, MM)

Anne Princess of Orange

Amelia

Caroline

Mary Landgravine of Hesse-Cassel

Louisa Queen of Denmark

GEORGE III — See TABLE III

Edward Augustus Duke of York and Albany

WILLIAM HENRY Duke of Gloucester and Edinburgh (167) ══ MARIA Countess Waldegrave (120–121)

Others

Mary dau. of George III ══ WILLIAM FREDERICK Duke of Gloucester and Edinburgh (167–168)

Sophia

250

Table II
Natural descendants of King Charles II and King James II

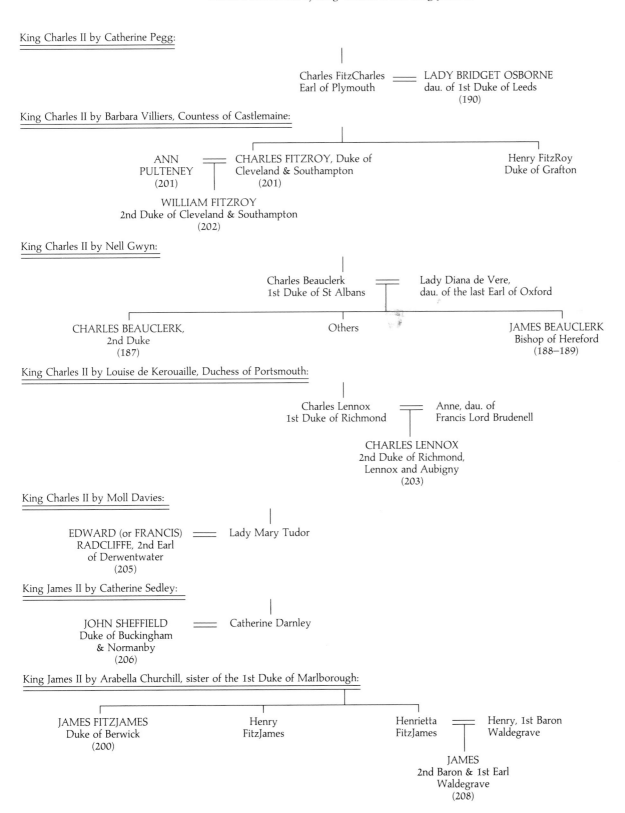

King Charles II by Catherine Pegg:

Charles FitzCharles ═══ LADY BRIDGET OSBORNE
Earl of Plymouth   dau. of 1st Duke of Leeds
                              (190)

King Charles II by Barbara Villiers, Countess of Castlemaine:

ANN ═══ CHARLES FITZROY, Duke of   Henry FitzRoy
PULTENEY   Cleveland & Southampton   Duke of Grafton
(201)   (201)

WILLIAM FITZROY
2nd Duke of Cleveland & Southampton
(202)

King Charles II by Nell Gwyn:

Charles Beauclerk ═══ Lady Diana de Vere,
1st Duke of St Albans   dau. of the last Earl of Oxford

CHARLES BEAUCLERK,   Others   JAMES BEAUCLERK
2nd Duke   Bishop of Hereford
(187)   (188–189)

King Charles II by Louise de Kerouaille, Duchess of Portsmouth:

Charles Lennox ═══ Anne, dau. of
1st Duke of Richmond   Francis Lord Brudenell

CHARLES LENNOX
2nd Duke of Richmond,
Lennox and Aubigny
(203)

King Charles II by Moll Davies:

EDWARD (or FRANCIS) ═══ Lady Mary Tudor
RADCLIFFE, 2nd Earl
of Derwentwater
(205)

King James II by Catherine Sedley:

JOHN SHEFFIELD ═══ Catherine Darnley
Duke of Buckingham
& Normanby
(206)

King James II by Arabella Churchill, sister of the 1st Duke of Marlborough:

JAMES FITZJAMES   Henry   Henrietta ═══ Henry, 1st Baron
Duke of Berwick   FitzJames   FitzJames   Waldegrave
(200)

JAMES
2nd Baron & 1st Earl
Waldegrave
(208)

Table III
King George III to Queen Victoria, with the Cambridge Family

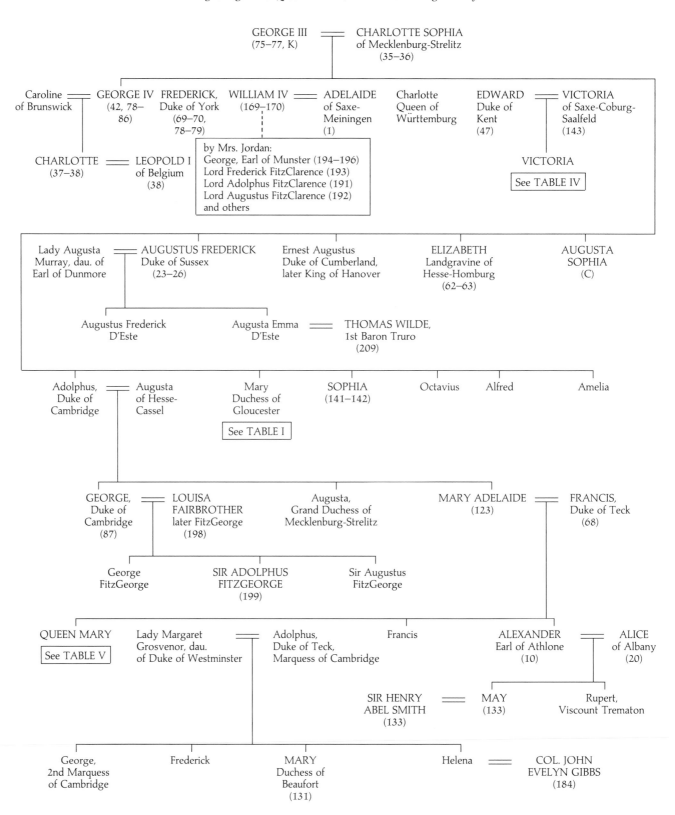

Table IV
Queen Victoria and Prince Albert, their children and grandchildren

VICTORIA (144–158) ═══ ALBERT of Saxe-Coburg & Gotha (2–9, A)

Friedrich III Emperor of Germany ═══ VICTORIA Princess Royal (159–161)

EDWARD VII (48–57, H) ═══ ALEXANDRA of Denmark (13–15)

Albert Victor, Duke of Clarence

GEORGE V — See TABLE V

LOUISE Princess Royal (119, R) ═══ ALEXANDER Duff, 1st Duke of Fife (183)

VICTORIA (163)

MAUD Queen of Norway (132)

KAISER WILHELM II of Germany (180)

HEINRICH (175) ═══ IRENE of Hesse & by Rhine (176)

MARGARETE, Landgravine of Hesse (177)

Marie of Russia ═══ ALFRED ERNEST, Duke of Edinburgh, Duke of Saxe-Coburg & Gotha (16–18)

Ludwig IV Grand Duke of Hesse & by Rhine ═══ ALICE (19)

Others

VICTORIA MELITA, Grand Duchess of Hesse, Grand Duchess Cyril (179) ═══ ERNST LUDWIG, Grand Duke of Hesse & by Rhine (174)

VICTORIA Marchioness of Milford Haven (162) — See TABLE V

Elizabeth Grand Duchess Serge

IRENE Princess Heinrich (176)

ALEXANDRA FEODOROVNA Empress of Russia (173)

Others

HELENA (41, 107–108) ═══ CHRISTIAN of Schleswig-Holstein-Sonderburg-Augustenburg (39–41)

LOUISE, Duchess of Argyll (117)

Christian Victor

Albert

HELENA VICTORIA (164–165)

Marie Louise, Princess Aribert of Anhalt

LEOPOLD, Duke of Albany (111–112) ═══ Helen, of Waldeck & Pyrmont

LOUISE MARGARET of Prussia (118) ═══ ARTHUR, Duke of Connaught (22)

CHARLES EDWARD, Duke of Saxe-Coburg & Gotha (34)

ALICE Countess of Athlone (20) — See TABLE III

Arthur of Connaught

Margaret Crown Princess of Sweden

LADY PATRICIA RAMSAY (135)

BEATRICE (29–31) ═══ HENRY of Battenberg (27–28)

ALEXANDER, Marquess of Carisbrooke (11–12)

Leopold

Maurice

VICTORIA EUGENIE, Queen of Spain (178)

253

Table V
The family of King George V and the family of Princess Victoria of Hesse

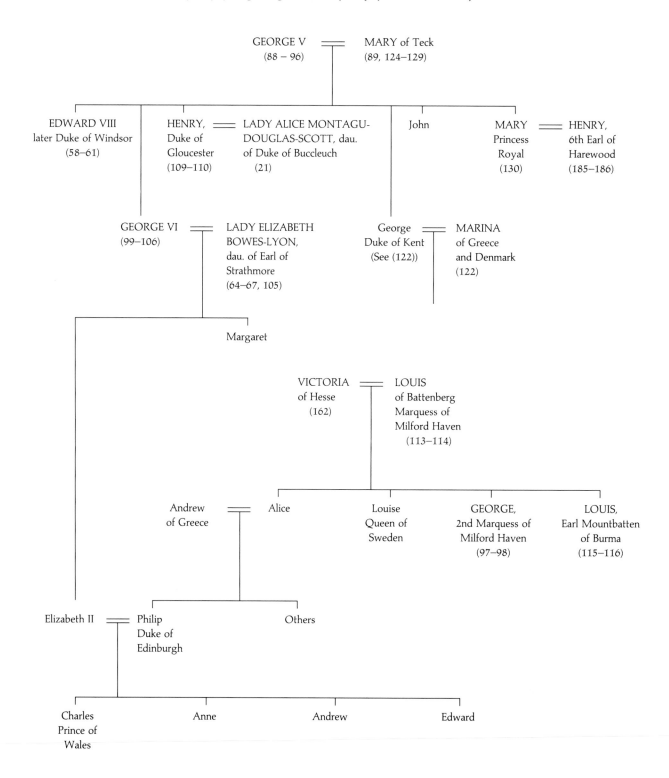

NB   Any bookplates of descendants of King George VI and Queen Elizabeth lie beyond the scope of this study.

Select bibliography

H.R.H. Princess Alice, Countess of Athlone, *For my Grandchildren*, 1966.

H.R.H. Princess Alice, *The Memoirs of Princess Alice, Duchess of Gloucester*, Collins, London, 1983.

Percy Neville Barnett, *Australian Book-plates and book-plates of interest to Australia*, privately printed, Sydney, N.S.W., Australia, 1950.

William Phillips Barrett, *LV Bookplates engraved on copper from designs by W. P. Barrett*, Bumpus, London, 1900.

Daphne Bennett, *King without a Crown (Albert, Prince Consort)*, Heinemann, London, 1977.

Arvid Berghmann, *Kungliga och Furstliga Exlibris*, Kungliga Biblioteket, 1955 (Svenska Exlibrisforeningens Utstallning).

Thomas Anthony Birrell, *English monarchs and their books: from Henry VII to Charles II* (the text of the Panizzi Lectures 1986, with preface and introduction), The British Library, London, 1987.

Charles Boutell, *Heraldry, historical and popular*, 3rd edition, revised and enlarged, 1864.

John Brooke, *King George III*, Constable, London, 1972.

Burke's Peerage, Burke's Peerage Ltd, 1970.

Egerton Castle, *English Book-Plates*, George Bell & Sons, London, 1892, new and enlarged edition 1893, reprinted 1894.

Phyllis M. Cooper, *The Story of Claremont*, published on behalf of Claremont, 8th edition, 1983.

The Church of England Yearbook.

Cyril Davenport, *Royal English Bookbindings*, Seeley & Co. Ltd, London, 1896.

Cyril Davenport, *English Heraldic Book-Stamps*, Constable, London, 1909.

A. C. Fox-Davies, *A Complete Guide to Heraldry*, edited by J. P. Brooke-Little, revised 1969.

The Dictionary of National Biography.

Campbell Dodgson, *Iconography of the Engravings of Stephen Gooden*, Elkin Mathews, 1944.

David Duff, *The Shy Princess (the life of Her Royal Highness Princess Beatrice)*, Evans Bros. Ltd, London, 1958.

David Duff, *Hessian Tapestry*, Frederick Muller, London, 1967.

Henry W. Fincham, *Artists and Engravers of British and American Book Plates*, Kegan Paul, Trench, Trubner & Co., London, 1897.

William Younger Fletcher, *English Book Collectors*, Kegan Paul, Trench, Trubner & Co., London, 1902.

Roger Fulford, *Royal Dukes*, Duckworth, London, 1933.

Roger Fulford, *The Prince Consort*, Macmillan & Co. Ltd, London, 1949.

Vicary Gibbs and others (editors), *The Complete Peerage*, revised edition, 1910–59 (reprinted photographically in reduced format in six volumes), Alan Sutton, 1982.

C. W. Scott-Giles and J. P. Brooke-Little, *Boutell's Heraldry*, Warne, London, revised edition, 1963.

Charles Hasler, *The Royal Arms. Its Graphic and Decorative Development*, Jupiter Books, London, 1980.

Olwen Hedley, *Queen Charlotte*, John Murray, London, 1975.

James Pope-Hennessy, *Queen Mary*, George Allen & Unwin, London, 1959.

Mary Hopkirk, *Queen Adelaide*, John Murray, London, 1946.

Simon Houfe, *The Dictionary of British Book Illustrators and Caricaturists 1800–1914*. The Antique Collectors' Club, 1978.

Richard Hough, *Louis & Victoria. The Family History of the Mountbattens*, Hutchinson, London, 1974.

E. R. J. Gambier Howe, *Catalogue of British and American Book Plates bequeathed to the Trustees of the British Museum by Sir Augustus Wollaston Franks*, three volumes, British Museum, London, 1903–04.

Kearsley's Peerage, 1796.

Norna Labouchere, *Ladies' Book-plates*, George Bell & Sons, London, 1895.

Brian North Lee, *J. A. C. Harrison Artist & Engraver*, The Bookplate Society and Forlaget Exlibristen, 1983.

Douglas Liversidge, *The Mountbattens. From Battenberg to Windsor*, Arthur Barker Ltd, London, 1978.

Elizabeth Longford, *Louisa, Lady in Waiting*, Jonathan Cape, London, 1979.

Jiri Louda and Michael Maclagan, *Lines of Succession. Heraldry of the Royal Families of Europe*, Orbis Publishing, London, 1981.

H.H. Princess Marie Louise, *My Memories of Six Reigns*,

Evans Bros. Ltd, London, 1956.

Hugh Montgomery-Massingberd (editor), *Burke's Royal Families of the World*, Vol. 1, pedigrees compiled by David Williamson, Burke's Peerage Ltd, 1977.

Hugh Montgomery-Massingberd, *Burke's Royal Palaces of Europe*, Burke's Peerage Ltd, 1984.

Roy Nash, *Buckingham Palace: The Place and the People*, Macdonald Futura, 1980.

J. F. and R. V. Pinches, *The Royal Heraldry of England*, Heraldry Today, London, 1974.

Sir Frederick Ponsonby, *Recollections of Three Reigns*, Eyre & Spottiswoode, London, 1951.

Christine Price, *Catalogue of Royal Bookplates from the Louise E. Winterburn Collection, San Francisco College for Women*, printed for the California Bookplate Society by the Saunders Press, Claremont, California, 1944.

Charles Davies Sherborn, *A Sketch of the Life and Work of Charles William Sherborn, Painter-Etcher*, Ellis, New Bond Street, London, 1912.

Robert Somerville, *The Savoy, Manor, Hospital, Chapel*, A. R. Clark, Edinburgh, 1960.

The Strand Magazine, George Newnes Ltd, London, 1894–95.

Philip Tilden, *True Remembrances. The Memoirs of an Architect*, Country Life Ltd, London, 1954.

H.M. Queen Victoria, *Leaves from the journal of our life in the Highlands from 1848 to 1861*, London, 1868.

The Times obituaries, various dates.

Francisco Vindel, *Ensayo de un Catalogo de Ex-Libris Ibero-Americanos*, Madrid, 1952.

George Heath Viner, *A Descriptive Catalogue of the Bookplates designed and etched by George W. Eve, R. E.*, The American Bookplate Society, Kansas City, 1916.

Karl Emich Count zu Leiningen-Westerburg, *German Book-plates*, An Illustrated Handbook of German and Austrian Exlibris (translated by G. Ravenscroft Dennis), George Bell & Sons, London, 1901.

W. H. K. Wright (editor), *The Ex Libris Journal*, A. & C. Black, London, 1891–1908 (in monthly parts).

Index

Sovereigns are listed under the name used; princes and princesses under their Christian names, with prince or princess; Royal dukes have their title added, foreign princes or princesses their territorial designation, and married princesses their title after marriage; British princes who dropped German titles in 1917 and adopted surnames, are under their British surnames or their titles as appropriate, with references from their original names; peers and peeresses are entered under their title, and commoners under their surnames. Since the principal section of the book details kings, queens, princes and princesses alphabetically and chronologically by birth, there is no need separately to cite bookplates bearing only initials except where these differ from ones later adopted.

'A' (Prince Albert) see King George VI   99
Abel Smith, Sir Henry and Lady
    May   133
Adelaide, Queen   1
Albany, Duchess of see Princess Helen
Albany, Duke of see Prince Leopold and
    Prince Charles Edward
Albert, Prince of Saxe-Coburg & Gotha,
    Prince Consort   2–9, A
Alexander, Prince of Battenberg see
    Carisbrooke
Alexander, Prince of Battenberg, Prince of
    Bulgaria   27
Alexander, Prince of Teck see Athlone
Alexander, William, engraver   45, 46
Alexandra, Princess, and Sir Angus
    Ogilvy   p. 8
Alexandra, Queen   13–15,   p. 9
Alexandra Feodorovna, Empress of
    Russia   173
Alexandra House, Kensington Gore   15
Alfred, Prince, Duke of Edinburgh and of
    Saxe-Coburg & Gotha   16–18
  attempt on the life of   17
Alice, Princess, Countess of Athlone
    20,   pp. 6, 9
Alice, Princess, Duchess of
    Gloucester   21,   p. 9
Alice, Princess, Grand Duchess of
    Hesse   19
Alix, Princess of Hesse see Alexandra
    Feodorovna
Anna, Princess of Montenegro and
    Battenberg   p. 9
Anne, Queen   B
Arctic Expedition, 1875   51
Argyll, George Douglas Campbell, Duke
    of   182
Army, The Queen (Victoria) to her   150
Arthur, Prince, Duke of Connaught
    22,   p. 9
Athlone, Alexander Cambridge, Earl
    of   10,   p. 3

augmentations of honour   p. 7
Augusta Sophia, Princess   C
Augustus Frederick, Prince, Duke of
    Sussex   23–26
Australian Ex Libris Society   17, 60,
    100,   pp. 9, 231

Badeley, Henry John Fanshawe, 1st Baron,
    engraver   11, 21, 31, 129, 135, 165,
    166,   p. 9
Baker, P. C., engraver   30, 176
Baldrey, Joshua Kirby, engraver   72–73
Balmoral Castle   154–155, A.1,   p. 8
Barnard, Sir Frederick Augusta,
    librarian   77,   p. 2
Barnett, Percy Neville, writer on
    bookplates   17, 60,   pp. 1, 231
Barrett, William Phillips, employee of
    Messrs J. & E. Bumpus   15, 58, 90, 99,
    118, 126, 130, 132, 163, 184
Bartolozzi, Francesco, engraver   K
Batchelor, Acheson, engraver   98,
    115,   p.9
Battenberg and Hessian arms   p. 15
Battenberg Princely Library   27–28
Beatrice, Princess, Princess Henry of
    Battenberg   29–31,   p. 9
Beauclerk, Charles see St Albans
Beauclerk, Lord James   188–189
Beaufort, Mary Somerset, Duchess
    of   131
Bell, Robert Anning, bookplate
    designer   181
Berghman, Arvid, writer on
    bookplates   pp. 1, 231
Berwick, James FitzJames, Duke of   200
Bilmann, A. Z., bookplate designer   18
bookbindings and book-stamps, note
    on   p. 2
Bowes-Lyon, Cecilia see Strathmore
Brand, Sir Thomas   p. 6
Brandon, Charles see Suffolk

British prisoners of war   105
Buckingham and Normanby, John Sheffield,
    Duke of   206
Buckingham Palace   36, 57, 147–148,
    p. 3
Bumpus, Messrs J. & E., booksellers and
    stationers   p. 9
  see also Barrett
Byfield, Mary, wood engraver   2–3, 151

Cambridge, Alexander see Athlone
Cambridge, Duke of see Prince George
Cambridge University Library, King
    George I's gift to   71–74
Campbell, George see Argyll
Canberra, Parliament House   100
Carelli, C., engraver   N
Carisbrooke, Alexander Mountbatten,
    Marquess of   11–12
Carleton House Library   80–83
Catherine of Aragon, Queen   L
Catherine of Braganza, Queen   D
Cavendish, William see Devonshire
Cecilia Lady Glamis see Strathmore
Chapels Royal see Royal Peculiars
Charles I, King   33, E,   pp. 2, 3
Charles II, King   F, G,   p. 2
Charles Edward, Prince, Duke of Albany
    and of Saxe-Coburg & Gotha   34,
    p. 3
Charlotte, Princess   37–38,   pp. 6, 8
Charlotte Sophia, Queen   35–36
Christian, Prince of Schleswig-Holstein-
    Sonderburg-Augustenburg   39–41
Clarence, Prince William, Duke of see
    William IV
Claremont House   pp. 4–6
Cleveland and Southampton, Ann FitzRoy,
    Duchess of   201
Cleveland and Southampton, Charles
    FitzRoy, Duke of   201
Cleveland, William FitzRoy, 2nd Duke
    of   202

Coburg   18, 34
Connaught, Duchess of *see* Louise
    Margaret
Connaught, Duke of *see* Prince Arthur
Cornwall, Duchy of   42–44
Cottrell, Sir Clement   p. 6
Crimean War bookplate   150
Culleton, Thomas, engraver   20
Cumberland, Duke of *see* Prince William
    Augustus

Davenport, Cyril, writer on
    bookbindings   p. 2
Dayrolles, Solomon   p. 6
Derwentwater, Edward Radcliffe, Earl
    of   205
Devonshire, William Cavendish, 1st Duke
    of   p. 6
Doepler, Professor Emil, bookplate
    designer   180
Downey, Alfred and Charles, engravers
    and their family   28, 113, 183
Downey, Alfred Dyer, engraver   28, 183
Duchess of York's Library *see* Mary, Queen
Duff *see* Fife
'D Y' *see* Frederick, Prince, Duke of York
    and Albany
Dyke, Sydney Margaret Eleanor, bookplate
    designer   10

Edinburgh, Duke of, *see* Prince Alfred
Edward VII, King   48–57, H,   p. 9
    Hospital for Officers   52
Edward VIII, King, later Duke of
    Windsor   58–61,   p. 9
Edward, Prince, Duke of Kent and
    Strathearn   47
Elizabeth, Princess, Landgravine of Hesse-
    Homburg   62–63,   p. 4
Elizabeth, Queen, Consort of King George
    VI   64–67, 105, 181
Ernst Ludwig, Grand Duke of Hesse and
    by Rhine   174
Eve, George W., etcher of
    bookplates   52–54, 91–96, 101, 156–
    158, 182–183,   p. 8

Feint, Adrian, engraver   60, 65, 100, 110
Fermor, Henrietta *see* Pomfret
Ferrier, Charles Anderson, wood
    engraver   19, 152–153
Fife, Alexander William George Duff, 1st
    Duke of   183
Fincham, Henry W., writer on
    bookplates   77,   p. 17
FitzCharles, Bridget *see* Plymouth
FitzClarence, Lord Adolphus   191
FitzClarence, Lord Augustus   192
FitzClarence, Lord Frederick   193,   p. 4
FitzClarence, George *see* Munster
FitzGeorge, Sir Adolphus   199
FitzGeorge, Louisa (Fairbrother)   198
FitzGeorge, Thos. Dunckerley   197
FitzJames, James *see* Berwick
FitzRoy, Ann and Charles *see* Cleveland
    and Southampton
Fletcher, William Younger, writer on book
    collectors   p. 2

Fölkersam, Baron Armin Eugene von,
    bookplate designer   173
Fourdrinier, Paul, engraver   J
Francis, Prince and 1st Duke of Teck   68
Franks Collection of bookplates   pp. 3, 16,
    231
Frederick, Prince, Duke of York and
    Albany   69–70, 78–79,   pp. 9, 16
    Osnabrugh, Bishop of   78
Frederick Louis, Prince of Wales   I
Friedrich III, Emperor of Germany   p. 4
Friedrichshof, home of the Empress
    Frederick   159,   p. 4
Friend, George Taylor,
    engraver   116,   p. 9
Furstlich Battenbergsche Bibliothek   27–28

Gambier Howe, E.R.J., cataloguer of the
    Franks Collection   p. 231
Gentleman Usher of the Green Rod   p. 6
George, Prince, 2nd Duke of
    Cambridge   87,   p. 6
George, Prince, Duke of Kent
    note on a bookplate design for
    him   122
George I, King   71–74
George II, King   J
George III, King   75–77, K, MM, p. 1
George IV, King   42, 78–86,   p. 9
George V, King   88–96,   p. 9
George VI, King   99–106,   p. 9
Gibb, Andrew & Co., Aberdeen,
    printers   4, 154
Gibbs, John Evelyn   184
Glamis, Lady Cecilia *see* Strathmore
Gloucester, Duchess of *see* Maria, Princess
    Alice
Gooden, Stephen, engraver   61, 66–67,
    102–104,   p. 8
Gray, Paul Kruger, artist   103
Gray's Inn   106
Green Cloth, Clerk Comptroller of the
    p. 6
Gull, Sir William   p. 7
Gull, Sir William Cameron   p. 7
Gunn, Revd William   p. 7

Halm, Peter, engraver   179
Harewood, Henry Lascelles, Earl of   185–
    186
Harrison, John Augustus Charles,
    engraver   15, 58, 90, 99, 108, 118,
    132, 164,   pp. 8, 9
Hasler, Charles, writer on the Royal
    arms   p. 3
Hatchards, Piccadilly, booksellers   14
Heinrich, Prince of Prussia   175,   p. 9
Helard, Miss C., bookplate designer   186
Helen, Princess of Waldeck and Pyrmont,
    Duchess of Albany   pp. 5, 6
Helena, Princess, Princess Christian of
    Schleswig-Holstein   41, 107–108,
    p. 9
Helena Victoria, Princess   164–165,   p. 9
Henry, Prince, son of King James I   p. 2
Henry, Prince of Battenberg   27–28
Henry, Prince, Duke of Gloucester   109–
    110
Henry Benedict, Cardinal York   M–N

Henry VIII, King   L
Henshaw, William, engraver   p. 7
Hessian and Battenberg arms   p. 15
House, Frank G., employee of Messrs
    Truslove & Hanson   108, 164
Howe, E. R. J., Gambier *see* Gambier

Ingrid, Queen of Denmark   11,   p. 9
Irene, Princess of Hesse, Princess Heinrich
    of Prussia   176,   p. 9

Jackson, William, engraver   139, 201,
    205–206, 208
James I, King   O,   p. 2
James II, King   P–Q
Johnson, Dr Samuel   77, p. 3
Jordan, Mrs Dorothy   169,   p. 4

Kent and Strathearn, Duchess of *see*
    Princess Victoria
Kent and Strathearn, Duke of *see* Prince
    Edward
Kent, Duchess of *see* Princess Marina
Kent, Duke of *see* Prince George
Kerby & Endean, Oxford Street,
    engravers   13
Kew Palace   p. 3
King's Library, British Museum   p. 2
Kirk, John, engraver   75, 78

'L M' *see* Louise Margaret and Louise
    Maximilienne
Lady of the Bedchamber   p. 6
Lancaster, Duchy of   32, 45–46, 106
Lane family of King's Bromley   p. 7
Lascelles, Henry *see* Harewood
Leighton, John, bookplate designer   89
Lennox, Charles *see* Richmond
Leopold, Prince, Duke of Albany   111–
    112,   p. 5–6, 9
Leopold, Prince of Saxe-Coburg-Saalfeld,
    later King of the Belgians   38,   p. 5
Levi, Isaac, engraver   197
Longford, Elizabeth, author of *Louisa Lady
    in Waiting*   p. 8
Longmate, Barak, engraver   77
Lord Steward of the Household   p. 6
Louis, Prince of Battenberg *see* Milford
    Haven, Louis
Louis-Phillippe, King of France   p. 5
Louisa *see* FitzGeorge
Louise, Princess, Duchess of
    Argyll   117,   p. 10
Louise, Princess, Duchess of Fife   119, R
Louise Margaret, Princess of Prussia,
    Duchess of Connaught   118,   p. 9
Louise Maximilienne, Princess of Stolberg-
    Gedern, Countess of Albany   204

Majendie, Henry William   p. 7
Margarethe, Princess of Prussia,
    Landgravine of Hesse   177
Maria, Duchess of Gloucester, formerly
    Countess Waldegrave   120–121
Marie-Amalie, Queen of France   p. 5
Marie Louise, Princess   39, 107, 164
Marina, Princess of Greece, Duchess of
    Kent   122

Marshall, Will, engraver   33, O
Mary of Modena, Queen   Q
Mary, Princess Royal, Countess of
    Harewood   130,   p. 9
Mary, Queen   89, 124–129,   p. 9
    Queen Mary's Dolls' House   127–128
Mary Adelaide, Princess, Duchess of
    Teck   123,   p. 9
Mason, Dame Anna Margaretta   p. 6
Master of the Ceremonies   p. 6
Master of the Revels   p. 6
Mathews, Elkin, Ltd, booksellers   61, 66–
    67, 102–104
Maud, Princess, Queen of Norway   132
Medina, Earl of *see* Milford Haven, George
Milford Haven, George Mountbatten, 2nd
    Marquess of   97–98
Milford Haven, Louis Mountbatten, 1st
    Marquess of   30, 97, 113–114, 162,
    175, 176,   p. 9
Milford Haven, Victoria Mountbatten,
    Marchioness of   162,   p. 9
Moore, John, Bishop of Ely, library of   71
mottoes   p. 14
Mountbatten, Lord Louis, Earl
    Mountbatten of Burma   115–116,
    p. 9
Mountbatten *see* Carisbrooke, Alexander
    and Milford Haven
Munster, George FitzClarence, Earl
    of   194–196
Murray, Lady Augusta   p. 7
Mussett, W. & A., heraldic office   106

Osborne House, Isle of Wight   134,
    149,   p. 8
Osmond, Robert, engraver   15, 64, 109,
    126–127, 130, 181, 184,   p. 9
Osnabrugh, Bishop of *see* Frederick, Prince,
    Duke of York
Ottway, engraver   140

Perkins & Heath, engravers   23–24
Pine, John, engraver   71–74
Plymouth, Bridget FitzCharles, Countess
    Dowager of   190
Pomfret, Henrietta Louisa Fermor,
    Countess of   p. 6
Ponsonby, Sir Frederick   15
Price, Christine, writer on bookplates
    pp. 1, 16–17, 231
Prince Consort *see* Albert, Prince
Prince of Wales's feathers   p. 14
Princess Royal
    note on the title   119
Private Library (anonymous)   172
Private Property, labels thus inscribed   88,
    129
Privy Purse Library, Buckingham
    Palace   136–137

'R H G' or 'R A G'   FF
Radcliffe, Edward *see* Derwentwater
Ramsay, Lady Patricia (earlier Princess
    Patricia of Connaught)   135

Regent, the Prince *see* George IV
Richmond, Lennox and Aubigny, Charles
    Lennox, Duke of   203
Romanov bookplates   p. 8
Royal arms, changes to since 1603
    pp. 11–12
Royal badges   p. 14
Royal crowns and coronets   p. 13
Royal Gardens, Windsor, Book
    Society   A.2–A.3
Royal household, bookplates indicating a
    position in   p. 6
Royal Library, gift to the nation   p. 2
    see also Windsor Castle
Royal Pavilion, Brighton   p. 4
Royal Peculiars   32, 139–140, 166,
    p. 10
Royal Yacht *see Victoria and Albert*

St Albans, Charles Beauclerk, 2nd Duke
    of   187
St George's Chapel, Windsor
    Castle   139–140
Sandringham House, Norfolk   55–56
Sattler, Josef, bookplate designer   160–
    161
Savoy, Chapel Royal of the   32
Scott, designer of bookplates   15
Shaw, Gerrard Gayfield, engraver   171
Sheffield, John *see* Buckingham and
    Normanby
Shepard, Ernest Howard, artist   128
Sherborn, Charles William, engraver   68,
    123–124,   p. 9
Silvester, R., engraver   81, 84–86
Smith, John Owen   63
Smith, Joseph, his books bought by King
    George III   p. 2
Smythe, Walter   207
Somerset, Mary *see* Beaufort
Sophia, Princess   141–142
Southampton *see* Cleveland and
    Southampton
Sparkes, Alfred, etcher and engraver   97
spine labels   4, 5, 48, 154
Stern of Paris, engravers   178
Stone, Reynolds, wood engraver   136
Strathmore, Cecilia Bowes-Lyon, Countess
    of   181
Sturt, John, engraver   JJ
Suffield, stationer and engraver   V
Suffolk, Charles Brandon, Duke of   p. 10
Sussex, Duke of *see* Prince Augustus
    Frederick
Sydney Sailors' Home, gift by Prince
    Alfred   17
Syson, John Edward, engraver   15, 163

'The Queen to her Army' *see* Army
Tilden, Philip Armstrong, architect and
    bookplate designer   59, 130
Treves, Sir Frederick, Bart.   p. 7
Truslove & Hanson, stationers   108, 164,
    p. 9

Truro, Thomas Wilde, 1st Baron   209
Tudor rose   GG

Ulrich, Heinrich Sigismund, wood
    engraver   94–96, 101

'V M' *see* Mary, Queen
Van Heylen, Gonzales, engraver   HH
Van Hove, Frederick Henry, engraver   II
Victoria and Albert Royal Yacht   15,
    138,   p. 10
Victoria, Princess   163
Victoria, Princess *see* Helena Victoria
Victoria, Princess of Hesse *see* Milford
    Haven, Victoria
Victoria, Princess Royal, the Empress
    Frederick   159–161,   p. 3
Victoria, Princess of Saxe-Coburg-Saalfeld,
    Duchess of Kent   143
Victoria, Queen   144–158,   pp. 5, 9
    her grandchildren of foreign Royal
    houses   173–180
Victoria Eugenie, Queen of Spain   178
Victoria Melita, Princess of Edinburgh,
    Grand Duchess of Hesse, later Grand
    Duchess Cyril   179
Viner Collection of bookplates   p. 16

'W H' *see* William IV
Waldegrave, James, Baron   208
Waldegrave, Maria *see* Maria, Duchess of
    Gloucester
Waldemar, Prince of Prussia   175, p. 9
Wale, Samuel, engraver   p. 6
Wellington College, Royal gift of books
    to   8–9
West, James, bookplate designer   19,
    151–153
Westminster Abbey   166
Whymper, Edward, artist and alpinist   29
Wilde, Thomas *see* Truro
Wilhelm II, Emperor of Germany   180
William, Prince, Duke of Gloucester   JJ
William III, King   HH, II
William IV, King   169–170,   pp. 3–4, 7
William Augustus, Prince, Duke of
    Cumberland   KK, MM
William Frederick, Prince, Duke of
    Gloucester   167–168
William Henry, Prince, Duke of
    Gloucester   167
Windsor Castle, Royal Library   171,
    pp. 3, 8
Windsor, Duke of *see* King Edward VIII
Windsor Royal Gardens Book
    Society   A.2–A.3
Winterburn Collection of bookplates
    pp. 1, 231

York and Albany, Duke of *see* Prince
    Frederick
York, Duchess of *see* Queen Mary, Queen
    Elizabeth
York, Duke of *see* King George V, King
    George VI